The Perfect Counselor

Break Through Your Past To Ensure a Healthy Future

By

Kimberly Davidson

Dear Friend —

You're a great blessing to me. I pray you have a blessed and amazing 2017!

Love —
Kimberly

The Perfect Counselor: Break Through Your Past to Ensure a Healthy Future
Copyright © 2016; Rev. 1 by Kimberly Davidson. All rights reserved.

All Scripture quotations, unless otherwise indicated, are taken from the Holy Bible, New International Version®, NIV®. Copyright © 1973, 1978, 1984, 2011 by Biblica, Inc.™ Used by permission of Zondervan. All rights reserved worldwide. www.zondervan.com The "NIV" and "New International Version" are trademarks registered in the United States Patent and Trademark Office by Biblica, Inc.™

Scripture quotations marked (MSG) are from *THE MESSAGE*. Copyright © by Eugene H. Peterson 1993, 1994, 1995, 1996, 2000, 2001, 2002. Used by permission of NavPress Publishing Group.

Scripture quotations marked (NLT) are taken from the Holy Bible, New Living Translation, copyright © 1996, 2004, 2007 by Tyndale House Foundation. Used by permission of Tyndale House Publishers, Inc., Carol Stream, Illinois 60188. All rights reserved.

Scripture quotations marked (TLB) are taken from The Living Bible copyright © 1971. Used by permission of Tyndale House Publishers, Inc., Carol Stream, Illinois 60188. All rights reserved.

Scripture quotations marked (GW) are taken from GOD'S WORD®. Copyright ©1995 God's Word to the Nations. Used by permission of Baker Publishing Group. All rights reserved.

Scripture quotations marked (ISV) are taken from the Holy Bible: International Standard Version®. Copyright © 1996-2012 by The ISV Foundation. All Rights Reserved Internationally. Used by permission.

Unless otherwise designated, all Scripture quotations are taken from the New International Version (NIV)

Interior Design by Kimberly Davidson

ISBN-13: 978-1539985235
ISBN-10: 1539985237

Contents

	Changes that Heal	5
1.	Wonderful Counselor	9
2.	The Expression of Our Emotions	30
3.	Exploring Painful Feelings	46
4.	Pain's Hidden Purpose	55
5.	No Place for Abuse	69
6.	The Grief We Call PTSD	85
7.	Insatiable Cravings and Addiction	109
8.	Healing Painful Memories	121
9.	You Mean I'm Not Stupid or Crazy?	136
10.	The Power of the Mind	158
11.	I Changed My Mind!	173
12.	Shame Off You!	188
13.	Set Yourself Free with Forgiveness	206
14.	Take Control of Your Life	228
15.	Love Like You've Never Been Hurt	244
16.	Personal Power	260
	Treasures by Janet Hansen	266

Please Note

This study is not intended to take the place of medical or psychological care. This study is the spiritual component of a comprehensive care plan. Licensed clinical counselors are trained to treat the difficulties associated with emotional pain.

Know when to seek professional help. Consider seeking pastoral or therapeutic help if your emotions seem out of control and cause you to do things you regret.

If you ever feel suicidal, seek help immediately. Call 1-800-273-8255 or 911. Ask for help. A professional will provide a safe place for you to talk and tend to your immediate needs.

Changes that Heal

> Forget the former things; do not dwell on the past. See, I am doing a new
> thing! Now it springs up ... —*Isaiah, speaking in Isaiah 43:18-19*

Today, millions of Christian women, of all ages, are trapped in pain, broken families, economic misery, depression, physical illnesses, emotional disorders, fear, and addiction, all of which create harmful thoughts literally embedded in their minds. Unaware they have hidden brokenness, pain, and repressed memories, their relationships with others and with God are compromised. Living a life they cannot sustain, and desperate for relief, they spend millions of dollars on mental health specialists and therapies, prescription medications, and vitamin supplements.

Women are searching today for direction and answers, but the answers are often difficult to come by, and change is hard. There is hope. Do you *genuinely* desire to change and grow? What lies and wounds do you hide? What accusations do you wear as your identity? What temptations are you continually enslaved to? You can break free and experience true and powerful change, restoring the mind and nature Christ died to give you!

My goal in this book is to give you the tools to help you discover two important relationships in your life: your relationship with your whole self, and your relationship with God. The objective is not simply to make your life tolerable again; it's to discover meaning, fulfillment, and joy. If you're afraid to go there, don't be. God wants to move within your soul and do an amazing work so you can respond to life's stresses and heal from the past.

Some of you will work through this book and find for the first time that you can identify painful feelings which have been locked away. Others will find validation for feelings and perceptions which they've been aware of for a long time, but wondered if they were crazy or way off base. Sadly, many will choose to bypass a recovery study like this because they fail to see this isn't about bringing up past mistakes or ongoing struggles; it is about participating in God's healing process.

What I've learned is that if I don't know why I respond a certain way to an event, I'll do it again and again. Therefore, I'll be directly challenging your thinking. We will be focusing on your different beliefs and thoughts—your interpretations of reality.

You may have concluded your situation is hopeless. Let me tell you that it's not. God is a God of miracles; of lifting off great and terrible weights. Carl Bard wrote, "No one can go back and change the past my friend, but anyone can start from now and make a brand new end."

Commitment

When you commit to work through this study, you begin a healing journey with the God of hope and healing. "Healing" literally means "to be made whole again." Recovery begins and ends with keeping our focus on God. There are no shortcuts to change, usually no overnight miracles. Change is difficult, uncomfortable work. It will likely be a painful rehabilitation process and will require mega-faith. Some counselors say, "Pick your pain." Both options are painful, but growth and recovery is productive. To not grow is to remain trapped in a distorted view of yourself, filled with lies, illusions, and denial.

My job as a counselor is to dive in with you and help you take God's hand, and support you as you untie the knots. You will come to:

- Understand your story. Events and memories need to be owned, grieved, and healed so pain can diminish.
- Acknowledge and understand the impact of your past and put it in perspective.
- Understand your responses to pain, and how your responses continue to impact your thoughts, feelings, and behaviors today.
- Update painful memories by bringing in new, relevant information, thereby enabling yourself to survive and thrive in future challenges.
- See where you've misunderstood the Bible's teachings about the character of God and suffering.
- Identify and expose false thoughts and beliefs, and wrong convictions through mind renewal.

The Perfect Counselor

God heals. *Increasingly research is showing a connection between religious beliefs and better mental health:* Greater well-being, less alcohol and drug abuse, less depression and suicide. He is *the* Great Physician. Our chief healing balm is God's Word and prayer. "Prayer" is an invitation to share deeply and honestly with God all our thoughts, feelings, longings, and needs.

God, through the Scriptures and through Jesus Christ, has revealed Himself to man. The whole Bible is about God delivering His people from oppression. The biblical stories are helpful because the people in them are like us. God can bring beauty out of the darkest secrets and piles of ashes. *You will* make it through to the other side. I'm living proof.

The process of healing is different for every person and goes by God's timetable, not ours. It takes the discipline of prayer, study, heart searching, and sensitivity to the Holy Spirit's leading. You'll acquire a great deal of good information and tools. But to heal emotionally and physically you must *experience* and *respond, and act on the truth of God.* Allow yourself to experience the material. When you do, something beneficial happens in your nervous system, brain, body, and spirit.

Now is the time for you to choose: to heal and change positively, or remain stuck trying to change everyone else. When you choose to move forward, the supernatural saving and healing power of God will invade your soul. You'll eventually experience joy and fulfillment. You may not be able to see God, but know His presence with you is a rock-solid reality. He loves you. He'll give you the courage to face the memories and fears. He promises you, *"Do not fear, for I am with you; do not be dismayed, for I am your God. I will strengthen you and help you; I will uphold you with my righteous right hand"* (Isaiah 41:10).

If you are uncertain about moving forward I have one question for you, *"Are you okay with living this way for the rest of your life?"* I think the answer is no which is why you are here. Hang in there. It will be worth it.

Frederick Douglass stated, "Without a struggle, there can be no progress."

Getting the Most Out of this Study

"The only way to make sense out of change is to plunge into it, move with it, and join the dance."—Alan Watts

Before you begin each day's reading pray. Throughout each chapter are *Reflect Questions and Exercises.* "Reflect" means to meditate, ponder, and think. I suggest writing out your answers. These activities provide a place to name experiences and feelings, which is an important part of healing. You may want to journal your feelings. Many find it helpful in coming to terms with the past, or processing fresh pain. Feelings and assumptions you didn't even know you had will slip out onto paper as your heart begins to unfold. Enter your thoughts and emotions, any physical sensations, and whatever comes to your mind. Journaling is a tool that enhances emotional growth and recovery. It will also become a record of your breakthroughs!

Spend time with the Perfect Counselor reading the Bible—His Word to you—every day. The Bible is not an unrealistic book, for it expresses the full range of human experience and emotion.

Always remember: *No matter how great your longing is for God, it will never compare to His longing for you!* Today is a new day—a new day when you can start afresh! Are you ready to let go of your past self and give God Almighty full freedom to live in you? Are you ready to get in touch with your personal story? *Take your time.* Simply do your best each day and leave the rest to God.

1

Wonderful Counselor

… And His name will be called Wonderful Counselor, Mighty God, Eternal Father, Prince of Peace (Isaiah 9:6) *… Then a cloud appeared and covered them, and a voice came from the cloud: "This is my Son, whom I love. Listen to him! —God, speaking in Mark 9:7*

At some time in our lives, each of us will feel overwhelmed and need help dealing with our problems. According to the National Institute of Mental Health, more than 30 million Americans need help dealing with feelings and problems that feel beyond their control, such as: problems with a marriage or relationship, losing a job, abuse, death, depression, trauma, divorce, stress, family drama, substance abuse, or suicide.[1]

Losses and stresses of daily living can be debilitating. Sometimes we need help from a trained professional to work through our problems. Therapists help millions of Americans of all ages live healthier, more productive lives. But how easy is it to find a great therapist?

In a 2011 *Psychology Today* blog, therapist Tracey Cleantis describes her first experience with a mental health counselor.

"The first time I went to therapy, my parents chose a psychotherapist quickly. My pediatrician thought she was a good choice because of her seemingly impressive pedigree. She did therapy on the Prime Minister from Israel. Even at age 10, I found this bit of information troubling and logistically dubious, as we lived in a beachside suburb in Los Angeles, and the Prime Minister from Israel lived in Israel. Here are just a few examples of her wacky behavior:

- She ate cottage cheese with her mouth open during our sessions. Her mouth full of curds gave me more nightmares.

- She read her mail during our sessions. While I get that my 10-year-old chatter was not very stimulating, she was getting paid to listen to me, and not to read what the latest edition of *Readers Digest* said about how to declutter your desk.
- She asked patients for a ride to the airport.

I wish I was making this stuff up. Should you ever find yourself in need of a therapist, know they can be harder to find than a good mechanic."[2]

For those seeking a great mental health counselor, I always say "do your homework." The good news is: We already have access to *the* greatest Counselor who ever lived. His name is Jesus Christ. He is *the Perfect Counselor.*

The life and work of Jesus provides us with deep insightful teachings, not only into how we should live in this world, but more importantly, into how to reap radical transformation and recover from our personal monsters. Jesus came to *make us* what He teaches us we should be. No human therapist can teach or touch or transform as Jesus Christ can.

Those touched by Jesus walked away from their old lives of pain, shame, bitterness, fear, guilt, and depression into new lives of peace and joy. Only Jesus can bring life to dead souls; to dead families and marriages. That's His job. Once He breathes life into us, we start removing our old grave clothes.

Just as we'd check the authenticity of a professional therapist's credentials, we too need to know about the one we are putting our trust in. Let's look at Jesus's credentials as the Perfect Counselor.

The Healer of Body, Soul, and Mind

Today we have a wide variety of prescription drugs designed to treat mental illness and ease emotional discomfort. *But what if the perfect anxiety or depression medication wasn't a medication at all?*

Many research studies have demonstrated that people of faith suffer less from anxiety disorders and depression, and they recover 70 percent faster from these illnesses than those without a strong religious faith. The suicide rate, even mortality rate, is lower for religious people than the non-religious.[3]

As we study the Gospels we see that whenever Jesus intervened in someone's life, they were cleansed, healed, restored, and set free from the moment He released His power. There is nothing Jesus cannot and will not do for those who seek Him. He frees us from the injuries and temptations of this life. He is the healer who can transform us into the people He created us to be. He is the friend who longs to be in a loving, intimate relationship with us. Everything we need can be found in Him.

While society at large often doesn't understand our personal experiences of pain, Jesus does. He's been called "the suffering servant." We may never know the reason we've had to suffer, but to God, it must be important. So, when you cry out to Jesus, you can be certain *He knows your agony.*

First John 1:1 tells us that Jesus is "the Word of life." Humans can speak and bring death; Jesus brings only life. He wants to bring life to you. When you come to Him with a broken heart and body, you can know with certainty you're speaking to the One who identifies and is the life-giver. *Do not lose hope—a plan is unfolding that you cannot clearly see yet.*

$$* * *$$

Did you know that Jesus is *the* most influential person in all of history? Entire cultures have been shaped, and multitudes of lives transformed because of His three-year ministry 2000 years ago. Why were His teachings so powerful? Jesus understood people and knew the best ways to communicate to them. He had an outstanding grasp of the human being, and that made them want to listen to Him. Jesus's teachings offered powerful psychological and spiritual insights. For centuries, people from all walks of life have benefited from His pearls of wisdom.

Scripture verifies that Jesus didn't come into the world to condemn mankind. He never approached people with the attitude, "You better change or you'll go to hell!" He came down here because He created us for Himself; He so *loved* the world (John 3:16-17). When Jesus first spoke in the Temple, He proclaimed His mission:

"The Spirit of the LORD is upon me, for he has anointed me to bring Good News to the poor. He has sent me to proclaim that captives will be released, that the blind will see, that the oppressed will be set free, and that the time of the LORD's favor has come" (Luke 4:18, NLT).

11 | **The Perfect Counselor**

What an encouraging passage of Scripture from the Wonderful Counselor and Bondage Breaker. Jesus brings the good news of the Gospel, to the spiritually lacking (the poor). He heals the brokenhearted and restores physical loss (such as blindness.) He brings freedom to the oppressed and those held emotionally, spiritually, and physically captive. *Jesus is the greatest therapist who ever lived!*

Jesus's ministry was powerful because He was unconditionally kind, understanding, patient, and sympathetic towards people. During His tenure on earth, He showed restraint, refusing to overwhelm people with a brash display of power. The people who encountered Jesus didn't need to do anything to earn His love, because He already loved them completely for who they were, despite their flaws, warts, and imperfections.

"Who Do You Think I Am?"

Like any other relationship, our connection to God can only exist when both parties know something about one another. *The route to knowing God the Father is to know His Son.* The Bible tells us that Jesus Christ, in the flesh, came down to earth as an exact likeness of the invisible Father (Hebrews 1:3). In the man of Jesus Christ, we see the very face of God. Jesus was like God—perfect and eternal—but became human for a period so He could enter the world and reveal Himself and His mission.

From the time Jesus started His public ministry to today, everyone agrees that Jesus was someone special. If you were born in America chances are you've been taught something about Jesus Christ. Jesus asked His disciples, *"Who do you think I am?" (Matthew 16:13)* How would *you* answer Him?

It wouldn't be unusual for you to know *about* Jesus, but not know Him *personally*. Maybe you've heard the Jesus miracle and healing stories in Sunday school. Perhaps all you know is the Christmas story. There's a lot of conflicting information about Jesus loaded with bias. Some teachings emphasize His love, mercy, and grace. Others accentuate His righteous anger. Some speak only of His majesty and power. More than a teacher or a prophet or a healer or a miracle worker, He was, and still is, the Messiah—the "anointed one," the living God.

For centuries prophets had been telling people that God had promised a way out of their miserable way of life. God had promised He would send someone to take the punishment for mankind's sin. That someone was Jesus Christ whom they called "Immanuel" which means "God with us."

Our lives are all about Jesus's relentless pursuit of us—to the point of dying on the cross so we might be intimately acquainted with God the Father forever.

The Man Named Yeshua

"In the Incarnation, God spanned the vast chasm of fear that distanced him from his human creation. But removing that barrier made Jesus vulnerable, terribly vulnerable."[4]
—Philip Yancey

In the Old Testament, we find God descending to speak to Abraham, to Moses, to the nation of Israel, and the prophets. After 400 years of silence, God took on a new form: He became a man, "the most shocking descent imaginable," as author Philip Yancey puts it. God found a way to approach humanity, a means they need not fear.

Two thousand years ago, the Son of the living God stepped into our world, earth (the only planet in the solar system that has human life), and lived a very real human life. His birth was not uncommon, nor was His name "Jesus." The proper name "Jesus" (or Joshua or Jeshua) was a common first-century name in Israel. In Hebrew "Jesus" is translated "Yeshua."

"Yeshua" the man is rarely thought of as a "man," in the sense of His masculinity. Yet He was a very real human man—the living God in a living man; a man who worshipped in temples, and walked the alleyways and marketplaces of ancient Israel. Even though He's holy and a God who transcends time and space, for 33 years He set aside His rights and privileges of divinity to become a human being like you and me. ("Kenosis" is the theological term used to describe this.)

I wonder how being born human felt to God? Just like any other fetus, Jesus began life in the womb of a human mother. As a baby, He wore diapers. He learned to walk and talk. He went to school and learned a trade. He had at least four brothers and several sisters (Mark 6:1-3). Like His siblings, He learned obedience to God the Father.

13 | The Perfect Counselor

I've often wondered about Jesus as an adolescent. The Bible is silent on this subject. Was it a difficult transition for Him like it is for scores of teens? What would it have been like to be in Jesus's peer group? Was He considered a sort of geek? After all, He had extraordinary knowledge and unusual talents. We don't know. We know He was just like other ordinary human beings—all the while He was God too. Mark Driscoll, author of *Vintage Jesus*, wrote,

"Jesus was a dude. Like my drywaller dad, he was a construction worker who swung a hammer for a living. Because Jesus worked in a day when there were no power tools, he likely had calluses on his hands and muscles on his frame, and did not look like so many of the drag-queen Jesus images that portray him with long, flowing, feathered hair, perfect teeth and soft skin ..."[5]

Considered a normal guy, Jesus did regular things that regular people do. He did blue-collar labor for most of His life. He spent six times as long working at a carpenter's bench as He did in His world-shaking ministry. He surely had a tanned, powerful physique, and dirt underneath His fingernails— contrary to the many paintings over the centuries that depict Him as scrawny and feminine, with creamy-smooth skin and scraggly legs; even freakish.

A real person, Jesus had a distinct personality. Ordinary like us, He experienced similar physical pangs and raw emotions: hunger, thirst, fatigue, exhaustion, sadness, playfulness, anger, distress, laughter, loneliness, disgust, joy, and agony. Those nails hurt!

When I study Jesus's three years of public ministry I see one long period of intervention in multitudes of people's lives. Philp Yancey wrote,

"Jesus used his powers compassionately to meet human needs, not for showy tricks. Every time someone asked directly, he healed. When his audience got hungry, he fed them, and when the wedding guests grew thirsty, he made wine. The real Jesus rebuked his disciples for suggesting that he avenge a resistant city. And when soldiers came to arrest him, he used his supernatural power only once—to restore the slashed ear of one of the arresters. In short, Jesus's miracles in the authentic Gospels are about love, not power."[6]

Jesus behaved and said what He did because He was on a mission to rescue His created—those who were completely deceived. Today He still intervenes. He doesn't throw the Bible at us, then tell us to deal with the world.

Jesus Christ became a man to show us the way. He brought the two worlds together—joining the spiritual and the flesh worlds in a way not seen since the Garden of Eden.

It's hard for us to comprehend that God became just like you and me. But it's true. If you sat next to Yeshua and shared a meal or conversation with Him, you would have, most likely, not have noticed anything unique about His appearance.

The Bible says, *"He had no beauty or majesty to attract us to him, nothing in his appearance that we should desire him"* (Isaiah 53:2). I've heard it said, "God loves ordinary-looking people. That's why He created so many of them." Yet, the psalmist speaks of gazing on *"the beauty of the Lord"* (Psalm 24:7).

The Alpha and the Omega

God's relentless love and mercy for us, has been and is still today, revealed in the Person of Jesus Christ—the Perfect Counselor. Wrap your mind around this: Jesus began His earthly life as a baby, yet He existed in the beginning with God (John 1:1). The virgin birth made possible the uniting of full deity and full humanity in one person—called the "incarnation." God did not merely send another prophet or angel to declare His unconditional love and truth for us—*He sent Himself.* Jesus is the incarnation of the compassionate Father. This is mind blowing!

I think of the incarnation like this: Pure gold cannot be used as a coin; it's too soft. To make the gold useable it must be mixed with another compound. To most of us, God Almighty is a mental abstraction—unless He can become real. This is exactly what God did. Think of God like the gold, and Jesus, the compound. Together God became the revelation of the Bible to mankind. Jesus was not pure divinity (gold). He was unique: divinity (gold) and human (compound). This was God's ultimate way to identify with us.

What we do know is Jesus was God in human flesh. Yes, the One who created the universe and breathed life into all creation; the Alpha and Omega, the beginning and the end. Not God dwelling in a man. Or a man made to be God. He was God and man, the two natures combined in one personality, baffling every possibility of explanation. This is how God chose to present Himself to the world.

A minister of considerable knowledge asked statesman Daniel Webster, "Mr. Webster, can you comprehend how Jesus Christ can be both God and man?" Webster said, "No, sir, I cannot. If I could comprehend it, He would be no greater than myself. I need a superhuman Savior."[7]

Who would choose to be born in a smelly barn (cave really)? He had all the power of the universe at His fingertips, yet during His ministry years Jesus was homeless (Matthew 8:20). Incredibly humble, every time the people wanted to make Him king, He'd slip away to where no one could find Him (John 6:15). Jesus's interest wasn't in receiving other people's attention; *His interest was in people.* He served.

There isn't one story in the Gospels where Jesus uses His power or resources for Himself. Instead He gives it away to people like you and me. Giving Himself away is who Jesus is.

Jesus didn't come to earth to recruit "special ops" Christians. He wanted to expand the kingdom and bring "salvation." (Salvation means deliverance from sin and its consequences, brought about by faith in Christ.) He brought it to *all*—not just the religious elite. He came for the lost: the large group of people no one else wanted to invite into their home.

The day came when He did lay His head down—on the back a wooden beam against a crown of mangled prickly thorns. Jesus did this to share our burdens and, ultimately, provide a permanent solution for the messes mankind made.

Is Jesus Really God?

"This is how the birth of Jesus the Messiah came about: His mother Mary was pledged to be married to Joseph, but before they came together, she was found to be pregnant through the Holy Spirit. Because Joseph her husband was faithful to the law, and yet did not want to expose her to public disgrace, he had in mind to divorce her quietly. But after he had considered this, an angel of the Lord appeared to him in a dream and said, "Joseph son of David, do not be afraid to take Mary home as your wife, because what is conceived in her is from the Holy Spirit. She will give birth to a son, and you are to give him the name Jesus, because he will save his people from their sins." All this took place to fulfill what the Lord had said through the prophet: The virgin will conceive and give birth to a son, and they will call him Immanuel" (which means "God with us")" (Matthew 1:18-23).

16 | The Perfect Counselor

In the man of Jesus, God Almighty took on a face, name, and address—
"God with us." Jesus was a God human beings could touch, smell, hear, see,
and have a conversation with. For centuries, people have been puzzled and
struggled with trying to understand how Jesus can be both God and God's
Son. The fact is: Jesus is co-eternal with God, which means that like God, He
has existed forever, yet for a period became human.

The Bible never records Jesus saying the precise words, "I am God." This
doesn't mean that He didn't proclaim that He is God. Take for example
Jesus's words in John 10:30, *"I and the Father are one"* and in John 14:9: *"Anyone
who has seen me has seen the Father."* In other words, "Whatever Jesus is, God is."
We need only to look at the Jews' reaction to His statement to know He was
claiming to be God. They tried to stone Him for this very reason (John 10:33).
The Jews understood exactly what Jesus was claiming—deity (divinity).

When Jesus declared, *"I and the Father are one,"* He was saying that He and
the Father are of one nature and essence. Jesus declared, *"I tell you the truth ...
before Abraham was born, I am!"* (John 8:58) (Note: *"God said to Moses, "I AM WHO
I AM. This is what you are to say to the Israelites: 'I AM has sent me to you.'"* Exodus
3:14). Jews who heard this statement responded by taking up stones to kill
Him for blasphemy, as the Mosaic Law commanded (Leviticus 24:16).

It's hard to swallow that God became just like you and me. This concept
doesn't fit our reality. Yet, Scripture clearly indicates that Jesus is God in the
flesh. The apostle John declared Jesus's deity (John 1:1, 14):

"The Word was God" and "the Word became flesh and made his dwelling among us."

Jesus's followers referred to Him as the "Word"—the ultimate
communication and bridge from God to humankind. Thomas the disciple
declared Jesus, *"My Lord and my God"* (John 20:28). Jesus received worship.[8] He
never rebuked people for worshiping Him. If Jesus were not God, He would
have told people to not worship Him.

There are many other passages of Scripture that argue for Jesus's deity.
To prove He was God, Jesus worked many miracles. The first was the
manner of His birth. The most important reason that Jesus must be God is
that, if He is not God, His death would not have been sufficient to pay the
penalty for the sins of the world (1 John 2:2).

When we human beings had fallen into sin and become subject to evil
and death, God, in His mercy sent Jesus Christ to share our human nature, to
live and die as one of us, to reconcile us to God, the Father of all.

17 | The Perfect Counselor

If Jesus were not God He'd merely be a created being. He could never pay the infinite penalty required for our sin against an infinite God. Matthew 8:17 states that Jesus *"took up our infirmities and bore our diseases."* This is only possible because Jesus is God.

Only God could pay such an immeasurable penalty.
Only God could take on the sins of the world and die.
Only God could be resurrected, proving His victory over sin and death.

As C. S. Lewis pointed out, Jesus was either God or else a madman.[9]

Reflect: This is how God chose to present Himself to the world—His real self. As we grasp His humanity, we find a person we can approach, know, trust, love, and simply adore. A picture of God's grace, *our existence is about Jesus's relentless pursuit of us—to the point of dying on the cross.* What is your reaction to this biblical narrative?

Jesus: The Author of "the Word"

It is impossible for us to know conclusively whether God exists and what He is like unless He takes the initiative and reveals Himself. History gives us some clues. We know in an obscure village in Palestine, 2000 years ago, a child named Yeshua was born. Today the entire world continues to celebrate His birth, and for a good reason. The other clues are revealed through the living Word—the Holy Bible.

Jesus is without a shadow of a doubt *the way* (to God), *the truth* (the Word) and *the light* (of truth about God and life). When Jesus declares, He is truth, what He's telling us is He is the author of the Bible. Scripture reads,

"In the beginning was the Word, and the Word was with God, and the Word was God. He was with God in the beginning. Through him all things were made; without him nothing was made that has been made. In him was life, and that life was the light of all mankind." (John 1:1-4)

In the Greek "the Word" is "logos" can be translated as "the incarnate Jesus Christ." There's no question, Jesus's words are life changing. Those words are sometimes hard to hear. They're often intended to produce sorrow over the

18 | **The Perfect Counselor**

way we've been living. It's easy to want to soften or discount those words.

Jesus said, *"It is written: 'Man shall not live on bread alone, but on every word that comes from the mouth of God'"* (Matthew 4:4). Jesus saw religion as a way to make relationship with God easier. He didn't come to set up a bunch of rules for people to use to make themselves feel good or bad. For Him, the Holy Scriptures were to be used to enhance relationships with God and others, not to give us power over others.

Jesus's words are 100 percent truth. Each word overflows with healing, love, encouragement, compassion, wisdom, and grace. His every word breathes life and resurrection into our weary hearts. God Himself tells us, *"This is my Son, whom I love. <u>Listen to him!</u>"* (Mark 9:7)

As *the Word*, imagine Jesus saying to you, "I'm living and powerful. My Word can touch your heart deeply and transform you thoroughly. The more of my Word you have in your mind, the more readily I can mold you to be more like Me. Yes, change is painful at times. It usually involves loss and may trigger anxiety. The remedy is to hang on to me—*the Word.* My Word is a lamp to your feet, a light for your path, and an anchor for your soul (Psalm 119:05; Hebrews 4:12; 6:19)."

Reflect: Do you have a set Bible and devotional reading plan? If you don't, start by committing to read Scripture five minutes a day. Get to know Jesus intimately by starting in the Gospels (the books of Matthew, Mark, Luke and John). Before you begin reading each day, remove all distractions (like the smart phone) and pray for clarity and wisdom.

The Ministry

Nothing about Jesus was selective and snobbish. Everything about Him and His followers was common and within the reach of the common person. It started with His choice to give up His heavenly rights and live among us in the same kind of flesh. He chose a nowhere place like Galilee to call home. He picked an unlikely crew to be His disciples (often called "the twelve Knuckleheads.")

When Jesus died, the temple curtain that had separated the Holy of Holies from every person except the high priest (and he could only go in once a year on the Day of Atonement), was ripped in half—from top to bottom.

What had been a symbol of the barrier between God and sinful people became a symbol of accessibility for *all*—for you and me. Jesus is still on a mission to save His created (Matthew 27:51).

The language of the New Testament was written in "Koine" Greek, which means "common" Greek. It was the language of the marketplace, in much the same way broken English is used around the world today. It wasn't the language of the educated or the elite. It was the language that everyone understood—Jews and Gentiles ("Gentiles" were perceived by the Jews as pagans who didn't know the true God; common folk).[10] Common Greek was the language God chose to communicate His message.

The religious elite didn't like Jesus coming and making accessibility to God so easy. After all, they had carefully constructed a complicated spiritual obstacle course of rules and traditions, and strict intellectual requirements—all to ensure that the best pedigree and most dedicated would make it through. Most of all, they were opposed to the types of people He included in His kingdom. Jesus refused to let them pick and choose who was going to be invited into the kingdom, and on what basis they'd be allowed in. So, they tried to get rid of Him by killing Him.

Jesus's ministry was radically different; counter-cultural. He sought only to please His Father. He wasn't concerned about projecting a "great guy" image and certainly wasn't paranoid about hurting anyone's feelings or stepping on any toes. He knew who He was. He permitted no one to stand in His way of being Himself and fulfilling His Father's mission.

The Perfect Counselor, He sought out people and drew people to Himself. Comfortable hanging around sinners, like prostitutes, adulteresses, tax collectors, and those who irritated the religious establishment, He made it easy for them to hear. Today, Jesus would ask homeless people to eat with him; and those from the IRS, and with AIDS. He'd welcome the attention of a prostitute. A gay couple could join him, and orphans looking for love and protection.

Jesus even healed people *before* they made a commitment to follow Him wholeheartedly … and one of those people was me (at age 34). His objective is to bond people to God *and* to one another in a healthy way. "Bond" refers to a feeling of connection. From His perspective, religion only existed to facilitate meaning and connection in life. Following Him was never supposed to be about "religion," but about human relationships and saving lives, as in *"the truth will set you free."*

Reflect: What emotions and beliefs might be getting in the way of bonding with God? Ask Him to show you if you're presently bonded to an object, or Person, other than Him. How are you drawing the essence of life from God?

Authentic Love

Can you imagine hanging out with God in human form? Can you picture gazing into His eyes and seeing 100 percent love, trustworthiness, tenderness, and faithfulness? Two thousand years ago, Jesus brought about a revolution—a radical and pervasive change in the world. Jesus doesn't merely refurbish the old creation—we are altogether a new creation. He transforms us into the very image of God; our minds are renewed by a spiritual revolution.

Jesus uttered these timeless and familiar words, *"Come to me, all you who are weary and burdened, and I will give you rest"* (Matthew 11:28). How Jesus longs to give people life! He is the Perfect Counselor. All we need to do is turn to Him. It's that easy.

Jesus loves everyone despite their motives and personalities because the very essence of His being, His personality and nature, is love. His love for us is not based on what we achieve, what we have, or what we look like. It's not based on how many members our church or youth groups have. He says, *"I have summoned you by name; you are mine"* (Isaiah 43:1). We are His! The most important decision you'll ever make is to accept His love.

Andrew Lloyd Webber wrote the song, *I Don't Know How to Love Him*, for the Broadway rock opera, "Jesus Christ Superstar (1970)." The lyrics in the first stanza beautifully depicts Jesus's effect on Mary Magdalene:

I don't know how to love him,
What to do, how to move him.
I've been changed, yes, really changed.
In these past few days when I've seen myself
I seem like someone else.

Many people have had a significant impact on our world. But no one has had a greater effect than Jesus Christ, whose birth, death, and resurrection have transformed countless lives for over 2000 years.

Reflect: What kind of impact has Jesus Christ had on your life? Does He fill your soul? Are you eager to learn more about Him?

Amos

In the book of Mark, chapter five, the apostle Mark tells three stories of three people desperate for the touch of Jesus. The first story is called "The Man in The Tombs" (Mark 5: 1-20). Jesus encountered a man who was naked, self-destructive, wild, and riotous, the very things that characterize our society today. Mark 5:3 says,

"This man lived among the gravestones and had such strength that whenever he was put into handcuffs and shackles, as he often was, he snapped the handcuffs from his wrists and smashed the shackles and walked away. No one was strong enough to control him" (TLB).

Mark doesn't tell us this guy's name. Pastor David W. Jones suggests we treat him as a person, not an illness. So he refers to the man as Amos—"Amos" means "burdened."[11] The man obviously had burdens.

Amos scared away anyone who dared to come near his home in the tombs. This scene seems made up to us who live in this society. But it would not be unreal on many mission fields. This story gives us some hints as to what the life of this man had been like. Ancient peoples, as well as us moderns, regard the tombs suitable for dead people, but not for the living. No one lived among the tombs, except as a last resort. In the tombs, he was free but he was also a dead man without hope or joy of life.

"Night and day among the tombs and in the hills he would cry out and cut himself with stones" (5:5). This man was in misery. Millions of people today are crying out by harming themselves with razors, glass, knives, cigarettes, and nails. "Cutting" has become a way to manage painful emotions. (An estimated one percent of Americans use physical self-harm as a way of coping with stress, anxiety, and depression.[12])

Jesus and His apostles came directly into this guy's space because of Jesus's heart for Amos. *"When he saw Jesus from a distance, he ran and fell on his knees in front of him"* (5:6). If anyone else came into his territory, he'd attack them like a wild beast. Not this time.

"Then Jesus spoke to the demon within the man, 'Come out, you evil spirit.'" The demon gave a shriek of fear and rebellion against God. "Then the evil spirits came out of the man…" (5:8, 13, TLB).

The demons had no power over Jesus. This tortured man's broken heart was replaced with a new one. Amos's tormented mind was replaced with mental clarity. The enemy intended to harm him, but God's intentions were for good (Genesis 50:20). Bob Benson wrote,

"When life caves in, you do not need reasons—you need comfort. You do not need some answers—you need someone. And Jesus does not come to us with an explanation, He comes to us with His presence."[13]

Amos begged to follow Jesus as a disciple, but Jesus told him to go back and join his community, and tell the people what great things God had done for him. Jesus commissioned Amos to be a witness of His mercy.

Reflect: "Vulnerability" is the key to empowering others. Are you willing to open up and admit your need for Jesus? Explain.

The Church in Laodicea

There are so many things I love and respect about Jesus, our Perfect Counselor. Let me share with you these words of Jesus which were directed to the church in Laodicea:

"I know your deeds, that you are neither cold nor hot. I wish you were either one or the other! So, because you are lukewarm—neither hot nor cold—I am about to spit you out of my mouth. You say, 'I am rich; I have acquired wealth and do not need a thing.'
But you do not realize that you are wretched, pitiful, poor, blind and naked. I counsel you to buy from me gold refined in the fire, so you can become rich; and white clothes to wear, so you can cover your shameful nakedness; and salve to put on your eyes, so you can see.

Those whom I love I rebuke and discipline. So be earnest and repent. Here I am! I stand at the door and knock. If anyone hears my voice and opens the door, I will come in and eat with that person, and they with me. To the one who is victorious, I will give the right to sit with me on my throne, just as I was victorious and sat down with my Father on his throne." (Revelation 3:15-21)

This passage was a revelation from Jesus Christ recorded by the apostle John after Jesus had left earth and returned to heaven (hence the book's name Revelation). Jesus is addressing a "lukewarm" church. "Lukewarm" means untouched by His gospel of love.

These folks were neither earnest for God, nor responsive to religion; kind of numb and uncaring. Jesus is saying He'd rather these people be hot or cold. He'd prefer they be open and profess their indifference or coldness. Then there's no disguise, no concealment, no pretense.

Laodicea was a bustling commercial city. The church was wealthy and complacent. The people were affluent, self-sufficient, and lacked Christ's presence. Unbeknownst to them, they had a huge soul hole they were attempting to fill with worldly pleasures. Jesus knocked at the door of their hearts, but they didn't hear Him knocking.

Reflect: When your days were dark and your heart bleeding, whose merciful hand was on the door of your heart?

The Hole in Our Souls

Whether we realize it or not, deep inside we all feel "something" is missing. People report feeling empty, a longing, which we can refer to as "a hole in the soul." They sense something is missing, but don't know what it is. At a point in their lives these sensitive souls stumble across an object which makes them feel better—a soul stuffer. Bertrand Russell said,

"The center of me is always and eternally in terrible pain—a curious wild pain—searching for something beyond what the world contains."[14]

Our secular society lies and tells us "things" and certain people will satisfy. Our need to be filled up is God-given because God created us to be overfilled by Him.

24 | The Perfect Counselor

We are designed to hold Him as the object of our deepest affections. When we don't, a hole in our soul is exposed. We can't stand for the hole to be empty so we stuff it with all sorts of things. Those things become the Lord of our lives. Yet we're never satisfied because only God can fill us sufficiently. St. Augustine pointed out, "Because God has made us for Himself, our hearts are restless until they rest in Him."

Jesus said He will spit these people out of His mouth if they don't get it together (His rebuke and discipline). These people were missing the mark, and had apparently been tepid for quite a while. They were messed up; arrogant, rich, and self-sufficient … as Jesus said, *"wretched, pitiful, poor, blind, and naked."* These people claimed to know and follow Him but didn't, at least not with the passion He desired. In other words, Jesus doesn't like it when we're unenthusiastic, indifferent, and uncommitted about our faith. When He called them lukewarm, it was like Judas betraying Him with a kiss.

Jesus called them to "repent"—to change their attitudes and ways. *Repentance* is a sorrow for the past, blended with resolve to begin writing a new chapter of life. It's a chance to start a new, fresh beginning.

His message sounds harsh but notice He wasn't writing them off, even though He left earth and was in heaven. *He continued pursuing them despite their lukewarm faith.* He didn't slam the door in their face. In fact, it's the other way around. He stands at their heart's door knocking—hoping at least some will open the door and let Him back in His own church.

Jesus "Knocks"

The pleasures of this world—money, security, material possessions, youthfulness, the perfect body—can be dangerous because they only temporarily satisfy. They can't compare to God's offer of lasting satisfaction. If we feel, or begin to feel indifferent to God, or the church, or to the Bible, then we've begun to shut God out of our lives.

Allowing Jesus in to "eat" with us is our only hope for lasting joy and fulfillment; the only way to enjoy the benefits of an authentic, real, and intimate relationship with the Father. Jesus's scolding is motivated by love, not hatred, wrath, or disgust. Proverbs 3:12 states, *"because the LORD disciplines those he loves, as a father the son he delights in."*

He was warning them one more time in the hope they'd come to their senses. The time would come when He would spit them out—but that time had not arrived yet.

Jesus wants us to open our hearts and lives to Him. Thankfully, He's patient and persistent. He'll never break down our doors. He allows us to decide which side we want to be on—His or Satan's. We can't sit on the fence. If we choose Jesus, He promises: *"Whoever believes in me, as Scripture has said, rivers of living water will flow from within them"* (John 7:38). However, if we shut our heart's door to Him, we automatically keep on eating with the world and Satan, whether we realize it or not.

"There stands amid the night dews and the darkness, the patient Jesus, one hand laid on the door, the other bearing a light, which may perchance flash through some of its chinks. In His face are love repelled, and pity all but wasted; in the touch of His hand are gentleness and authority."

(McLaren's Expositions; Revelation 3:20)

Reflect: Notice in the painting of Jesus knocking on the unopened door, there is no door handle. The door must be opened from the inside. Answer these questions:

How often has Jesus tapped, even boomed, at the door of your heart? How often have you neglected to open it?

Do You Believe?

Jesus said to Martha, *"I am the resurrection and the life. The one who believes in me will live, even though they die; and whoever lives by believing in me will never die. Do you believe this?" "Yes, Lord,"* she replied, *"I believe that you are the Messiah, the Son of God, who is to come into the world"* (John 11:25-27).

People are saved based upon what they believe. The door is closed and Jesus will stay outside unless we take definite action to open it. To do nothing is to keep the Savior and Perfect Counselor out. Recognize who it is that pleads with you to open the door. It is God Almighty Himself.

Romans 5:8 reads, *"God demonstrates his own love for us in this: While we were still sinners, Christ died for us."* Jesus came and died so you "may have life, and have *it* abundantly" (John 10:10). Do you realize that if you were the only person in the world Jesus would have died just for *you*? Do *you* believe that what Jesus said about Himself is truth?

"I am the resurrection and the life. The one who believes in me will live, even though they die; and whoever lives by believing in me will never die. Do you believe this?" (John 11:25-26)

If we truly desire a personal relationship, now and forever, with God, and if we truly want to be living off the power of the Holy Spirit, then we must know and go through Jesus Christ. Jesus said, *"I am the way and the truth and the life. No one comes to the Father except through me"* (John 14:6).

There's no such thing as a 12-step program in God's world. There's just one step—accept Jesus Christ as your Lord and Savior. Only Jesus can fill us with a sense of belonging like we've never known before.

Come just as you are—you don't have to be healed, perfect, or addiction-free. Today, by faith, invite Jesus Christ into your life. He said, *"If anyone is thirsty, let him come to me and drink. Whoever believes in me, as the Scripture has said, streams of living water will flow from within him"* (John 7:37-38). Jesus invites you to partake in the abundant life He offers. If you don't feel ready, you can come back when the Holy Spirit prompts you to. Eventually, a time will come when you'll want to give Him complete control.

Pray, "God, I do believe Jesus is your Son, and that He died on the cross to pay for my sin, and then rose three days later. Forgive my sin and make me part of your family. I acknowledge I've been living separated from you. I now pledge to turn from living my own way. Thank you for this gift, for eternal life, and for your Holy Spirit who has now come to live in me. In Jesus's name, Amen."

Imagery Exercise

"The Father is in me; I in the Father." —Jesus, speaking in John 10:38

As soon as Peter and John received word of Jesus's empty tomb, they ran to reach the tomb (John 20:3-4). Peter got there first. Peter—the denier of Jesus, failure as a friend in His hour of need, a coward before a servant girl in the courtyard; this same Peter ran to Jesus. Peter is among a group of biblical tawdry characters who were not paralyzed by their past response to Jesus. Tossing aside their guilt and shame, they ran, clung, and jumped to meet Jesus. And Jesus welcomed them with loving open arms.

Knowing the truth about Jesus is very important to healing. Recognize that Jesus meets us in our sin, but never leaves us there. You may be a person who *knows intellectually* the truth about Jesus, but you're not *experiencing* His truths, thereby not being transformed. The lie or lies must be exposed.

People always *feel* that their reality is true. So initially when I'm told that God Almighty has been fully revealed in the person of Jesus Christ, this may seem unreal to some people. For some, to imagine Jesus as a caring, loving, empathetic Father and Perfect Counselor seems unrealistic. Yet if we can create a truthful vivid and concrete image of Jesus, He will be real to us.

I suggest you block out about 30 minutes per day to help you experience the true God, revealed in the Person of Jesus Christ. If you have some soft and lyric-free music, put it on. You may want to light a scented candle and turn off the lights. Settle in.

Start by asking the Holy Spirit to help you remove all lies, and empower you to see the true Jesus. Second, pull up a peaceful and beautiful scene in your mind. It may be a place you previously visited, or a place you'd like to visit, like Hawaii—some place that will evoke a pleasant and peaceful feeling.

Now imagine Jesus in this place. You can see Him far off and He's running towards you. He's been desperately searching for you. Remind yourself this is the Person who died for you; that everything you need to know about God is found in Jesus.

Look into His face. See His perfect love for you in His eyes. He's coming towards you. Then He tenderly embraces you. He's ecstatic He's found you. Consciously see, hear, and feel what Jesus is personally communicating to you in this letter:

"My precious daughter, I love you more than you could possibly imagine. I couldn't love you more than I do right now. You're not only my beloved child, but my radiant bride! I rejoice that I've found you. I will never leave you—never! You've been lost and I've hurt and suffered for you. I considered it a joy to give my life so we can be together eternally. Don't lose hope. I know your struggles and your wounds. Your life may be in shambles, and it may not have turned out as you've dreamed. Don't lose hope. The same power that kept me nailed to the cross and brought me out of the grave, is the same power I will use to transform you, and one day forever destroy evil. My power is available to you right now. Together we're going to conquer the struggles and heal your wounds. You will shine like the sun as you recover and discover the truth. Don't lose hope! My divine power has given you everything you need for a godly life" (Peter 1:3).

You must believe that God has something great for you. Remember, He'll never be late or too early—always on time. You may hear an internal voice say, "This isn't real … You know this can't be true."

Or you may feel a sense of shame. In the upcoming chapters, we will align these lies with truth. Simply tell yourself, "On God's divine authority, I receive Jesus's words as true."

Do this exercise regularly as you encounter new Scriptures about God.

Finish this sentence: "I have hope in a new life because …"

2

The Expression of Our Emotions

Praise be to the God and Father of our Lord Jesus Christ, the Father of compassion and the God of all comfort, who comforts us in all our troubles, so that we can comfort those in any trouble with the comfort we ourselves receive from God. *–Paul speaking in 2 Corinthians 1:3-4*

Marcella was told by her pastoral counselor that she was addicted to anger. The endorphin rush that came with each burst of rage gave her a euphoric feeling of power and control, and the confidence to deal with her problems. Whenever her security or self-worth was threatened, Marcella took to her drug of choice—anger. This way she didn't have to deal with feeling insecure or insignificant for very long.

As a kid, Marcella's dad wasn't there for her. He traveled a lot and when he was home he busied himself with projects. Her mother, trying to compensate for her dad's lack of presence, became over protective. Consequently, Marcella felt insure on both sides: she didn't feel she had her father's approval, and her mom's overprotectiveness made her feel that she didn't believe Marcella could do anything for herself. She was afraid to try new things despite the fact she was a good student. Marcella hated feeling this way most of the time.

The only time Marcella felt alive was when she was angry. She didn't feel good about herself which made her vulnerable to getting her feelings hurt. This would send her into a rage. Then she'd feel worse about herself which made her even more susceptible to hurt feelings, fueling the cycle.

It is easy to see her anger was an attempt to cover up personal feelings of insecurity and inadequacy. It calmed her down and worked for her time after time. Unfortunately, the anger became an addiction. Marcella felt so alone.

There'd never been anyone she could trust and turn to for help and support. Therefore, she took the weight of the world upon her shoulders.

When Marcella began counseling she let her counselor take some of the weight off through her guidance. She pointed Marcella to Jesus, the ultimate Burden Bearer. Her angry outburst lessened as she developed a genuine relationship with Jesus. Then she became confident enough to reach out to her church family for help and support. Her outbursts stopped.

We can all learn to "soothe" ourselves when we are being soothed by the Perfect Counselor, and others who care about us.

How You Feel Matters

"Be open to your emotions, to people you want to meet, and to all situations—without closing down; trusting you can do that. Then you'll understand Jesus's teachings."
–Unknown

"I am watching my husband sleep. This is not how he wanted to end his life. He was so active and enjoyed life so much. Now he's bedridden and can't walk without help. He needs help in everything he does. This is terrible for him, but he doesn't complain. He says he's ready to die. Jesus, please take him in your loving arms and welcome him to Heaven. I ask for the strength I will need when he is gone. I have shed, and will shed many more tears. I will feel so alone. I will need you more than ever to help me. Please give me what I need, and my family, to get through this. I love him so much and will miss his daily presence. Sixty-four years together. When you're ready to take him, please do it quickly so he doesn't suffer. When my time comes to die, help us find each other so we can be together forever. Amen." –Janet Hansen

This lament was written by my mother about my father. A wise psychotherapist once said, "To know what you want, you have to know how you feel."15 My mother acknowledged the pain, uncertainty, and loneliness. She knew what she needed—Jesus.

How you feel matters. We can't afford to ignore our emotions. They are God-given and the spice that gives life flavor. Emotions provide important survival and relationship-based data so we might release the appropriate responses in any given situation.

31 | The Perfect Counselor

Our socially-based emotions serve two purposes: to signal to others, and to signal to ourselves, what we feel and need. This allows individuals to co-participate in each other's feeling, which is the intimate connection God intended.

Our emotions drive our wills. They connect us to the very core of how we experience ourselves—our vitality and purpose in life. Therefore, we need to learn to develop a competence for reflective self-awareness and exploration. Emotions have the potential to connect us to the deep parts of ourselves. Emotions are:

- Part of the inner prompting that tells us what we need.
- The basis of how we relate to ourselves and how we get to know ourselves.
- An important part of the connection to our inner spirit, which is connected to God's Spirit. Those who are unable to connect with, and name, and communicate their emotions are often dubbed the "walking dead," which is often associated with trauma.[16]

Are God's Emotions the Same as Ours?

"From the Old Testament we can gain much insight into what it "feels like" to be God. But the New Testament records what happened when God learned what it feels like to be a human being. Whatever we feel, God felt. … Only the Suffering God can help. Because of Jesus, we have such a God." –Philip Yancey

God is a personal God who has chosen to engage intimately with His creation. He loves us in ways we cannot even gauge. Therefore, we come to know Him and relate to Him as a feeling Person who loves, hates, gets angry, grieves, laughs, etc. This is how He felt about the destruction of Moab: *"I wail over Moab, for all Moab I cry out, I moan for the people of Kir Hareseth. I weep for you, as Jazer weeps"* … *(Jeremiah 48:31-32).*

Quite often we'll be required to put our emotions aside to do what is right in God's eyes. But let's not forget, emotion is evidence of life. God has emotions. We see through the incarnation that Jesus felt the same emotions as us regular human beings. He had no fear of showing His true feelings.

The gospel portrait of Jesus is that of a man who was attuned to His emotions and expressed them. One moment He was meek and gentle; in the next, His passionate zeal turned into anger, and no one dare interfere with the Father's business (Mark 11:5). Jesus wept (John 11:33-36); got angry (Mark 3:5); was touched by our infirmities (Hebrews 4:15); "deeply moved," His Spirit "groaned" (John 11:33, NKJV). Jesus got so tired that even violent tossing waves didn't wake Him (Mark 4:38).

We can assume as God-man He had fleshly desires since Hebrews 4:15 states Jesus had been tempted in every way. Yet, He rejected the thoughts and temptations because they interfered with His desire to please His Father. Hebrews 4:15 says,

"For we do not have a high priest who is unable to empathize with our weaknesses, but we have one who has been tempted in every way, just as we are—yet he did not sin."

Jesus Christ became one of us—and lived and died as one of us. In his book Disappointment with God, Philip Yancey wrote,

"If I wonder how God views deformed or disabled people, I can watch Jesus among the crippled, the blind, and those with leprosy. If I wonder about the poor, and whether God has destined them to lives of misery, I can read Jesus's words in the Sermon on the Mount. And if I ever wonder about the appropriate "spiritual" response to pain and suffering, I can note how Jesus responded to his own: with fear and trembling, with loud cries and tears."17

The prophet Habakkuk wrote this about God, "… In your anger, remember your mercy" (Habakkuk 3:2, NLT). The Hebrew word "mercy" is a form of the same word used for "womb," and signifies a warm love of great depth. In the Greek (New Testament), the word "mercy" is linked with the inner depths of a person's being (translated "bowels"). The word is used to consistently describe the way Jesus was moved with "compassion" in the face of all kinds of human conditions.

The difference between God and us is God has no mood swings, no bad days. Our emotions cloud our judgment; His don't. His emotions are always righteous and predictable; ours aren't. Unlike us, His emotions are rooted in His Holy nature and are always expressed without sin. God's feelings towards us never change; we can be fickle.

---

33 | The Perfect Counselor

What is wonderful about having a relationship with an emotional God is He understands our feelings and reactions. He created us with the ability to feel them. He also created us with the ability to transform any toxic emotions into healthy ones.

Reflect: Scripture demonstrates the triune God has the same emotions we experience. You may choose to do a Bible study on this topic.

- *Anger* – Psalm 7:11; Deut. 9:22; Romans 1:18
- *Love* – 1 John 4:8; John 3:16; Jeremiah 31:3
- *Laughter* – Psalm 37:13, 2:4; Proverbs 1:26
- *Compassion* – Isa. 49:15; Ps. 135:14; Judg. 2:18; Deut. 32:36; John 11
- *Grief* – Genesis 6:6; Psalm 78:40; John 11:35; Ephesians 4:30
- *Sorrow*—Isaiah 53:3
- *Deeply moved in spirit & troubled:* John 11, Matt. 26:38
- *Hate* – Proverbs 6:16; Psalm 5:5; Psalm 11:5
- *Indignation*—Zephaniah 3:8
- *Jealousy* – Exodus 20:5, 34:14; Joshua 24:19
- *Joy* – Zephaniah 3:17; Isaiah 62:5; Jeremiah 32:41
- *Pleasure*—Matthew 3:17
- *Laughter:* Psalm 2:4
- *Victory*—1 Corinthians 15:54

Experiencing Our Emotions

Dr. Dan Allender stated, "Emotions are like messengers from the front lines of the battle zone. Our tendency is to kill the messenger. But if we listen carefully, we will learn how to fight the war successfully."[18]

Emotions themselves are neither amoral. It is what we do with them and how we respond to them that can be judged as good or bad, righteous or evil. Most of our feelings about ourselves are built into us in childhood. If we were fortunate to have loving parents who conveyed our worth, and if we grew up in a safe environment with positive relationships with peers, teachers, and role models, then it's likely we will feel reasonably good about ourselves. We will have an emotional intellect that serves, rather than enslaves, us for the rest of our life.[19]

34 | The Perfect Counselor

However, if we grew up faced with negative influences, such as ongoing rejection or teasing or issues of abandonment, we're most likely to have a flood of negative emotions and experiences, such as fear of rejection and low self-esteem.

If toxic emotional memories pile up in early childhood, physiologically, brain chemicals hijack the rest of the brain by flooding it with strong and inappropriate emotions. In this case, our emotions will tend to enslave us.

It is important we learn to experience our emotions openly and honestly. It's difficult to have interpersonal relationships if we don't—as well as peace, joy, and good health. Some people can express their emotions freely. Some can't. Perhaps they have been taught that showing emotion is a sign of weakness or being whiney, rather than evidence of life and strength. None of us should discount our feelings.

Reflect: Are you able to express your emotions openly and honestly—to your family, friends, or professional? Explain.

When Emotions Don't Work

Suppressed emotions don't go away with time. They can turn into prolonged physical pain. When we chronically suppress and block emotions and memories, the intricate psychosomatic network in the brain is destabilized. Emotions are God-given, yet they can lie to us.

God wants us to believe based on evidence. We need to learn to separate our feelings from fact; emotions from biblical evidence. Therefore, we need to *look for proof and inquire deeper*. To believe something without sufficient evidence is unreasonable. *Is there biblical truth to support this belief and emotion?*

People mistakenly believe that if it *feels* right, it must be right. *Not true.* Our actions should not be made solely on feelings themselves, but on the facts, evidence, and truth associated with the circumstance. Feelings are data that we must allow *reason* and *conscience* to evaluate, then act upon.

After Christ's resurrection, two disciples were walking on the road to Emmaus, mourning the loss of Christ. They were joined by a stranger, who unbeknownst to them was Jesus. Jesus could have performed a miracle to prove it was Him, but instead He took them to the Word. He opened biblical evidence to them, and their hearts "burned within them" (see Luke 24:13-32).

Biblical evidence resulted in a change of emotion for the disciples, and not the other way around. The best decisions are made with *all* the available data—from both the head and the heart. If we are feeding ourselves the Word of God each day, the available data will help us choose correctly.

Daddy Holes

"God's hand that holds the ocean's depths can hold my affairs; His hand that guides the universe can carry all my cares. Our work is to cast care; God's work is to take care."
—Unknown

Carmen became emotionally, relationally, and spiritually stuck because she kept hoping both her Dad and husband would finally love her the way she needed and wanted to be loved. Many women have a "daddy hole." Some misguided and wounded parents have a way of getting us to believe we are flawed, and therefore unworthy of love and belonging. *Recognize: Just because someone is unwilling or incapable of loving us, that doesn't mean we are unlovable.*

Father hunger is a term that expresses the emptiness experienced by women whose fathers were emotionally absent. That void often leads to destructive behaviors. Studies support there is something unique in the bond between fathers and daughters. Yet there's only one Daddy who can fill our soul-hole completely.

The fact is: *No one human being can completely fill our love tanks. Only one spiritual being can—Jesus.* Therefore, our restoration is built on knowing everything we can about our Perfect Counselor. And it begins with worship; with desiring to put Him first in everything we do. He'll show us what we need to know about ourselves, the ones whom He created in His amazing image (Genesis 1:27).

God made us relational beings. We have a deep-seated need to connect not only with others, but with God. He created us to be filled by Him *first* so He may meet our deepest needs. When we don't fill ourselves with God, we will find something or someone to fill the void: men, pleasing others, work, family, money, sex, food, substances, ministry—things we feel give us value or make us feel loved—things to cover the pain.

Reflect: Are you willing to offer your thoughts on your childhood wounds and/or daddy hole? Expressing these thoughts is an important part of healing and feeling validated.

Distorted Impressions of God

"Those who look to him for help will be radiant with joy; no shadow of shame will darken their faces. … the LORD will redeem those who serve him. No one who takes refuge in him will be condemned." –Psalm 34:5 & 22 (NLT)

Seeing God as our Almighty Father does not sit well with many who've had a chaotic upbringing, experienced abuse, and/or have a big daddy hole. To them, He never had their back and they feel suspicious and distant from Him.

Some think of God as unloving and waiting for them to mess up so He can punish them. Others had a parent who misused Scripture to belittle, shame, manipulate, and criticize them, or press them to work harder to be a "good Christian."

Many believe deep down they don't deserve God's protection; that they're not special and loveable; only worthy of criticism and reprimand. Others believe since He is holy and majestic, and cannot be in the presence of sin, then He cannot be in their lives. They don't feel free to approach God or worthy of receiving love from Him. Some people have childlike expectations of God. They see Him as Santa Clause, or a genie, or Grandpa, or a policeman, even an abusive parent or enemy.

And others turn Him into a god who is understandable and predictable. Others don't see God—only His silence.

For a child, caregivers are the first picture of God. It may be hard to accept God as your Father, especially if you have a broken or abused relationship with your earthly dad. Many perceive what God is like by the way significant people in their lives have mistreated and failed them—husband, boyfriend, mother, father, and other family members.

If you have (or had) an earthly dad (or father figure) who didn't represent the character of God the Father, then God the Father becomes guilty by association. The parental voice becomes God's voice, with all its inherent negative authority.

Since most children develop their sense of God as a heavenly Father from their experiences with their human fathers, we'll start here. If you had a father who was:

- *Distant, impersonal, and uncaring*, you may see God as passive. You believe He's disinterested in you with more important things to do.
- *Abandoned you*, you may believe God has left you completely, or is present but continually threatens to leave.
- *Rejecting, manipulative, and/or cruel*, you may not trust God.
- *Pushy, controlling, didn't believe in you, and/or discouraged you*, you may see yourself as a failure deserving God's criticism and wrath.
- *Demanding, critical, and hard on you*, you may feel God won't accept you unless you meet His demands and commands which seem unattainable (which has driven you to become a perfectionist).
- *Weak, passive, and undependable*, you may believe God cannot help you, therefore, you must rely on yourself.
- *A narcissist*, you may see God as a monarch who demands you bow down and worship Him (my personal distorted image).
- *Verbally abusive*—he alleged you were bad, an evil sinner, or deserved God's wrath, then you feel worthless in God's eyes.

If we have been abused, the abuse usually magnifies these perceptions because at the heart of abuse is the misuse of power and control. And since God is *the* Power and Authority figure in the universe, He represents an abuse victim's greatest fears.

If mothers committed the abuse, the fatherhood of God can be problematic too. In these cases, survivors don't fear God will actively harm them, but they may believe He is passive: "If my earthly father didn't stop the abuse, then the heavenly Father won't be responsive either."

These perceptions of God are not factual. Far too many women believe God is angry at them. John declared that "God is love" (1 John 4:8). Because God *is* love—He is unable to *not* love. It may be hard for us to believe this because we've never experienced unconditional love.

The good news is: God's *love* can free us of the pains of life. If our earthly dads didn't validate us, show us love, or hurt us in some way, there's a good chance we'll expect the same from our heavenly Father.

Reflect:
- Have you ever doubted that God loves you; that you must try to be good enough for God?

- Do you have difficulty receiving love and mercy from Him?
- Have you ever felt fear or guilt when you think about getting close to God? If you answered yes to any of these questions, what do you conclude?

God and Our Brains

"Come near to God and He'll come near to you." –James, speaking in James 4:8

Did you know that knowing the truth about God has an impact on our brains (thereby, our lives)? It does! Everyone worships something or someone. And it's a fact: Our characters will become transformed to reflect that which we worship and admire (2 Corinthians 3:18).

The human brain is a magnificent, living super-computer. Scientists have made significant breakthroughs regarding the brain. Brain imaging today gives us a picture of what our thoughts and beliefs look like. It confirms that *what you believe about God changes your brain—either positively or negatively.*

One of the leading Christian psychiatrists in this country, Dr. Timothy Jennings, states in his research that when we consistently believe fear-based lies—for example, lies about God, such as, "He is a tyrant and doesn't care about me;" or "He can't wait to send me to hell;" or lies about ourselves, such as, "No one could ever love me," what happens is:

- *Unhealthy neural circuits* in the brain fire up and grow stronger. →
- The prefrontal cortex of the brain is damaged (where thoughts and actions are coordinated). →
- The amygdala part of the brain (processes memory, decision-making, and emotional reactions) fires up continuously. →
- *Fear* circuits are activated and *stress circuits* are reactive. →
- The result is a *selfish, fear-controlled brain.* →
- *Stress* levels rise and produce chronic inflammation and damage to our brains and bodies. →
- Love, growth, development, and healthy thinking are impaired. →
- Relationships are damaged. →
- We are prevented from living the lives God desires. →
- Destructive patterns of living and ill health.

Brain scans show that if our minds are filled with fearful and stressed thoughts and beliefs, those thoughts literally look like ugly, mangled thorn bushes. Due to structural changes in the brain, they become "strongholds," and look like cancer or abscess. The good news is, *this cycle can be reversed when we choose to worship and saturate our minds with the truth about the real God.*

When we exercise our free will and choose right, God fills our minds with His divine energy that gives us strength to break free from destructive patterns of living (2 Peter 1:4). The neural circuitry in our brains is changed positively. *"God has not given us a spirit of fear and timidity, but of power, love, and* <u>*sound mind*</u>*"* (2 Timothy 1:7, KJV).

✳ ✳ ✳

The truth is: *What we do influences how we feel; and how we feel influences what we do.* Proverbs 3:8 says to, *"fear the LORD and turn away from evil."* In other words, "Run to God; run from evil" … because … *"Then you'll have healing for your body and strength for your bones"* (NLT).

Through the Bible, God invites us to take a journey into the heart and life of Himself—to meet the God who loves us unconditionally—the God who forgives us of every sin—the God of mercy and grace—the God who wants to be our Papa and friend. *When we believe this our brains grow healthier, fear is gradually overcome, and we will live longer!* When genuine Love and Truth pours into our lives and minds, not only does fear, guilt, and shame decrease, but growth, character development and healthy thinking improves!

When we worship *the real God*—the God who loves us wholeheartedly and wants to lavish His favor, love, and grace upon us—the God who wants to heal us—*our brains, characters, and lives are changed!* Science confirms this! An enriched environment of thinking positive, healthy thoughts can lead to significant structural changes in the brain's cortex. On a brain scan positive thoughts look like beautiful, lush, and healthy green trees, and our brains are changed positively.[20]

Reflect: You are the gardener of your thought like. You can either create a beautiful flower-filled garden, or a toxic garden of weeds and thorns. What one powerful thing can you do to begin to create a beautiful flowery garden in your mind?

I Want You!

*"God has been rushing toward us with reckless love, arms flung wide to hug us home. …
So while we are crying out, "Where are you, God?" the divine voice echoes through our
hiding places, "Where are you?""—Howard Macy, Rhythms of the Inner Life*

True or False? God longs for *your* company and wants *your* love.

This is true! I bet you've never thought of God as the "jilted Lover." The Old Testament is filled with images of God as just that. The first commandment, *"You shall have no other gods before me,"* is like a marriage contract. So, when God's beloved ones break that contract, this causes Him great pain (read the book of Hosea). We all understand the tortured emotions of being loved and not loved; of being totally devoted to someone who toys with our hearts. The surprising thing is, God experienced this too.

God desires a deep, loving and personal Father-daughter relationship. He longs to draw us into a state of restoration with Himself. Remember, God doesn't hoard power over us and take our freedom of choice away as some people do. That would be less than love.

God's character always represents the opposite of power and control. God's love is unbelievable and so different from human love. Most of us cannot even fathom what it means to be loved by God Almighty. I can't. All I know is His love exceeds human love—and He loves me despite what I've done and who I was for so many decades. And today I trust God completely.

You are so loved! Yes, *you*! The truth about God is that He is never mean, cruel, or abusive. People are—not God. We must separate the character of God from the actions of bad and evil people. *He does care. He's not mad at you. He's madly in love with you!* 1 John 4:18 says, *"There is no fear in love. But perfect love drives out fear, because fear has to do with punishment."* The New King James version reads, "fear involves torment." What this verse is saying is, "There is no fear or torment which comes from God."

As you read the Bible, you'll see it is one big book telling one great story of how God has reached out from eternity into time to give us a place in His story! God says, *"Oh, how can I give you up, Israel? How can I let you go? My heart is torn within me, and my compassion overflows"* (Hosea 11:8, NLT).

When we don't understand God's ways, we need to trust His unchanging character. Replacing negative perceptions about God with perceptions which are true (reframing) is an integral part of healing and understanding God as a power we can trust.

Reflect: What experiences have you had that make it difficult to receive love and nurture from God?

Jesus Loves Me This I Know

"So we fix our eyes not on what's seen, but on what's unseen, since what's seen is temporary, but what's unseen is eternal." –Paul, speaking in 2 Corinthians 4:18

There is a story of a minister who was assigned to provide counseling in a state mental institution in Oregon; to minister to deranged, barely clothed patients. He said the stench of human excrement filled the room. He couldn't even communicate with the patients. The only responses he'd receive were groans, moans, and demonic laughter.

Then the Holy Spirit prompted him to sit in the middle of the room for an hour and sing nothing but the song, *"Jesus loves me this I know for the Bible tells me so. Little ones to Him belong; they are weak but He is strong …"*

Nothing happened, but he persisted. For weeks, he'd sit and sing the same melody and words with greater conviction each time. As days passed, the patients began singing with him one by one. Amazingly, by the end of the first month, 36 of the severely ill patients were transferred from the high-dependency ward to self-care. Within a year, all but two were discharged.

This story is an example of what scientists have found—that thoughtful meditation is associated with positive brain and life changes. *Studies have shown the greatest improvements occurred when participants meditated specifically on a loving God for at least 12 minutes per day for 63 days.*[21] The prefrontal cortex of the brain grew; there was an increase in empathy, sympathy, compassion, and selflessness; thinking and memory improved.

No fitness or self-help or medical program can do this! *We have power over what we believe. And what we believe holds power over us—the power to either heal or the power to destroy.* Will you make a commitment to do this exercise?

42 | The Perfect Counselor

Good versus Evil

Every story needs a hero and a villain, whether it's in a novel, a film, a sermon or just office gossip. The battle between good and evil is the essence of all storytelling because it is the essence of the world we live in. As an audience, we need someone to root for and someone to hate.

There's an old saying that goes, "Good and evil can't exist if one goes away." Good versus Evil is the story structure of life. The corruption of good by evil is fascinating in storytelling because it gives the audience a chance to root for redemption and take that hope into their everyday lives.

The good of God, and the evil of Satan are very real forces in our lives—not some Hollywood story. The Bible records that long ago, God's kingdom was challenged by a created being named "Satan" or "the devil," the most powerful of fallen angels. Scripture reveals very little about his fall. His act of rebellion against God's sovereign authority was sin. At his fall, Satan established a counterfeit kingdom. His motive was, and still is, to claim kingship and authority over this earth. Therefore, the Bible calls him the "god of this age" (2 Cor. 4:4), and Jesus called him "the ruler of this world" (John 12:31). Every ruler needs subjects. To gain a following, Satan tempted the first human couple and successfully carried out his scheme to bring about their demise.

Satan is also referred to as Lucifer, the adversary, the great deceiver, the tempter (Matt. 4:3), the destroyer (Rev. 9:11), accuser of the brethren (Rev. 12:10), and evil one. He is like a terrorist out to demolish, even kill, believers (John 10:10; 1 Peter 5:7). His objective is to corrupt God's holy name and the human mind. He does this by somehow perverting all God has created as good, beautiful, and moral. He hates all that God loves, which is us.

The Bible states, *"Satan, who is the god of this world, has blinded the minds of those who don't believe"* (2 Corinthians 4:4, NLT). Satan has ingeniously kept people from seeing and experiencing God's truth. Adam and Eve believed lies about God. What happened was the flow of love and trust with God broke. The result: selfishness, fear, shame, and guilt infected their hearts and minds.

Because of the fall, every person is born with a sin nature, and will experience distorted, twisted, and perverted ideas about God—which only incites more fear. Through lies, deception, and accusations, somehow Satan blocks out God's truth from our hearts and minds, thereby, controlling our minds and hearts. The result: we disobey God and promote self.

Scripture says, *"the world around us is under the control of the evil one"* (1 John 5:19). This world has its own wisdom, standards, and earthly rulers—all at cross-purposes with the plans and values of the all-good God. Therefore, we're told *"do not copy the behavior and customs of this world"* (Romans 12:2).

Where God's goal is to give us an abundant life; the god of this world's goal is to steal, kill, lie, destroy (John 8:44), and lead us astray. He uses despair to shame and destroy, to make us do things God didn't create us to do. The Bible states,

"For we are not fighting against flesh-and-blood enemies, but against evil rulers and authorities of the unseen world, against mighty powers in this dark world, and against evil spirits in the heavenly places" (Ephesians 6:12, NLT).

Few Christians in America take the Bible's teaching seriously. They believe Satan and his kingdom are irrelevant. This is like saying you believe some of the Bible is truth, and the rest is made up. If you believe in Jesus Christ, then you must believe what He said. Jesus spoke of the devil and hell more than He did of heaven or any other person.

When we believe that Satan controls the entire world, we look at the question: "Why do bad things happen to good people?" in an entirely new light. We're kind of amazed there's any goodness left at all in the world.

Jesus teaches that when we know the truth, we are set free (John 8:32). The reverse is also true. When we believe a lie, we're in bondage. Score Satan! The apostle Peter warned, *"Stay alert! Watch out for your great enemy, the devil. He prowls around like a roaring lion, looking for someone to devour"* (1 Peter 5:8, NLT). The enemy wants to eat us, and when we separate ourselves from our Christian family and God, we make his job easier.

Reflect: What have you been previously taught about Satan? If you are one of the many who haven't taken the Bible's teaching seriously or you have been skeptical, what are your thoughts now?

It's All About Choice

We all have a choice about how we will live. We can live centered on ourselves, or centered on others. We can live enslaved, or free. We can live gratifying our physical desires, or we can walk with the Spirit. We can live honestly, or live in a world of deception, manipulation, and illusion.

I encourage you, as you move through this healing study to regularly pray and journal through your emotions. A way to begin breaking down our walls is through *journaling*. Many find it helpful in coming to terms with the past, or processing fresh pain. Feelings and assumptions you didn't even know you had will slip out onto paper as your heart begins to unfold. (No one will read what you write except you, so grammar and spelling don't count!).

Enter your thoughts and emotions, any physical sensations, and whatever comes to your mind. Journaling is a tool that enhances emotional growth and recovery. It will also become a record of your breakthroughs! For example:

- What am I feeling? What am I reacting to?
- How am I responding to my interpretation of the situation?
- What are my options?
- Weighing all options, I choose to…

Reflect on what Henry Nouwen wrote: "The question is not "How am I to find God?" but "How am I to let myself be found by him." The question is not "How am I to know God?" but "How am I to let myself be known by God?" And finally, the question is not "How am I to love God?" but "How am I to let myself be loved by God?" God is looking into the distance for me, trying to find me, and longing to bring me home."

45 | The Perfect Counselor

3

Exploring Painful Feelings

It is shameful even to mention what the disobedient do in secret. But everything exposed by the light becomes visible—and everything that is illuminated becomes a light. This is why it is said: "Wake up, sleeper, rise from the dead, and Christ will shine on you."
–Paul, speaking in Ephesians 5:12-14

Jasmine wrote, "As a child I was betrayed, bullied, and rejected continuously. I believed God and most people were untrustworthy and unsafe. How could I know any different?"

Jasmine experienced a lot of painful rejection as a child. She indicated she felt loved by no one in the world, and couldn't feel love for anyone—parents, siblings, a man, or friends. The pain was so great that she constructed a great protective wall to keep others out, which also prevented her from feeling love. In fact, she could feel little besides depression.

Lysa TerKeurst wrote, "It only takes a teaspoon of rejection to drown an otherwise very alive soul with sorrow. Its poisonous flow has such a sharp potency that cuts through the skin and bone."[22]

Science proves we are all wired for love. We all want to know, "Am I lovable and beautiful?" Sadly, broken people and unequipped parents, even this culture, have a way of implying, "There's nothing about you which is beautiful or lovable." Since love is learned by being loved, it's difficult to experience it if you've grown up in an environment with barriers to giving and receiving love.

Every person's heart cries, "Love me!" Many of us are trying to cope with unresolved feelings stemming from our need for love and affection. Others are reaping the consequences from trying to connect and fill that hole.

Consequently, we have a warped picture of what connectedness looks like. When our cry is ignored or mistreated then the potential for any addiction or destructive behavior springs up because it distracts us from the pain of feeling unloved. Since we don't have a clear picture of what "normal" is, we end up wandering down many heartbreaking roads.

Starved for Love

My weekends as a young adult were spent in bars looking for Mr. Right, followed by nursing hangovers and my dignity. I cannot count how many times I woke up with a strange man, staring at the ceiling, pretending to be loved and needed and desired. *Will he want to get to know me; perhaps ask me to spend the day with him? Or is he simply another "smooth operator?" Will he, like the others, promise to call only to dismiss me? Might he actually want to start a relationship—a meaningful love relationship my soul craves?*

Then my mind switched tracks. Being repeatedly rejected in the past fueled cynical and destructive feelings: *I can't believe I'm in this place again. I feel used, abused, and embarrassed. I hate myself. This keeps happening because I'm bad.*

It's interesting how we get into relationships we don't truly want to be in, but the acceptance factor is so great (which is why people join gangs). It's all about jumping through hoop after hoop to be accepted and loved. We don't know what it's like to be loved unconditionally with no strings attached.

My parents grew up in a generation where parents didn't show their children much affection. I only remember them telling me one time they loved me, and that was when I got grounded for sneaking out. Like so many other kids who didn't feel loved, I came to associate love with pain.

If we don't feel we are getting the love and acceptance our soul craves, we'll search for it in a community or situation, like I did. What I longed for was to be seen and loved, but my quick fixes only proved to be catastrophic. The longing to be chosen becomes a life force. Once we find it, it's very hard to let it go.

For girls, if we were never hugged, then we have the tendency to run to the first guy that will hug us and stay with us. We become willing to suffer the consequences just to get a hug, a kiss, and hear the words which confirm we're important and beautiful.

Sadly, when we get into a meaningful relationship we become needy and demanding, *"Please love me!"* This is how we get into disastrous relationships so easily. What happens so often in childhood is, we have a painful or traumatic experience, but we're too young to be able to process the event—yet, it is still in our memory bank. These memories, like all memories, shape our emotional experiences, self-image, and relationships. We rarely realize they're influencing and guiding our moment-to-moment life experiences. These wordless, emotional memories come to life in adulthood in either positive or negative ways.

Reflect: Our brains have a scrap book of how our parents related to us. Close your eyes and think back to a childhood image: What facial expressions did you see? What did their eyes communicate? Their voice tone?

Self-Sabotage

One of my greatest discouragements as a pastoral counselor is when a woman chooses to halt her healing journey. Many of us (unconsciously) sabotage any progress we're making toward wholeness. You ask, "Why would anyone want to self-sabotage healing?" There are three common reasons:

"I feel unworthy" identity. A common subconscious belief I've seen surface in women is the "I do not deserve …" pattern, which comes from the lack of self-love and holding onto old hurts.

Fear of the new identity. Many of us fear losing *what we know and/or what we have.* It is the direct opposite of embracing change.

"Attention and disease" identity. Being a victim, or being labeled with a certain condition, might give us the attention we crave, which gives us a feeling of being loved.

All self-sabotage is born from the misbelief that we are less than, not good enough, do not deserve, and not worthy of love and abundance. We are all born with an innate God-given need to be loved—to have our "love tanks" filled. (Many professionals refer to our basic need for love as a need to fill our *love tanks.*)

48 | The Perfect Counselor

Self-sabotage comes from a desperate need to be loved and belong. If we didn't receive that necessary love and acceptance in our early years, a sense of rejection and hurt may be present for the rest of our lives. This creates a sense of instability and insecurity in who we are as a person.

Mark Buchanan wrote, "the perpetual delusion of humanity is thinking we are better off hiding than confessing, avoiding rather than facing, clinging to our sickness instead of taking the remedy that's freely given and readily available." The remedy is Jesus.

Reflect: Describe a time when you self-sabotaged.

Empty Love Tanks

The first people who must fill our love tanks are our parents. If we don't receive their love, then we'll feel something isn't right. We need to see that even though our genetics played a big part in the development of our brains and personalities, so did the quality of our earliest experiences with our mothers and other caregivers. We know a baby's early relational experiences, positive or negative, are literally imprinted into the baby's brain circuits. It is through these relational experiences, of whether we feel loved or not, that we come to view ourselves the way we do.

The problem is, if parents aren't keeping each other's love tanks replenished, they usually can't fill their child's tank adequately. When our love tanks aren't filled, our self-worth deteriorates. These experiences and feelings impact how we relate to others—even how we feel about God. Yet, *feeling* unloved has nothing to do with our worth—we just interpret it this way.

Unconsciously we hunger for full acceptance in our present relationships. Hence, we can become deeply hurt at even the slightest hint of what we think is rejection—even when it's not intended.

Is there hope for someone who hasn't received their full measure of love and acceptance? Yes! It begins when we run to Jesus and let Him fill our love tanks first. Only His unlimited and unconditional love can fill our tanks entirely, and thereby, correct and heal our faulty self-images. Secondly, we were designed to love ourselves. Loving ourselves is to take the time to nurture our relationship with Jesus; allowing Him to fulfill our own needs and desires.

49 | The Perfect Counselor

Reflect: Jesus said, *"You did not choose me, but I chose you ..."* *(John 15:16)* How does it make you feel to know *you* have been chosen by the One who will *never* unchoose you?

The Four Personality Types

Part of the healing process is recognizing what personality type we tend to be, and identifying our dysfunctional ways of relating so we may work to change them. Human beings generally have four ways of relating to others. Four different personality types have been identified:

Passive Personality

Linda and Tom were married (their second marriages). Tom was domineering and Linda allowed him to make all the decisions. She accepted his verbal abuse. The more she withdrew, the more controlling Tom became. Linda was very good as second-guessing every idea she had, and actions she took. One-day Tom got so angry that he hit Linda and knocked her to the ground. Her son happened to be there and moved Linda into his home. He talked her into divorcing Tom. Tom told her since she left him that legally she wasn't entitled to anything, which was a lie. Linda wasn't aware of the law, and once again, assumed Tom had the right to take everything from her.

Linda has a "passive" personality, which is defined as: "receiving or enduring without resistance; submissive." This person yields readily to someone's authority, and in doing so, does not respect herself. Some women are passive, mistaking passivity for godly submission to their husbands. Healthy, godly husbands want the respect of their wives, but they also want them to have opinions and be confident in themselves.

Passive people don't realize they have the power to control their thoughts, and instead give in to them. They often spend sleepless nights nurturing critical thoughts and indulging in self-pity. Their heart's desire is to hear positive compliments. When they compare themselves to others, they always come up short. They struggle with low self-esteem and anxiety. Studies show women with passive personalities are most likely to be raped—even though they tend to wear body concealing clothing. We tend to believe that

50 | The Perfect Counselor

women who dress provocatively draw attention and put themselves at risk of sexual assault. Not necessarily so.

Reflect: You are passive if, for example, you regularly try to gain approval by being compliant; try to avoid people who have hurt you; act helpless and let others tell you what to do.

Aggressive Personality

In the previous story of Linda and Tom, Tom was the "aggressive" personality. Most aggressors are attracted to a mate who is passive. The dictionary defines aggressive behavior as "reactionary and impulsive behavior that often results in breaking rules or the law." The behavior happens quickly without consideration for the effect it has on others. They look for people to hold power over. The aggressive person simply reacts according to how he or she is feeling. They don't respect others, and defend themselves with powerful nasty behaviors. Pride and arrogance are common attributes.

Reflect: You are aggressive if, for example, you regularly feel you need to win every argument; tell people off if they offend you; take charge when someone else is leading; regard others feelings as irrelevant to your point of view.

Passive-Aggressive Personality

Samantha (Sam) is a 16-year-old "spoiled brat." She wanted to go to a concert which her mom wouldn't let her go to because these concerts had a reputation of being "wild." First, she gave her mom the silent treatment. Mom didn't change her mind. Then she was especially nice and did extra chores. Mom didn't change her mind. They had a big fight about it one morning. Sam lost it and shoved Mom into the wall.

Mom didn't change her mind. Angry, Sam stomped out, quickly devising a new plan. On the day of the concert, Sam went to the local police station and filed a complaint that her mother had been physically abusive. Mom was picked up, arrested, and spent the night in jail. Sam was released to her grandmother's custody. On her way to the concert, Sam gloated, feeling powerful and proud for outwitting her mother.

Sam has a "passive-aggressive" personality, which means, "displaying behavior characterized by the expression of negative feelings, resentment, and aggression in an unassertive, passive way." These people don't respect others but aren't openly disrespectful. They may appear to be your friend while they're with you, but away from you, they hurt you in some way.

They express their feelings often by sabotaging. For example, Ariel's boss asked her to work late to get a job out. Instead of expressing her disapproval, she made many typographical errors, trying to mess up her boss's goals. The aggressive part wants to hurt; the passive part doesn't want to be responsible.

Reflect: You are passive-aggressive if, for example, you regularly give a person the silent treatment; enjoy seeing others fail if they offend you; hold grudges and bring up old issues; destroy someone else's property to get even.

Assertive Personality

Monica had been coerced by her aggressive boyfriend into prostitution, then got pregnant by him and was forced to have an abortion. She found some good friends who came alongside her. They took her to church and introduced her to Jesus Christ. The church offered classes for new believers and taught the elements of faith. She loved being able to explore a new meaning of life.

Monica learned about the concept of "assertiveness," which is defined as "the ability to state your own needs or defend your own personal worth or convictions firmly, without devaluing the needs and feelings of others." She took steps to escape the relationship with her abusive boyfriend using the tools she learned. She did this by asking him to sit down and discuss the issues. She told him she forgave him for the abuse, but reiterated to him that this didn't mean they could have a relationship. After "asserting his aggressiveness" he abruptly left. Monica has never seen him since. Today she is a happy adult growing in her relationship with God and healthy people.

To be assertive is to stand up for ourselves in a respectful way, while at the same time, seeking to understand the other person and their point of view. God supports assertive behavior.

Reflect: You are assertive if, for example, you regularly confront issues in a calm matter; can say no without feeling guilty; use "I feel" sentences which are firm yet loving; take responsibility for your mistakes.

The Bible Supports Assertiveness

The ongoing question Christians face is, "To assert yourself or not to? To stand up for yourself or go along with someone else's wishes?" I believe that if we examine Scripture carefully, we will see that being assertive is the most mature, biblical way to behave.

Assertiveness is so important because it affects every aspect of our lives—how we feel about ourselves; how we interact with others; how we relate to God. I recognize there are times when it is appropriate to be passive, even aggressive. (Being passive-aggressive is never appropriate.)

- Ephesians 4:15: *Instead, speaking the truth in love, we will grow to become in every respect the mature body of him who is the head, that is, Christ.* We are to speak the truth which may be hard to hear at times, but when we do it respectfully, it is easier.
- Matthew 7:12: *In everything, therefore, treat people the same way you want them to treat you.*
- 2 Corinthians 3:12: *Therefore, having such a hope, we use great boldness in our speech.* We are to be in control of our emotions and speak boldly.
- Matthew 5:37: *Let what you say be simply 'Yes' or 'No.'* We need to own our lives, and break free of others' control and expectations.

There is a classic saying that goes, "You can't stop a bird from flying over your head, but you can stop it from building a nest in your hair." One of the main objectives of this book is to give you the tools to be assertive.

Growth Goals

This healing journey will help us learn to bring our emotional needs out, and become less dependent on the other unhealthy things we've chosen to survive toxic feelings. In some cases, a doctor may need to prescribe an antidepressant or mood stabilizer as a temporary aid in the transition.

Over time, as we heal, our children can begin the journey as well. With every change, our children become more secure. The kids will see what it's like for a person to be freed from bondage and danger. As we heal, we'll become models of courage and bravery. *We can break the generational curse!*

Alan Watts said, "The only way to make sense out of change is to plunge into it, move with it, and join the dance." In the forthcoming chapters I will give you some good tools to help you do this. You will learn to:

- Grieve the losses and the past.
- Acknowledge and express toxic emotions.
- Embrace and change distressing memories.
- Become self-aware; value and protect yourself.
- Assert yourself; set boundaries; say no to what's not working.

Other things we can do is join a recovery group in our community. I suggest meeting with a Christian therapist who has experience with your specific issue. She/he can give you the tools to re-parent. Consider enrolling in a self-defense class.

Take courage. 2 Chronicles 20:15-17 gives us hope:

This is what the LORD says to you: 'Do not be afraid or discouraged because of this vast army. For the battle is not yours, but God's. You'll not have to fight this battle. Take up your positions; stand firm and see the deliverance the LORD will give you, Judah and Jerusalem. Do not be afraid; do not be discouraged. Go out to face them tomorrow, and the LORD will be with you.'

54 | **The Perfect Counselor**

4

Pain's Hidden Purpose

He reveals the deep things of darkness and brings utter darkness into the
light. *–Job, speaking of God, Job 12:22*

Renita wrote, "I'm a broken and bruised soul whose heart has become very
cold. I cry and cry. I wish I could erase the past and do it over."

When we become a Christian, God deletes the file marked "sins," but
there isn't a delete key for the files in our memory banks. Everything stored in
our minds before Jesus Christ entered our lives is still in there, written on our
brain's hard drive. A traumatic or hurtful event may have occurred in the past
(*past* merely means having occurred any time before the present); however,
the emotions about the event are still alive right now. This is because they're
etched in our brains. Think of them as video-clips that are recorded as
sensory and bodily experiences.

Our memory encodes and stores experiences that when we recall them
we re-experience them; we feel them. We literally experience again what we'd
experienced earlier. We recall them with all our senses. For example, the
effects could be fear, heart racing, sweating, dilated pupils, flushed skin,
sweaty palms, etc.

No wonder those in pain say, "Just let sleeping dogs lie! Let the horrible
memories remain buried and forgotten." It's natural to want to guard against
letting the demons from the past enter our conscious. The problem is, the
demon sleeping dog eventually wakes up!

Repressing toxic feelings and memories is the flesh's only way of dealing
with trauma and pain and sin. Yet these painful memories remain stored up in
multiple centers in the brain. They remain alive and affect what we do and
who we are. They continue to bubble up as an ongoing series of problems
and disruptions in life.

55 | The Perfect Counselor

This is when we turn to a coping mechanism—anything to push down negative feelings and memories. Suppressed emotions don't just go away with time. They can turn into prolonged physical pain. When we chronically suppress and block emotions and memories, the intricate psychosomatic network in the brain is destabilized. Our immune system is undermined and hindered from doing what God created it to do.

Going Forward: Brain Science

In this book, I frequently reference brain science (the study of the brain and mind is called "neuroscience"). It is no exaggeration to say there's nothing in the entire universe that compares to the sophistication of the human brain. I know most of us aren't scientifically minded, yet I believe knowledge changes everything. Knowledge gives us the power to change—*if* we so desire. *If you understand something, you can begin to control it instead of letting it control you.* When we understand our brains and minds, we can come to understand why we do what we do; why we respond the way we respond.

I trust God will enable you to understand and process the precise information He wants you to You may feel like you're on "information overload." Take away the main principles and ideas from the material. Don't get lost in the details. My goal is that you *respond* to the material and begin to *experience healing*.

Purpose in Pain

"Not only is it natural to expect that we will have problems in living, it is also natural to expect that we all can cope adequately with these problems. If we did not have the inherited ability to cope, human beings would have died out a long time ago."
–Dr. Manuel J. Smith

"I don't feel like functioning. Drugs didn't help deal with life. Hurting others—sharing the misery—didn't ease the pain. But I know now that with God's help and His love, I will recover." –Lanelle

Empty love tanks produce pain, which comes in a lot of shapes and sizes. And it attacks our identity. As much as we want to believe the past is gone, old hurts and empty love tanks haunt and trap us. People ask, "Why me?" The fact is difficulty, discomfort, and pain are not signs of unworthiness, devalue, or lack of love. They're part of life. If Jesus had problems, why won't we? If Jesus was beloved and still struggled, why shouldn't we?

We can go through "dark nights of the soul," yet what we have in common is our suffering forces us to face the fact that we're limited and must depend on something else to get through it. The Bible has a lot to say about pain. Emotional and physical pain, at the hand of God, has a precise impact in our lives. *The problem isn't that God has abandoned us in our pain, but that sometimes we refuse to face it with Him.* First Peter 5:10 says,

"The God of all grace, who called you to His eternal glory in Christ, after you have suffered a little while, will himself restore you and make you strong, firm and steadfast."

God is still with us—even if our troubles are due to our own willfulness and bad choices. It may feel like God is hiding, but He is very close to you. Chances are He's leaving a trail of bread crumbs for you to follow: Encouragement from an unexpected source; an accident diverted; strength to get your work done; a gentle whisper in your heart. Look for the bread crumbs.

Reflect: Pain: We must face it, feel it, grieve it, and move forward into the truth. Restoration involves healing, which is usually associated with talking through problems. It includes taking ownership for the pain we've caused others. How does it make you feel to know you must face the pain head-on? How does it make you feel to know God is with you through the process?

Addicted to Emotional Pain

Emotional pain can become an addiction!

Emotional pain addiction (also called *emotional dependency*) is when a negative feeling, such as anger, guilt, worry, grief, fear, or depression, can become so entrenched and habitual that a person cannot live without it, leading to a paralysis of life and faith.[23]

When a person is continuously stressed by emotional pain, there are subtle changes in the body which create a dependency on stress-related circumstances. Some women become addicted to physical beatings. A beating brings on the same feelings and/or euphoria that a self-harming method, such as cutting, induces.

Many mental health experts say changing habitual patterns of pain can be as difficult as giving up an addictive substance. The emotional pain addict unconsciously seeks out situations that are sure to result in pain.[24] Some are risk-takers; some self-harm. Others are addicted to pain because of the attention they receive. And I know others who use it as an excuse for a cleaning crew to come in once a month. Heck, why get well?

In cases of a broken love relationship, a study published in the May 2008 issue of *Neuroimage* suggests the normal grieving process turns into an addiction. As the griever ruminates obsessively over the events leading up to the loss, she/he may express symptoms of obsessive thinking, crippling anxiety, and a yearning for the absent person—which gives the person some type of pleasure or satisfaction.

Our Natural Response

Lysa TerKeurst, founder of Proverbs 31 Ministries, wrote,

"The pain isn't the enemy. Pain is the indicator that brokenness exists. Pain is a reminder that the real enemy is trying to take us out and bring us down by keeping us stuck in broken places. Pain is the gift that motivates us to fight with the brave tenacity and fierce determination knowing there's healing on the other side."[25]

Not recognizing how we *feel* is one of the most common and troubling blind spots we have as humans. This means our emotions manage us, rather than the other way around. Feelings are important to pay attention to since they show us how we have interpreted our experiences.
The following words may describe what you've experienced. They are all normal responses to pain. *You're not crazy!*

Fear: A state of debilitating fear follows post-traumatic stress, which can set off responses such as panic attacks, and those listed here.

Grief: A strong many-sided, sometimes overwhelming emotion, stemming from a significant loss. Abuse victims often lose: familial and romantic relationships, seasons of life, a sense of self-worth, their virginity, the ability to bear children, and their voices.

Intrusion: When a survivor of trauma vividly remembers traumatic events in flashbacks—while awake; or nightmares—while asleep. Some survivor's nightmares are bits and pieces of the event woven into an ordinary dream. Others replay, often night after night, the literal memories of the event.

Flashback: A very powerful memory that feels as if you are back in the time and place of the event. You literally can feel it happening over and over. You hear the sounds, smell the smells, and feel the touches. It can be terrifying and disorienting. It's hard to hear anything in the present. Flashbacks can occur because of a trigger.

Disassociation: Is like *compartmentalizing,* which occurs when you shut off different parts of yourself to protect a part of you from experiencing the feelings or awareness of the trauma. It's like turning your thoughts, emotions, and behaviors into compartments that you open and close at will, even though the compartments are part of your whole person.

Numbing: This involves the shutting down of all feelings. Instead of feeling pain, or fear, or grief, she feels nothing.

It takes time and work to begin to feel again. Think of your God-given emotions as hibernating. It is normal to be afraid of feeling again. Therefore, it's important we find a safe person or group to talk to. More important, we must trust the Perfect Counselor with our feelings. These symptoms can also be reduced through counseling (individual and group), education, self-care, and/or medical intervention. Dr. Manuel J. Smith said,

"Not only is it natural to expect that we will have problems in living, it is also natural to expect that we all can cope adequately with these problems. If we did not have the inherited ability to cope, human beings would have died out a long time ago."

God doesn't say we won't have bad days. He does promise,

"I will be with you; and when you pass through the rivers, they will not sweep over you. When you walk through the fire, you'll not be burned; the flames will not set you ablaze" (Isaiah 43:2).

Reflect: What do you expect to happen when you start exploring and talking about your pain? What are your expectations for healing?

Coping Mechanisms

"Life, what's life that it is so easily taken away? freedom gone. what's it in your life you're tryin' to forget? cuz getting high ain't cutting it."—Julianna

Years ago, I met a woman who walked with a pronounced limp. She fell down her basement stairs and broke her leg, yet she didn't know it was broken. She let it heal on its own and consequently had a bad limp. I asked if doctors could restore her. She replied, "Yes, but … it would be horrible. They'd have to break my leg all over again. I'd be in a cast and on crutches with a brace for 6-months, followed by 9-months of grueling physical therapy." Then she said, "I can manage just fine the way I am."

The pain of a limp is like pains that arise when we try to cope with an unmanageable event. The woman who has survived abuse must somehow make sense of the abuse she experienced. If the environment is dysfunctional, which means it is chaotic, disorganized, and doesn't function in a healthy manner—*she must alter her thinking to fit her environment to minimize further trauma.* She develops "coping skills" to help her gain relief of the tension, work through her feelings, and get through interactions with the offender. Frankl wrote, "The one thing you can't take away from me is the way I choose to respond to what you do to me."

Denial is one way we try to keep the abuse experience from surfacing. It helps us to cope and makes survival possible. For example, our mind responds with a denial technique to absolve an abusive loved one so we can feel safe and cared for. Most common techniques are:

- *Minimizing:* The event was not abuse and/or not important.
- *Hostility:* Defending the event by becoming angry.

- *Diversion:* Changing or avoiding the subject. For example, staying away from people or situations that would confront you or cause you to admit abuse is causing you pain or problems.
- *Double-minded & Rationalizing:* We hold in our minds two inconsistent thoughts at the same time. "My dad was a good man and provider. He also terrified me because he'd drink and hit me."

Other coping mechanisms to escape from unbearable anguish include: *substance abuse, disassociation, isolating, numbing, an eating disorder, self-injury, misdirected anger, envy, secretiveness, people-pleasing, codependency, rationalization, projection, controlling, minimizing, perfectionism, depression, even abuse.*

Deception and *dishonesty* are also coping mechanisms. It isn't just lying to others. To cope with pain, it's not uncommon to lie to ourselves, deny our true feelings, and pretend we feel one way when we feel another.

Delusions may also surface. Delusions are marked by a set of false beliefs in which the person *misinterprets* their experiences and/or their perception of the experience.

Darkness may produce good mushrooms, but it doesn't produce beautiful, healthy flowers! To recognize and acknowledge our coping mechanisms is acceptance —*radical acceptance.* This means admitting there's something stinky going on in our lives and deciding to do the hard work of getting the stink out. Change begins when we prepare our hearts and minds to accept the truth and consequences, no matter how unpleasant. As we accept truth and reality, and start to feel our feelings and ask questions, we begin to heal. Be aware, feelings of denial or deception or delusions may re-surface to self-protect.

Reflect: Make a list of the techniques you have used most frequently to deny the truth about your abuse and/or coping mechanism. Do you use these techniques for other life problems? If so, explain.

On the Other Side of Fear

1962: Our family made the voyage from Cedar Rapids, Iowa to London, England. My father got a new job, and we all got new lives. Although I was only in grade school, I remember certain events with great clarity. Many of those incidents evolved around listening to ghostly and ghoulish tales. That's London, known as "Haunted London."

One supposing true story I'll never forget. Our babysitter's friend, who was a live-in nanny, came over one evening. It was just us three girls sitting in the living room. She was quite upset and sad. The baby she cared for died the day before. According to her, everyone in the house was asleep when this young nanny was woken by the baby's cry. The mother was in such a deep sleep she didn't respond, so the nanny went into the baby's room. She said she observed a cloud-like figure holding a smaller cloud-like figure. The entire image looked like a cloudy cross. The baby had stopped crying. The nanny thought she was dreaming and went back to bed. In the morning, the mother found her child's lifeless body. Cause of death: SIDS (*Sudden Death Infant Syndrome*).

I'll never forget how "creeped out" I felt. I couldn't sleep that night, certain that some ghoul might show up in our house—maybe even take my baby brother! I heard more ghostly stories at school. Combine them with the nightly shrieking cat fights in the back alley, and you have a 9-year-old who is terrified of the night. I'd plead with my mom to sleep with me. Eventually we moved back to America and that was the end of my ghost phobia.

"When they had rowed about three or four miles, they saw Jesus approaching the boat, walking on the water; and they were frightened. But he said to them, "It is I; don't be afraid" (John 6:19-20).

Can you imagine being out on the lake fishing with your companions, then you notice one of them is walking towards you—on the water! No wonder they were afraid. They thought Jesus was a ghost. If a ghost was approaching me I'd be shaking in my boots! Then they heard the calming and reassuring voice of an extraordinary friend, "It is I; don't be afraid."

"It is I." Jesus told His disciples how to combat their fear: Focus on Him. He also said, *"Do not worry about your life …."* (Matthew 6:25). In other words, our Perfect Counselor is saying, "Get rightly related to me first." It is He who can calm our souls and minds as we traverse the rough waters; thereby, diminishing any feelings of terror. When we trust our souls to Jesus for His safekeeping, He will give us peace in any storm.

The Face of Fear

So much is going on around us today: wars, conflicts, persecution, violence, crime, natural disasters, rioting, abuse, terrorism, economic uncertainty, unemployment, divisions, disease, and death. We fear for our children's future, for our families, for our financial future, for our safety. The list goes on and on. Fear is one of the enemy's most popular weapons that he uses against us. Worry, anxiety, fear—they can each overwhelm us with a thick cloud of darkness, controlling our every move and decision. Yet reality tells us that so much of what we spend our time worrying about never happens.

The word "fear" comes from the English root word "peril." It is a reaction to something we interpret as a threat to our well-being. As a response to loss and anxiety, fear can arise. And for many, it becomes a way of life. It's an incapacitating emotion with enormous psychological power. The person feels trapped and unable to do anything about it. It also cuts off the body's flow of energy, and the daily function of living is diminished. For example, a person may retreat into an apathetic, lethargic condition, ready to give up.

Control, dishonesty, negativity, denial, dependency, and defensiveness are all born out of fear. Also, consider that fear, is often the reason women choose to stay in unhealthy relationships. It is a common response to powerlessness and helplessness. The problem with fear is we don't outgrow it. Instead, we tend to hide or bury it, and then try to be strong.

Fears are often expressed through nightmares and sleep disturbances. Experiencing anxiety, panic attacks, phobias, patterns of obsession and compulsion, is common. Fear evolved as a survival mechanism, but it may require clinical intervention when the person is unable to function normally. Talking about what happened can have a huge therapeutic benefit.

Types of Fear

We have two important groups of mindsets: *positive faith-based* emotions and *negative fear-based* emotions. *Positive fear* is God-given. Human beings have an instinctual response to potential danger, which is important to survival. It motivates us to buy home insurance—fear of fire, to follow the law—fear of incarceration, and to obey—fear of discipline.

Toxic fear is the most disintegrating enemy of the human personality. It's from Satan. Satan's plan is to instill deadly, incapacitating fear. If he can get you to fear, it makes you incredibly vulnerable to all his other strategies. He knows we make choices based on fear.

Three kinds of fear threaten healing:

1. *Fear about haunting and unbearable past experiences.*
2. *Fear of lack of control in the present over something upsetting.*
3. *Fear of the unknown.* Fear most often relates to future events. Abandonment and rejection are two of those great fears.

Only when we acknowledge and then give our fear to God will these deadly emotions begin to dissipate.

Reflect: Which one of these do you relate to? Or do you fear something else? Name your fears and talk about it with a safe person.

"Don't Be Afraid!"

Jesus, matter of factly exclaimed, "Don't be afraid!" This phrase appears multitudes of times in the Bible. There are more than 365 parings of the "fear not," "do not be afraid," and "do not fear." This tells me that we flawed human beings have fear-filled hearts. When some of the disciples got caught in a storm, Jesus asked, *"Why are you so afraid?"* (Mark 4:40; Matthew 26).

Human beings live storm-tossed lives. There are times when life is overwhelming and stormy for us, when there are anxious and threatening circumstances. We petition God, we seek out friends, we read the Bible, we fast and pray, hoping God will turn things around. Yet it seems He's asleep.

The most difficult question that Christians and non-Christians alike ask is the question of suffering. How can God be all-powerful and all-loving and allow His people to live in fear and anguish? Jesus said,

"Do not be afraid of those who kill the body but cannot kill the soul. Rather, be afraid of the One who can destroy both soul and body in hell. Are not two sparrows sold for a penny? Yet not one of them will fall to the ground outside your Father's care. And even the very hairs of your head are all numbered. So, don't be afraid; you are worth more than many sparrows" (Matthew 10:28-29).

Satan schemes and attacks God's children with more than fear. Condemnation in the form of oppression and depression; shame, guilt, and low self-worth are some of his greatest weapons. This world is a war zone, a battle raging against the abundant life Jesus promised us (John 10:10).

Jesus's words affirm that He won't let one of His precious children "fall to the ground" where predators lurk, without His consent. Often, He allows us to fall when we're being stubborn, rebellious, and disobedient. You say, "That's not me. I did nothing wrong. Why did Jesus let this person damage my soul?"

First, Satan is the one who leads us to abuse our freedom to hurt others and ourselves—then he deceives us into believing it is a result of God punishing or not caring about us. The devil trembles at the thought we might realize that God chooses not to control our actions and still loves us at the same time. If he could, Satan would destroy love itself.

God isn't the creator of evil. Scripture says, *"Your [God] eyes are too pure to look on evil; you cannot tolerate wrongdoing"* (Habakkuk 1:13). It is *people* who withhold love and kindness, who choose to inflict pain and abuse, when God commands them not to. Is that God's fault? Might we be sabotaging God's purpose and joy in our lives simply by believing God is to blame? One thing I know is that one day God will put everything right. Scripture says, *"Trust in the LORD with all your heart and lean not on your own understanding"* (Proverbs 3:5).

Reflect: As you studied the face of fear, what was the most important concept for you? How will you use it in your life now?

Understand Your Feelings —Understand Yourselves

Feelings are like lights on a dashboard of a car. They tell us what's going on in the engine under the hood. If the light flashes and we don't pay attention, the car will eventually break down. Therefore, if we want to understand and change ourselves, we must understand feelings.

65 | The Perfect Counselor

Neuroscience has documented that human beings are driven by what we experience through our senses—what we see, hear, smell, taste, and touch. The brain then takes this sensory experience and turns it into an "image," or what neuroscientists call a "map" or "brain map." It becomes a memory. *I will be using the word "image."* The images we collect live in us and shape us. These images are like individual puzzle pieces linked together to make a complete puzzle picture.

We're constantly weaving everything we encounter through our senses into an organized story, which becomes our "beliefs" (our opinions and convictions). The images we create early in life shape what we perceive to be good or bad, right or wrong, normal or abnormal, accurate or inaccurate.

These images are used by our minds to make sense of the world and guide our behavior. For example, when a child grows up seeing their parents constantly fighting, that will become an image which says to the child, "This is normal behavior for parents."

Think about this for a minute: *Our brains process and install falsehoods with the same efficiency with which it processes truth.* This explains why I'm a sucker for infomercials!

Images Bring About Feelings

Our brain stores conclusions it has reached about an experience, and treats the new image as reality—until it's instructed to do otherwise. Each image we collect in our brains is associated with a real feeling or feelings. Important to recovery work is understanding what feelings are. They have three characteristics:

1. *Perception:* How we see an experience we have with people, places, and things.
2. *Personal values and judgments* we develop based on those experiences.
3. *Learned responses:* With each experience, we create an image or memory in our brains, and act on them when we need to use them.

For example, Joe hurt me badly. When I see him walk into the room, or when I think of him, the feeling of anger, fear, and panic comes over me. In other words, all the images that we experienced and then downloaded into our brains are tagged with emotions.

In the case of abuse, if my image maps from childhood tell me it is normal for a husband to beat his wife when she doesn't do exactly what he asks, I may unconsciously conjure up acceptance-based feelings, even positive feelings, toward men who beat their wives. This explains why some women end up partnered with abusive men.

Bad experience → *Produces emotions* → *Creates an image.*

For example, emotions such as hopelessness, rejection, worthlessness, or not belonging, are forever attached to these images. The result: deadly thinking takes over and structures our entire world.

When we have an experience, our brain automatically takes a snapshot of what we see and finds the images (puzzle pieces) in our head that will in some way match what we are experiencing in the present. The closer the new experience connects to an existing image of what we think is good or bad, pleasing or displeasing, the more we will see the new experience to be either good or bad, pleasing or displeasing.

Take for example watching a documentary on a Stone Age Tribe. In one scene, they show the children and adults combing through the hair of the other tribe members, and then picking out bugs and eating them. For that tribe, this is a tasty treat (and for my cats). Their images tell them *Yummy!* For us—not so yummy. Our images tell us that hair bugs don't make a meal!

Good news: *Our image brain maps are changeable.* We don't have to be slaves to them, and can develop new ones.

Reflect: What do you conclude from this as it applies to you?

Feelings Are Learned & Often Confusing

What we can conclude is: We've trained ourselves to feel certain ways.
For example, you may feel a certain kind of person is dangerous because in some way this person resembles someone who in your past hurt you, or resembles a person you've associated with a bad experience.

Tara stays away from any man who has a moustache. A mustached man triggers horrid feelings associated with her last boyfriend who constantly groped her. His rough moustache left skin burns on her face causing her pain and embarrassment. For some people a certain phrase, or nickname like "Babe," can elicit the same kind of response.

For a healthy relationship to be possible, such feelings must be reshaped. Tara, most likely, won't move forward into a successful love relationship until she addresses this.

Some feelings are trying to get our attention. Feelings that persist and won't go away may be telling us that something is awry in our lives and needs attention. Maybe there's something going on in our physical bodies? Our feelings change us physically. It may take time, even counseling, for us to figure out what God wants us to see in our lives through these feelings.

We need to ask God why we feel like we feel, and ask Him to help us get to the root of the issues, if possible. If we can't figure it out after prayer and trying for a while, we acknowledge this is how we feel *without panicking* about it. We remember: He's got us! We give our feelings to the Perfect Counselor every time.

Reflect: How will you apply this material to your life?

68 | The Perfect Counselor

5

No Place for Abuse

There is a time to weep and a time to laugh, a time to mourn and a time to dance ... —*Solomon, speaking in Ecclesiastes 3:4*

"**K**imberly, there's a guy I want you to meet. His name is Bill and I think you guys will hit it off. He's charming and adorable. You'll love him!" This suave and good looking guy, that my dear friend wanted me to hook up with, was extremely toxic and dangerous. This is the guy who walks into your life, charms you into trusting him, then causes paranoia and panic, and then intently watches you fall further and further down a black hole, leaving you alone to pick up the pieces. You end up questioning your sanity.

I spent two years in this abusive relationship. Why would I stay? I didn't know at the time it was abuse. I remember thinking I deserved to be called insulting names. The criteria most people use (like I did) to determine abuse, is if your mate or another person physically harms you. It's so much more. Think of abuse as an umbrella. Each rib represents a different type of abuse.

I have included this chapter because I know many of you reading this don't recognize you're in an abusive relationship, or that you carry the scars from childhood or some type of abuse. I urge you to continue to read this chapter, if not for yourself, for someone else. You could save a life.

* * *

Were you aware that rape and abuse goes back to biblical days? You might be surprised to know there is a story of incestual rape is found in 2 Samuel 13. As the beautiful royal princess, and daughter of a highly respected godly king, Tamar's life should have been a fairy tale. Instead, it became a nightmare.

She had a spoiled and deceitful half-brother, Amnon, who lusted after her and then raped her. His lust quickly changed to hatred.

Today abusive relationships are surprisingly common—from childhood abuse, to intimate partner violence, to date rape and sexual assault. If you're not an abuse victim/survivor, chances are you know at least one person who is. If you've been blessed to not have experienced abuse, I encourage you to read this chapter as you can to use the information to help someone else.

Tamar's story doesn't end there. Scripture says,

"Then Amnon hated her with intense hatred. In fact, he hated her more than he had loved her. Amnon said to her, "Get up and get out!" "No!" she said to him. "Sending me away would be a greater wrong than what you have already done to me." But he refused to listen to her. He called his personal servant and said, "Get this woman out of here and bolt the door after her." (2 Samuel 13:15-17)

Rape was, and still is, strictly forbidden by God (Deut. 22:28). In that culture the law mandated when a man raped an unmarried woman he pay a dowry, marry, and never divorce her. Tamar was telling Amnon that by sending her away and not marrying her, he was destroying her future. Grieving, she tore her robe (a symbol of her virginity) and wept loudly.

Tamar's father, King David, was furious at Amnon, but did nothing; no rebuke or punishment. I find it interesting that Absalom, another brother, discounted her emotions by saying, *"Be quiet now, my sister, he is your brother. Don't take this thing to heart"* (13:20)—yet, later he took matters into his own hands. Absalom avenged Tamar by killing Amnon, though it resulted in many problems for himself. Absalom lived away from his family for five years before seeing his father's face. He would later seek to seize his father's throne, resulting in his own death.

This tragic story highlights some of the problems associated with sexual sin and its aftermath. *No one* should experience what Tamar endured. It is important to respond to such situations with truthfulness and justice. King David neglected justice, and Absalom implemented his own justice, creating additional problems in the process.

What happened to Tamar? Being raped by her brother and called "this woman" instead of her given name, and then being physically thrown out by a servant, no doubt, made her feel like damaged goods. A gigantic stronghold of shame, perhaps even hate, possibly consumed her. We assume she took this to her grave.

Despair often involves a crisis of faith and trust in God. The Bible says she lived in Absalom's house a ruined and desolate woman. She never married or had children. *Ruined. Desolate.* Tamar lost hope. Did she suffer from PTSD? Did she ever know God had a wonderful plan for her life?

The story of Tamar begs us to reflect on rape myths of today, such as, *She wanted it. Guys can't control their urges. If she didn't scream or fight back, it wasn't rape. She didn't say no. Her clothes said she was willing.* The voice of the enemy fans the flames of despair: *Look at what you did! Can there be anything worse? There's no hope for you now. You are nothing—beyond redemption.*

Reflect: What is your reaction to this biblical story?

Abuse Is Trauma

Abuse is trauma. Abuse comes from a place or power, or *perceived* power. The abuser need only be *perceived* as someone who has power and authority, and is in a place of leverage, whereby their actions and words wound. "Trauma" is defined as any *experience or situation that is emotionally painful and distressing, overwhelming the person's ability to cope, leaving her/him powerless.*

Many of you can identify with Tamar. You can relate to her feelings of powerlessness; of silence. You know what it's like to be victimized in the place which should have been a place of safety and security. You know what it means to have those who should have protected you hand you over to save themselves. You know what it feels like when an abuser transfers their guilt and shame onto you—it gets twisted into despair. *You are not alone!* The facts and statistics are staggering:

- 1 in 3 females is sexually abused by the age of 18.
- A woman is beaten every 15 seconds in America.
- 1 in 5 females have been assaulted.[26]
- 1 in 5 females are raped (compared to 1 in 71 males).
- 48% of all rapes involve a young female under the age of 18.[27]
- 1 in 4 females experience Domestic Violence (a.k.a. Intimate Partner Violence); women ages 20 to 24 are at the greatest risk.[28]
- Abusive men who kill their partners often do after they're separated or divorced.

- *Over* 39 million adults in the US survived childhood sexual abuse.
- Every 47 seconds a child is abused or neglected; every 5.5 hours a child is killed by abuse or neglect.[29]
- 10 million children witness domestic abuse each year.
- Female child abuse survivors are more likely to be re-victimized in adulthood.
- Childhood sexual abuse is a contributor in child prostitution.[30]
- Physical and sexual abuse are primary factors in adolescents running away and becoming homeless, and contributes to youth suicide.[31]
- 52% of abused victims consider suicide.
- The abused make more (20-26%) suicide attempts.

These numbers represent reported and confirmed experiences. Far more suffer in silence. For example:[32]

- 84% of rape victims do not report the rape to police.
- Only 5% of college women reported a sexual assault.

Reflect: As you think about your own abuse experiences, how do these statistics speak to you?

Different Forms of Abuse in Relationships

One of the main reasons abuse is so damaging is because God wired human beings for relationships. Human beings are designed to be social, and driven to stay connected to family, friends, and God. Our identities are formed from the groups we belong to. In fact, the pleasure centers of our brain light up when we're in nurturing relationships! Research shows that rejection and abuse in a relationship leaves a lasting imprint in our minds and bodies. This drive to stay relationally connected is so strong that it can lead to dysfunctional thinking and behaviors that only make sense to the person.[33]

Abuse is real. When I use the term "abuser" I'm speaking of a person who has recurring problems with disrespecting, controlling, insulting, or devaluing their partner or another person. Whether his/her behavior involves obvious verbal abuse, physical aggression, or sexual misconduct, these behaviors have a serious impact on a person's life.

Abuse can lead a girl/woman to feel confused, depressed, anxious, afraid, and even suicidal. It's a subtle trap in which the ones who perpetrate the abuse on others are just as trapped in unhealthy beliefs and actions as those they knowingly and unknowingly abuse. Abusive people take a victim's mind captive. They don't allow them to disagree with or criticize them. Over time abusers teach victims new information, and the victim's mind falls into their subtly devised traps. The cumulative effect of repeatedly rejecting one's own desires, and the continual pressure to conform causes severe pain and emotional distress.

God is against whatever destroys us, which includes abuse of any kind. *Abuse is sin.* God is outraged because His divine law, and the human soul and personality which He created, *in His image*, are dishonored and violated. To recover from abuse, the person needs to hear and believe the truth.

Exercise: As you go through each type of abuse, either highlight or underline your experiences.

Emotional/Psychological Abuse

When learning about the different types of abuse, keep in mind that each one overlaps with *emotional abuse, which by far causes the greatest harm.* Emotional abuse tactics are *non-physical* and *non-verbal behaviors* intended to manipulate, coerce, intimidate, threaten, undermine, and confuse—anything that interferes with our independence, and is aimed at discrediting and silencing us. It is a pattern of intentional affliction of emotional hurt onto another person. Emotional abuse is difficult to prove and is *often mistaken for normal marriage conflict*, but is the opposite of love.

"Brainwasher" is a word that describes an emotional abuser. "Terrorist" is another. A pastor described a woman suffering from emotional abuse, "Inside her soul the woman has black eyes, bloodied lips, and broken bones. She is being ignored. Overlooked. Rebuked. Shamed. Chastised."

Common behaviors include: constant monitoring, stalking, watching, harassing; threatening to hurt or kill family members, controlling what one does, trying to make one think she/he is crazy by playing mind games, withholding intimacy, giving out the silent treatment. Other behaviors include minimizing, denying, blaming, humiliating, or using children.

73 | The Perfect Counselor

An abuser may use visitations to harass you, use your kids to relay messages, tell them horrible things about you, or threaten to take the children away; or make you feel bad about your parenting skills.

Manipulation is common. Comments like, "You're too sensitive," "You're angry because you're not getting your way, so you say I'm hurting you," You think everyone is abusing you," are tactics to get the victim to doubt herself.

Guilt is a powerful motivator. Once an abuser plants seeds of guilt, he doesn't need to physically prevent a person from certain actions, like leaving, because their own guilt will do this. In other words, the victim turns her guilt against herself.

Digital abuse uses technology to control, such as excessive texting, sexting, and using social networking to bully, harass, stalk, manipulate, or intimidate.

Abandonment/Neglect: When we think of abandonment, we think of neglect; when a parent or guardian fails to meet a child's basic physical needs. 1 Timothy 5:8 says, *"If anyone does not provide for his relatives, and especially for his immediate family, he's denied the faith and is worse than an unbeliever."*

Abandonment can also be emotional abuse—and can cause the same emotional damage as all the other types of abuse. This kind of abuse, called "emotional abandonment," involves someone in a position of power and responsibility failing to act morally and legally, and failing to provide the child or adolescent with adequate emotional support. Emotional abandonment can be difficult to recognize. Children are good at convincing themselves they don't need anything, and their home is just fine.

Isolation: Using manipulation to keep a person away from all healthy connections such as family and friends, or preventing them from participating in work, school, church, or other independent activities. An abuser usually wants the person home where she can be watched and controlled; where she becomes more dependent upon him.

Financial/Economic: Using money or access to accounts to exert power and control; interferes with the ability to get or keep a job, or go to school.

Verbal Abuse

"Each verbal battle with an abuser is a walk through a minefield, and each field is different" (Lundy Bancroft).

"With the tongue we curse human beings, who have been made in God's likeness" (James 3:9). A "curse" is an offensive and/or a profane assertion intended to hurt the person. Abusers tend to verbally attack their partners in disturbing, degrading, and revolting ways. The words assault the person's dignity and humanity.

All criticism is destructive. Vicious verbal attacks shame and make a person unable to think things through, or see issues clearly. The abuser may call it "constructive criticism," but she hears it as destructive judgment.

The Bible speaks about the destructive power of words as having *"the power of life and death"* and *"crushes the spirit"* (Proverbs 15:4). The Bible says, *"There must not be even a hint of ... obscenity, foolish talk or coarse joking"* (Ephesians 5:3-4). Verbal abuse always leaves scars. Studies indicate the brain cannot distinguish emotional pain from physical pain. Words can hurt as much as sticks and stones. Literally, words can either intensify or relieve stress. Verbal abusers use words which attack, interrogate, injure, criticize, insult, confuse, threaten, demean, and degrade (yet they may be charming in public). Often a critical attitude or "wicked tongue" is a mask for a deep sense of despair.

Physical Abuse

Would it surprise you to know that many men say they feel *entitled* to use violence?[34] Physical abuse is the use of physical force with the intent to cause fear or injury; like hitting, shoving, biting, strangling, kicking, or using a weapon. Research states that physical experiences lead to changes in every part of our bodies (bones, blood, muscles, tissue and brain structure). First Corinthians 6:19-20 says, *"... your body is a temple of the Holy Spirit within you, whom you have from God."* (See also: Psalm 11:5; Proverbs 1:15-19.)

Research indicates a woman's intuitive sense of whether her partner will be violent with her and/or her children is a substantially more accurate predictor of future violence than any other warning sign. So, listen closely to your intuition.

Property and Intimidation: Destroying property; hiding, or throwing out personal things; slamming doors, using threatening body language, not allowing a person to speak; kicking, throwing, hurting a pet in any way, or threatening to do so. (Behavioral specialists say if an abuser kills a pet, consider the person very dangerous.)

75 | The Perfect Counselor

Sexual Abuse (includes Rape and Sexual Assault)

Sexual abuse is the exploitation of another person through sexual contact, or coerced non-consensual sexual contact. It is ignoring someone's refusal to engage in sexual activities by repeatedly using emotional, verbal, or physical pressure. Sadly, rape/sexual assault is so stigmatizing that many women do not report it. If your partner doesn't physically or verbally assault you, but does rape or sexually coerce you repeatedly, it is sexual abuse.

Sexual abuse includes: unwanted touch or forcing the victim to touch the abuser's sexual parts, affairs, sexual jokes, pornography, exhibitionism; insisting the person dress erotically, prostitution. It also includes restricting access to birth control or condoms, non-disclosure of STD/HIV status, forcing or terminating a pregnancy.[35] It has been said that 10 people are affected by one person's sexual abuse.

Sexual sin (includes sexual immorality) causes damage far beyond anything else. Demanding sexual acts which are offensive is disrespectful and demeans a person's dignity. A woman who was sexually violated carries a burden she wasn't designed to carry. It's too heavy. I can tell you from personal experience, once that sacred boundary has been crossed, there's no un-doing what she's been forced to do; no going backwards. As she moves in adulthood it becomes hard to separate love from sex. She will often gravitate toward emotionally and abusive unavailable men because they are sickeningly familiar to her.

Many women say their husbands for them to have sex with them. Forced sex is just another kind of abuse. *The Bible makes a strong differentiation between sex that enriches the human spirit and that which degrades it.* Sex is the most powerful bonding activity (Matthew 19:6). It must be used reverently and with caution. It is one of God's greatest gifts. For it to be a blessing between two people it means that both people are fully consenting, and that it takes place in a context of respect, choice, and regard for each other's well-being. The Bible is clear that each partner holds power over the body of the other. Each is to show respect for the other (1 Corinthians 7:3-4).

The sexually abused feel a great deal of shame. The victim, not the offender, carries the guilt. The feelings of shame are amplified each time the person is emotionally and/or verbally abused; such as being degraded or condemned in some way.

Sex Trafficking: The recruiting, transporting, transferring, holding, and/or receiving a minor for exploitation; sex is exchanged for money and amenities.

Dr. Stephen Tracy stated that trafficked girls are sexually exploited and sexualized in more extreme ways. He stated,

"They are repeatedly sexually and physically assaulted (often by a trusted adult), dressed, and taught to act in sexual ways, unprotected from pornography and other media images that depict women in sexually subservient roles to men, and often prostituted."

He stated, "It doesn't' take long for this sexualization to become her new identity and she in effect goes on to sexualize herself."[36]

Spiritual Abuse

Spiritual abuse is a real phenomenon that happens in the body of Christ. It is any kind of deception and manipulation that damages a person's relationship with God; it harms or overloads people with spiritual weights. When God, the Bible, and/or faith is used to distort, weaken, or destroy a person's sense of self, spiritual abuse is present.

A spiritual abuser may or may not be a religious leader. Spiritual abusers feed people lies and take away their choices. The motivation is not spiritual enlightenment but spiritual enslavement.

Abuse occurs when a *person in a position of spiritual authority,* such as a minister, misuses that authority to control, degrade, shame, coerce, or manipulate for seemingly God's purposes, which are just their own. One manipulation method is when a leader imparts "words of knowledge or wisdom from God." Their words do not carry the same authoritative weight as those of the Bible authors, which are the very Word of God. And the fact that someone reads the Bible to us doesn't mean they have a specific word from God for us. Any word from God, whether from Scripture or other, will be confirmed by the Holy Spirit who lives in us. Until He confirms it, we should be reluctant to take "the word from the Lord."[37]

My husband and I left a church in crisis for these very reasons. Sadly, many of the "sheep" didn't have the know-how or tools for overcoming persuasive, deceptive teachings, and practices, and fell to leadership's tactics.

The second type of spiritual abuser may be a *non-clergy person* who, for example, disallows attending church/faith services, questions the person's

Salvation and beliefs, misuses and quotes verses out of context to manipulate, or makes false accusations to the pastor. God's Word is often misused to minimize a person's pain and excuse their offender.

Abuse and Alcohol/Substances

The role that alcohol, drugs, and other addictions play in abusive behavior is often misunderstood. Most abusers are not addicts, and of those who do abuse substances still mistreat their partners, even when they're not under the influence. Abusers who successfully complete an addiction recovery program continue to abuse.

However, we do know alcohol and drug abuse can make matters worse. When an abuser is under the influence, the risks of abuse are quite often amplified, leading to a more deeply troubling situation. Alcohol encourages people to let loose what they've had simmering below the surface. It can act like "truth serum." Addiction can certainly contribute to cruelty and volatility.

Lundy Bancroft, has counseled over 2000 abusive men. He is the author of a bestseller, *Why Does He Do That?* As an expert in this field, he is adamant,

"Addiction does not cause partner abuse, and recovery from addiction does not cure partner abuse. ... Alcohol does not directly make people belligerent, aggressive, or violent. There is evidence that certain chemicals can cause violent behavior—anabolic steroids or crack cocaine, for example—but alcohol is not among them. In the body, alcohol is a depressant, a substance that rarely causes aggression. Marijuana similarly has no biological action connected to abusiveness.

"Alcohol does not change a person's fundamental value system. Abusers make conscious choices even while intoxicated. For example, after a few drinks, he turns himself loose to be as insulting or intimidating as he feels inclined to be, knowing he can say, "Sorry. I was really trashed last night." He uses his alcohol abuse as an excuse. People's conduct while intoxicated continue to be governed by their core foundation of beliefs and attitudes."[38]

While substance addiction does not *cause* a person to become abusive, it ensures the abusiveness *remains.* Far too often substance abuse blocks the self-examination process. An abuser will most likely not make any significant changes in his behavior until he simultaneously deals with his substance abuse. These are two distinct problems which require two distinct solutions.

* * *

Controlling people fall on a spectrum of behaviors. Let's say your partner's behavior doesn't fit any of the definitions of abuse, it may still have a serious effect on you. Any coercion or disrespect by an intimate partner is a problem. One of the best ways to tell how deep a person's control issues go is by observing how he/she reacts when you demand they treat you better. If they accept your grievance and take steps to change, prospects are good.

Reflect: What is the value of learning about these types of abuse and highlighting your own personal abuse experiences?

Stockholm Syndrome

Why do people remain in abusive relationships? It's a common question. Have you ever been to a circus and seen an elephant restrained by a piece of rope to a small wooden stake? This is only possible because the elephant has been held captive since a baby.

Eleven-year-old Jaycee Lee Dugard was abducted from a school bus stop (1991). She went missing for over 18 years. Jaycee had two daughters by her abductor. Most people wonder why she didn't run away when she had the opportunity. The answer: she couldn't—not without help. Psychologists have a term to explain this phenomenon: *Stockholm syndrome.*

Stockholm syndrome is a psychological response described as *an emotional bonding with an abuser as a survival strategy.* A victim who was abducted and then sexually and emotionally abused may see the captor as a great person with whom she's formed an emotional bond with. It is also called "loyalty bonds," "trauma bonding" or "betrayal bonds." These bonds are extremely heavy-duty and resilient. If someone holds your life in their hands, they are a very powerful person to you. Pleasing this person, the abductor, becomes critical. The abductee doesn't resist and shows signs of loyalty or caring for the person who took them. They do so despite the dangerous and harmful things the abductor does to them. At times, she believes the captor is protecting her instead of harming and dominating her.

We can use this term, Stockholm syndrome, to understand why a person doesn't leave or report their abuser. The abductor makes the person do many things she doesn't want to do by taking hold of her mind (brainwashing). She feels powerless. And the abductor offers her a false sense of protection.

79 | **The Perfect Counselor**

The person held captive creates an identity around the abductor. She won't let go despite the fact the abuser is harmful, even potentially lethal. She'll even defend him/her when other people show concern. Over time she believes the abductor is helping, not hurting her. In a perverse way, the more severe and dangerous the abuse, the stronger the loyal bond is. The person may even continue in this mode long after the events pass.

Reflect: If you have been abused, what did your abductor promise you? What did he/she steal from you (emotionally, relationally, physically, or spiritually)?

Three Levels of Trauma

"Trauma shocks the brain, stuns the mind, and freezes the body. It overwhelms its unfortunate victims and hurls them adrift in a raging sea of torment, helplessness, and despair."[39] –Dr. Peter A. Levine

Abuse in any form causes a crisis in a person's life. It makes her feel overwhelmed, powerless, and out of control. All the familiar ways of managing and dealing with the world don't work any longer. Sexual assault and rape can be the worst life crisis a person ever faces because sexuality is so sacred. It violates every facet of the person's soul. The abused usually experience three levels of trauma:

Level 1: The original trauma, for example, sexual assault.

Level 2: Secondary wounding or compounded trauma, such as your loved ones not believing or discounting, or even blaming you (lack of social and emotional support). Each person's action in Tamar's story "added injury to insult." Then you believe you did something to deserve the assault. On the other hand, if we don't tell anyone we wound ourselves with self-condemnation and fear. The people around you may think the abuser is the greatest person and refuse to believe you, but remember—*God knows the truth.*

Level 3: Society's view of the trauma, which holds the victim responsible for what has happened and/or treats her as 'contaminated.'

Responses number 2 & 3 can add to the damage of the actual abuse, called "re-victimization."

Reflect: What actions happened to you after your situation that you consider to be secondary wounding? How did this make you feel damaged?

Abuse and Abuse of Power

"Abuse" is a repetitive act of violation and domination to maintain power and control over a person. With abusers, the act of abuse is not their goal—*power and control* is their goal. It's what makes them feel good and entitled to.

"Abuse of power" is when someone in a position of authority violates another person's freedom and rights. Tactics include: intimidation of physical size, confinement, isolation; restricting and controlling privacy, relationships, and personal belongings.

Can you say your experience has made you feel like you've gone crazy? Yes! You're not alone. "Crazy making" through power and control is one popular abuser tactic. This is when a person intentionally distorts reality, often through lies and deception, all to bring about a reaction—and then deny that it ever took place. They suck you into petty, ridiculous, and pointless conversations that make you feel insane.

"Domestic violence," also known as *intimate partner violence,* or *domestic abuse,* or *family violence,* is a pattern of coercive and abusive behavior used by one person to control and oppress another person in an intimate relationship. Some studies state that one in four women, others say one in three women, have experienced domestic violence in an intimate relationship. Regrettably, this number is no lower in our church communities.

Let's define "violence." Violence is behavior that does:

- Physically hurts or frightens; uses contact with your body to control or intimidate.
- Takes away freedom of movement and independence, such as locking you in a room.
- Causes you to believe you will be physically harmed.
- Forces you to have sexual or other unwanted physical contact.

You ask, "Is it violence if he says he'll slam my head into the wall, but never does?" Yes! You say, "He was verbally abusing me so I slapped him. He then punched me in the face and said it was self-defense." It was not self-defense; it was revenge. Abusive men in intimate relationships are more likely to abuse when they perceive their partner's behavior as threatening their damaged sense of self. They have a greater tendency to use force when they perceive their power is challenged.

Many men who "batter" experienced or witnessed abuse in their own childhood and have developed distorted values. Most people don't understand the complexities of domestic abuse, like why women stay in a relationship with an abuser. Women stay for a multitude of reasons. One chief reason is their *inability to recognize that abuse is killing them*. Like sandpaper, an abuser will wear away at a person's self-esteem through a calculated cycle.

Victim's excuse their abuser's behavior, unable to acknowledge the painful truth that something is very wrong. The picture that develops is one of a *powerless person* and an *abusive system* that fit together. She is literally powerless to leave and is trapped. Often the victim's standards fall so low that she becomes grateful for mediocre or bad treatment.

The Boiling Frog

The cycle of abuse is like the boiling frog story: place a frog in boiling water, it will jump out. But if you place it in cold water that is slowly heated, it won't perceive the danger and will be cooked to death. Once an abused woman gets to the point where she recognizes its devastating effects, she's usually already experienced a great deal of pain and loss, and the harder it is to remove herself, for these reasons:

- The more time the abuser has to break down her self-worth, the more she believes she doesn't deserve any better treatment.
- The more emotional, physical, relational, and spiritual damage that is done, the more likely her energy and initiative is to diminish, then she is too drained to get out.
- The more damage the abuser does to her relationships, the less support she will have for the hard process of ending the relationship.
- The longer she lives in the cycle of abuse, the more attached she will feel to the abuser.

Reflect: How do you relate to the boiling frog story? Name some ways you've blamed yourself for any abuse you've incurred. What kind of self-talk messages has this created? List them. These are your unspoken beliefs; your reality. The reality is, these are lies which have come out of the mouth of a master manipulator.

How Do I Know When My Partner Is Being Abusive? When is It Abuse?

Most couples yell at one another at some time, or call each other a name, or interrupt, or act selfish and insensitive. These behaviors are worthy of looking at, but are not necessarily "abuse." However, these behaviors are abusive when they become part of a *pattern*; when controlling, disrespectful, or degrading behavior happens repeatedly.

Recall, abuse is about power, which means that one person is taking advantage of a power imbalance to exploit or control another person. The point of abuse begins when one person starts to exercise power and control over another person in a way that causes harm to her, and creates "entitlement" or status for the abuser.

Do you show signs of being abused? Answer these questions:[40]

- Are you afraid of him? Has he ever threatened you?
- Are you getting distant from your friends or family because he makes those relationships difficult?
- Is your level of energy and motivation declining (feel depressed)?
- Is your self-opinion declining; you're always fighting to be good enough and to prove yourself?
- Do you find yourself constantly preoccupied with the relationship and how to fix it?
- Do you feel like you can't do anything right?
- Do you feel that all the relationship problems are your fault?
- Do you repeatedly leave arguments feeling like you've been messed with (crazy) but can't figure out why?
- Has he ever trapped you in a room or another place?
- Has he ever raised a fist as if he was going to hit you?

- When you feel hurt or confused after a confrontation, what do you think he was trying to get out of it (the benefit for him)?

If you answered yes to any of the questions, you're probably involved with an abusive partner.

It's not always easy to figure out who has the power in a dysfunctional system. Remember this: The abuses committed against us, whether physical, sexual, verbal, or emotional, are not our sins. Those sins belong to the offender/abuser. Despite what your abuser, or a person covering for the abuser, may have told you, *you did not deserve the abuse, or do anything to warrant it. You're not responsible.* And let me also say, anyone, Christians included, has the right to question authority. Galatians 5:1 states,

"It is for freedom that Christ has set us free. Stand firm, then, and do not let yourselves be burdened again by a yoke of slavery."

84 | The Perfect Counselor

6

The Grief We Call PTSD

Then they cried to the LORD in their trouble, and he delivered them from their distress. He brought them out of darkness and the shadow of death, and burst their bonds apart. Let them thank the LORD for his steadfast love, for his wondrous works to the children of man! *–Psalm 107:13-15*

On a cold night in November, 2004, six teenagers in New York bought a 20-pound turkey with a stolen credit card. While driving on a highway, 18-year-old Ryan Cushing threw the frozen bird out the back window for a thrill. The turkey hit Victoria Ruvolo's car, crushing the windshield and then her face. She sustained life-threatening injuries. She needed countless surgeries to rebuild her shattered face.

When a traumatic event like this happens it's natural to ask God the "why" questions. Most often, there are no answers.

It's no secret the Bible speaks powerfully to trauma, and has done so for thousands of years. If you're familiar with the Bible's text you know there are difficult passages. From Cain's murder of Abel (the first family) to the crucifixion of Jesus, to the persecution of Christians, the Bible features people dealing with life's most profound crises: Noah and his family survive an epic flood; Abraham was asked to send his oldest son, Ishmael, out into the barren desert with his mother. He was then asked to give up his other son, Isaac, as a sacrifice; Jacob was nearly murdered by Esau and later wrestled God; young Joseph was sold into slavery by his brothers; Moses was abandoned as a baby by his mother.

The ancient people of Israel suffered trauma after trauma in the Old Testament, from slavery and the killing of male children in Egypt to oppression by Assyria and destruction of Jerusalem and exile by Babylon.

The list goes on to include Jesus, the apostle Paul, and the remaining disciples dealing with traumas imposed by Rome — imprisonment, torture, and execution. The Bible, in short, is a story of struggle for survival in the midst of devastating circumstances.

You are not alone. Suffering can be an opportunity for transformation. The Bible presents trauma as an opportunity to focus more intently on God alone. There is no return to a pre-trauma "normal." This is one of the up-and-down struggles of the trauma survivor. Those around a victim can be impatient with the survivor's failure to put it all in the past. The Bible recognizes the abiding impact of traumatic events. Jacob fights God and leaves with a limp. Jesus is resurrected after death, but still wears bodily scars.

The entire Bible features fallible heroes who work through and survive it. There is "stubborn and stiff-necked" Israel who survive 40 years of threat and death in the wilderness. There are the often-clueless disciples who find their way forward in the wake of Jesus's death and resurrection. These are the people who populate the sacred drama.

Survivors of trauma often struggle with the way their survival seems arbitrary and could have gone differently. The soldier whose buddy is shot down next to him. The burn survivor who saw the patient in the neighboring bed die of his injuries. The Bible frames the survival of Israel's ancestors and the church as the result of God's choosing them for a greater future. Survival, then, is not random, but has a purpose. This affirmation of God's purpose for individuals on the other side of trauma fails, of course, to explain why the event happened and why others did not survive. But the Bible can give crucial guidance and meaning to those finding their way forward after trauma. This is what Victoria Ruvolo did.

Victoria's Story: Continued

Ryan Cushing was charged with assault. The prosecutor was ready to seek maximum punishment—25 years in prison for a crime he rightly denounced as "heedless and brutal." He said, "This is not an act of mere stupidity. They're not 9-year-old children." But at Victoria's insistence, prosecutors granted him a plea bargain. He got 6 months in jail and 5-years' probation.

Cushing left the courtroom after pleading guilty and then came face to face with Victoria for the first time. He said he was sorry and wept. He begged her to forgive him. She did. She cradled his head as he sobbed. She stroked his face, patted his back, and then said, "It's okay. It's okay. I just want you to make your life the best it can be."

The *New York Times* titled this story, "A Moment of Grace." The reporter wrote, "Ms. Ruvolo gave and got something better: the dissipation of anger and the restoration of hope, in a gesture as cleansing as the tears washing down her damaged face, and the face of the foolish, miserable boy whose life she single-handedly restored."

We live in an evil world. We may not be able to avoid bad circumstances but God gives us the ability to choose how we will react. Victoria acted with grace. How did Victoria come to forgive such an unforgivable act? How would you have reacted?

PTS and PTSD

Traumatic experiences, such as death of a loved one (or sudden abandonment), a bad car accident, abuse, rape, job or financial loss, serious illness, terrorism, war, or natural disasters, are often referred to as "Post-Traumatic Stress" (PTS) or "Extreme Stress." The letters PTSD stand for "Post-Traumatic Stress Disorder." Whatever you call it, it's a deeply distressing or disturbing experience; an intrusive injury to the soul.

According to the National Center for PTSD, the National Institutes of Mental Health, and the PTSD alliance, 50 percent of the population will experience a traumatic event at least once in their lives. About 15 percent will develop symptoms that meet the medical criteria. It is also thought that women develop PTS twice as often as men. The theory is because they are more likely to be subject to interpersonal violence.[41] (To be a clinical case of PTSD, the symptoms must last more than a month, and lead to difficulties functioning socially, on the job, and in other areas of life.)

Despite the attention on returning vets, it's important to realize that a grieving or distressed person may have come through their own PTSD war zones. For example, the National Women's Study reported 33 percent of all rape victims develop PTSD sometime during their lives.[42]

The impact of PTSD is always based on the severity of *the response* to the event versus the severity of *the traumatic event*. This explains why some people are "fine" after a trauma. Their brain managed to process it. What we need to know is: Trauma images in our brain may not surface as a conscious memory, but as *emotions, sensations, and bodily responses* long after the event is over.

PTSD is different than "dissociation." PTSD victims relive the severely stressful memory, and try to avoid situations that remind them of it. With a normal experience the brain processes an experience and turns it into a memory. However, with a traumatic event the brain can't process it correctly. It doesn't form a memory. Instead it lives in the present. Even when the person is no longer in danger, the memory and emotions connected to the traumatic event can take on a life of its own. *Symptoms are:* numbness, feeling of disconnect, flashbacks, triggering memories, aversion to love and sex, feeling of two "yous" and isolation.

Reflect: Do you believe you suffer, or have suffered, from PTSD? Explain. Never forget: There are no burdens too heavy for God to lift, or a problem too hard for Him to solve, or a request too big for Him to answer. God does things no one else can do.

Trauma and Substance Abuse

Trauma is a risk factor for substance abuse. Because of the profound distress and impairment in the lives of those affected by PTS, many people abuse drugs or alcohol to cope; as an attempt to manage distress associated with the effects of stress symptoms.

It would not be unusual if you turned to alcohol and/or other drugs to self-medicate—to manage the intense flood of emotions and traumatic reminders, or to numb yourself from the intense emotion. (Studies show a direct link between alcohol use and engagement in risky behaviors in which a person may get hurt and traumatized either for the first time, or re-traumatized.)

Reflect: Did you use substances to cope with your pain? How was it your friend? How was it your enemy?

Abduction: Kimberly's Story

"I will repay you for the years the locusts have eaten— the great locust and the young locust, the other locusts and the locust swarm … You'll have plenty to eat, until you are full, and you'll praise the name of the LORD your God, who has worked wonders for you; never again will my people be shamed." –God, speaking in Joel 2:25-26

If you had told me at 16-years-old that soon I'd be living a captive in my own prison of food, booze, men, vomit, shame, guilt, and fear, I'd have told you that were crazy! For 40 years, I was defined by the "god of this world" and my dysfunctional parents—and not by God. I had downloaded into my mind lies, beliefs, thoughts and emotions—that I didn't choose, which kept me a prisoner of this world.

"You can't have that—you're fat!" Dad snatched the plate of food away as I reached for seconds. "I bet you weigh 150 pounds. Get on the scale and let's see," he barked. The humiliation crushed my soul. *If my dad thinks I'm fat, then everyone else does.* Add to that: I never felt attractive growing up.

What started as a diet, and a quest for love and acceptance, ended up being a near 20-year battle with bulimia, substance abuse, and promiscuity. I lived a double life which looked pretty good to outsiders. I became a master at lying and faking it; a pro at hiding behind the suits and leather boots. I always felt that I wasn't pretty enough or thin enough I just wasn't enough. Unbeknownst to me, I had a daddy hole; a craving for love, affection, attention; basic emotional needs I didn't receive from Dad. In the quest to fill this hole I headed down a dark and dirty road which led into an abyss.

By day I camouflaged myself as a medical sales rep; by night you'd find me one of two places: either in my apartment bingeing and purging, or getting plastered at my local "Cheers," stalking a potential prince. I put myself into high-risk situations. I'd meet a guy, enjoy getting to know him, and then sex was assumed and subtly forced upon me. I didn't say no or stand up for myself. In fact, I believed if I stopped him then he'd never want to see me again. After all, he may just be *the* prince! If he asked me out again I might actually feel good about myself for a moment. But typically, there'd be no second date. Then the truth would slam me upside my head: I'd been used and thrown out like a piece of garbage—again.

I did find "love" with four guys, only to be deceived, devalued, cheated on, and rejected by each one. (I spoke of the damage done by Bill, the

89 | **The Perfect Counselor**

psychopath, in chapter 2). The shame of being abandoned and experiencing sexual boundary violations increased my self-hatred and self-doubt, fueling the addictions. I did everything in my power to prevent these kinds of events from ever happening again—from excessive dieting and beauty treatments to ungodly submission. *This wasn't how my dream was supposed to go!*

To cope with the emotional pain, I'd retreat into my apartment for days with my friend "Ed," my eating disorder. Spending days at a time bingeing enabled me to detach emotionally. Unconsciously I'd get rid of all bad memories by flushing them down the toilet. Ed, the "god of this world," stole my dignity and dreams, lied endlessly, and slowly destroyed my body. I believed my god Ed was helping me, not hurting me. Ed allowed me to cherish and protect my sin.

Alcohol was a secondary addiction. I convinced myself I was just a social drinker, only interested in having fun. Unbeknownst to me, I was deeply invested in not feeling bad; in medicating myself against painful feelings.

I died and didn't even know it. I had no clue my lack of self-worth was a red flag; the very thing a guy quickly manipulated to satisfy his sexual needs. One of the many consequences was getting pregnant. I justified abortion. I also got picked up for shoplifting, then got a DUI and went to jail. More shame!

"I turned away from God, but then I was sorry. I kicked myself for my stupidity! I was thoroughly ashamed of all I did in my younger days. ...

How long will you wander, my wayward daughter? For the LORD will cause something new to happen..." (Jeremiah 31:19, 22; NLT).

"The waves of death swirled about me; the torrents of destruction overwhelmed me. The cords of the grave coiled around me; the snares of death confronted me. "In my distress I called to the LORD; I called out to my God. From his temple he heard my voice; my cry came to his ears" (2 Samuel 22:5-7).).

The day came when God showed me a way out of ungodly and abusive relationships. A godly man (my present husband) entered my life. I couldn't understand why he wanted to stay in a relationship with a party girl. Apparently, he was the prince God chose for me! He saw the ugly parts and chose to stay.

* * *

90 | **The Perfect Counselor**

Control is a big issue for many of us. There is healthy control: we want to protect our children, instill order into our homes. But often control moves into a manipulative and potentially dangerous place. Even though the first four decades of my life were spent as a slave to my pain-filled past, this did not determine *how I would continue to live*. I was created to be free! The good news is that what the enemy intends for evil, God can use for good (Genesis 50:20). Developing this study *for you* is one example. This is the key to healing from pain: Do something about it by acting on your purpose in life.

Romans 8:28 tells us, *"We know that in all things God works for the good of those who love him, who have been called according to his purpose."* Paul is saying that our pain has purpose *if* we love and live for God; our pain is a doorway to our destiny. If we choose not to live for God, our pain has nowhere to go. Instead, it will rot us from the inside out.

Sadly, life in this world is a perpetual cycle of negative experiences and triggers, which we didn't choose to install in our minds. *God created a way to break this cycle.* No matter how evil and damaging something may be, He can bring about good if we love Him.

The deeper our pain, the deeper the meaning of life. Not only can we survive our past experiences, we can flourish with purpose. As Paul puts it, we can become "more than conquerors" (Romans 8:37).

I was taught how to install truth into my mind. I learned to love, trust and accept my parent's weaknesses. And my beliefs about myself and others started changing when I aligned myself with God's Word and His Spirit.

As I look back on my life, I can see God's loving and merciful hand leading me out of the world and exposing the falsehoods, one by one. It was not His will that all these negative events took place. His heart grieved for me, as it does over tragic events you've experienced. Remember: No matter what the enemy does to define us, and rob us of our dignity, or destroy our hopes and dreams, in God's strength we can rise from the darkness!

"The LORD is my rock, my fortress and my deliverer; my God is my rock, in whom I take refuge, my shield and the horn of my salvation. He is my stronghold, my refuge and my savior— from violent people you save me" (2 Samuel 22:2-3).

Reflect: How do you relate to my story, the Scriptures, and to God's providence (means: the foreseeing care and guidance of God)? If you are in a class, tell your story of hope about when you saw God use some painful experience for His glory and your destiny?

Psyche Damage

When we experience a traumatic event, something significant, violent, and horrible happens, often suddenly, outside of our control. The result: We sustain an injury. Our bodies may be injured, but even when they're not, our psyches (the mind, soul, and spirit) are injured in a way that often creates severe physical, mental, emotional, social, and spiritual symptoms.

Trauma affects the family system, and changes the way a person views the world (one's awareness of reality). Trust and a sense of safety are broken. A person who's been violated learns she's powerless, and seeks to cope by finding some way to take back power and control.

I believe psyche damage occurs because God wired us to love and be loved, first by Himself, then by others. Blaise Pascal said, "There is a God-shaped vacuum in the heart of every person which cannot be filled by any created thing, but only by God, the Creator." We need to understand that our behavior is largely driven by our need for God. Suffering results when we try to fill that God-shaped hole with something other than Him.

Neuroscientists state there are areas of the brain designed to create deep bonds between individuals to ensure their wellness. These are particularly strong in infancy, and continue throughout life. Because the need for love and relational acceptance is so deeply imbedded in us, when those types of relationships are not present, or when a significant relational break occurs (by either rejection, abandonment, or physical/verbal abuse), *the brain registers the emotional pain the same way it registers the pain of a physical injury.* Therefore, we say we're "heart-broken," or "That really hurt my feelings," or, "I felt like I was punched in the gut." In other words, when our need for love and acceptance is destroyed or betrayed, trauma occurs.

For this reason, I don't particularly like the term *Post-Traumatic Stress Disorder.* The word "disorder" implies an illness, disease, or mental problem. I believe symptoms stemming from abuse are normal and necessary responses to this type of atrocious injury. A mild injury like a paper cut causes minor symptoms, while an extreme injury like a compound leg fracture causes severe symptoms. The severe symptoms of *Post-Traumatic Stress (PTS)* are normal and necessary. *Whatever your PTS is, it is unique to you and a natural reaction to the serious injury you sustained.*

92 | The Perfect Counselor

Survival Instincts

When Deana was 12-years-old she witnessed her father's murder. Today, this past event (whether consciously remembered or not) raises in this 28-year-old woman, *a present day threat of violation* whenever she comes across a man of the same stature and race. Deana stiffens, retracts, collapses in fear and revulsion. This man's presence brings up all the emotional subject matter Deana had attached to her father's murder. When this happens to Deana:

- She is reacting to the combined triggers of men, race, and build. →
- Her mind is confused between a safe and a dangerous person. →
- When a kind and well-meaning man who fits this description comes near to Deana or tries to speak to her, she goes into a survival-based mode assuming danger, when there is no danger. →
- Deana freezes and folds.

For us whatever meaning our brains gave to an experience when it first occurred is re-experienced as true in the present. When a person is traumatized, they instinctually go into "survival mode." The instinct is to either *fight, flight, freeze,* or *fold.* The dictionary defines this response as "a physiological reaction that occurs in response to a perceived harmful event, attack, or threat to survival."

1. *Flight:* We may try to escape. We are surprisingly strong and fast when we feel threatened. The brain pumps adrenaline and other chemicals through our body, giving our muscles lots of power. The chemicals also cause us to be more resilient to pain so we can function, even if we're wounded.

2. *Fight:* We may choose to attack. Again, the chemicals surging in our bodies give us increased strength.

3. *Freeze:* If we can't run away or fight, or had previous traumas that precondition us not to even try, our brains will cause us to freeze.

4. *Fold:* If the threat is perceived as inescapable or possibly subject to death, we may "fold." We collapse in a profound state of helpless mobility and hopelessness. The body and spirit collapses while our metabolic processes (digestion, respiration, circulation, and energy production) shut down.[43]

When the incident subsides, ideally, we return to a *state of relaxed alertness*. (Often freezing and folding, as in "scared stiff," will make us feel shamed and defeated, further compounding a trauma experience.) What Deana learned to do when a man fitting this description came into her presence was to reframe what was happening to her. She'd repeat this to herself,

"I have a problem with this man, but *it is not him*. It is the past experience I had with father. I'm not that 12-year-old girl anymore. I'm a grown woman. I need to refocus on the good qualities in this man and realize he is a totally different person. He is not a murderer."

Deana linked positive material into the negative image, softening her reaction to her husband, thereby, helping her gain a sense of meaning and control over this past traumatic experience. She also brought Jesus into those painful experiences. In her brain, she developed new neural pathways that helped circumvent the bad father memory.

Reflect: How has learning about the different kinds of survival instincts helped you put words and validation onto your experience?

The Fear Factor

Fear is an emotion we all experience at one time or another, but for the distressed and traumatized it can be lethal. Fear is a basic response to injury and threat of danger. To survive, the body's internal stress system works 24 hours to keep itself safe; the stress reactions never stop.

Traumatic events create a unique two-part grief experience. The first is focused on *the event* itself; the second is focused on *the different losses* the event caused. The first part which is focused on the actual event is a source of fear-based symptoms, such as flashbacks and anxiety/depression.

With trauma, bodily responses to fear can be harmful because our brains move resources away from thinking and toward survival. The brain basically shuts down as the body prepares for action. The *prefrontal cortex* (the brain's center for reasoning and judgment) becomes impaired when the *amygdala* (the brain's response center) senses fear. The ability to think and reason decreases as time goes on. So, thinking about the next best move in a crisis can be a hard thing to do, which is why some people "freeze."

94 | **The Perfect Counselor**

Some people "fold," which means they collapse, associated with feeling helpless and hopeless. Others experience feelings of time slowing down, tunnel vision, or feeling like what's happening is not real. Fine and complex motor skills like finding your car keys and starting your car, or handling a knife, become less effective. All these symptoms can make it hard to stay grounded and logical in a dangerous or threatening situation.

Reflect: What fears do you have about opening up an abusive experience and memory?

The Body's Response

Picture it: It's 11:00 PM and you're alone at home. You hear a loud noise. You hear it again. You know it's coming from the room across the hall. How do you react? People who haven't experienced trauma have a balanced and resilient nervous system that says to the emotionally charged fearful brain, "False alarm. Chill out and relax. It's not a burglar—it's the wind blowing the window shutter." They can stand back, observe, and reduce the intensity of fear and anxiety. They can switch off the survival response and then relax.

On the other hand, many trauma victims live in an ongoing anxious, fear-driven mode of survival, like a combat war zone. Their intense emotions and bodily responses to trauma becomes *chronic* (means occurs frequently; long term). The very emotions God created to serve, guide, protect, and defend turn against them.

Often when people hit the "fold" mode of survival, they become stuck and are left in the realm of hell, paralyzed with terror, while experiencing fits of rage, yet lacking the energy to act.[44] These physical responses occur:

- Feels hyper-anxious and unsafe. → Fear kicks in.→
- Heart rate increases; blood pressure goes up. →
- Breathing gets quicker. →
- Stress hormones such as *adrenaline* and *cortisol* are released.

Adrenaline and cortisol are the primary chemicals of the fight or flight response, and help deal with stress by increasing energy. In the last decade, scientists have become aware that chronic exposure to adrenaline causes our systems to be overstimulated and leads to anxiety and depression, obesity, and memory problems.[45] →

- The blood flows away from the heart and out towards the extremities, readying the arms and legs for action—for fight or flight.

For some people, the fear triggers flashbacks and nightmares from the unconscious. This explains why some war veterans hit the ground if they hear a car backfire. It is why Dianne recoils when her husband touches her.

Reflect: What do you conclude from this information as it pertains to your life and experiences?

PTS or Grief?

Recovery from trauma is about grief recovery. With trauma comes innumerable losses. *Grief is intense emotional suffering caused by a significant loss.* It's not always about death. It happens with relationship breakups, in abusive relationships, in business and life transitions, with disaster or any kind of misfortune. Grief involves a complex set of emotions which come in waves and cycles, which is perfectly normal.

In his book *The PTSD Solution,* Dr. Alan Wolfelt considered, "What if post-traumatic stress is really a form of grief?" His theory is that when we experience a traumatic event, we experience profound losses.[46] Grief is not an illness or disorder. It's what we think and feel inside when we lose something or someone we value. Loss is a normal and unavoidable part of life, which means having a response is also normal.

Loss = injury. Grief is our natural and necessary response to the injury and its successive losses. For many who have been abused, since abuse occurs over a long period, the person experiences many traumatic events. Grief affects our whole being—the physical, relational, emotional, and spiritual. The griever's sense of security has been threatened, and naturally asks, "Am I going to be okay? Will I get through this?"

Grief isn't merely measured by sadness, but also by feelings of shock, anxiety denial, disorganization, confusion, fear, depression, regret, panic, guilt, and explosive emotions like anger. One therapist said *anger* is the emotion we use to avoid the less comfortable feelings of confusion, fear, and sadness.

If you find yourself angry a lot, there's a good chance its roots are buried in grief.

With grief, symptoms can be mild, extreme, or somewhere in between. Their severity often depends on the degree of attachment the person felt to the person or thing that was lost. Traumatized women often experience feeling "empty." They often let go of dreams and goals which are important; they don't know what their gifts and talents are—basically no purpose to life.

For example, Kathie lost her home and all her belongings in a fire; Janice's beloved Labrador died; Aimee lost her virginity when her uncle raped her; Cindy's confidence in herself vanished when her mother repeatedly told her she was stupid, ugly. All huge losses. For each big loss, we all suffer secondary losses such as:

- Trust in others.
- Sense of safety.
- Some aspect of our health.
- A financial cost.
- Self-identity and self-confidence.
- Hopes and dreams for the future.
- Joy and contentment.

The many losses naturally give rise to grief. To face our history means to face our losses. *There are many losses which need to be recognized and then mourned.* For example: the loss of freedom, our childhood, particular season of life, our home, health, a parent's love (including divorce), the loss of joy, peace, and happiness, expectations and dreams, job opportunities. Or, the loss of something we never had, like a healthy intimate relationship with other family members.

God is all about restoring life. He reminds us that our pain is not our identity. Oswald Chambers wrote, "When Jesus Christ emancipates the personality, individuality is not destroyed, it is transfigured."[47] As you come alive in Christ the feelings of hopelessness, emptiness, and lack of purpose will begin to disappear, even if slowly.

As surely as you pass through the painful emotions, you'll in time come out of the dark valley into the light, and into the Sonshine. Grief, although seemingly unbearable at times, causes us to grow in ways that might not be possible otherwise. The Bible tells us God is close to the person who grieves (Psalm 34:19).

Reflect: God will *"comfort all who mourn, and provide for those who grieve—He'll bestow on them a crown of beauty instead of ashes, the oil of joy instead of mourning, and a garment of praise instead of a spirit of despair"* (Isaiah 61:2). How has God spoke to you personally through this verse?

Expressing Grief

"A man, when he does not grieve, hardly exists." –Antonio Porsche

"My physical outside appearance was always more important than my inside appearance—because if people saw what was inside they'd only see darkness and emptiness. I'm learning how to let Jesus's Light in by mourning my losses." –Tiffany

Everything you've been doing so far has been preparing you for the grief process. It wouldn't be unusual to fear confronting your grief—like you'll get lost and never come out of it. Yet, feelings, such as grief and fear and anger, which aren't exposed and expressed, are merely buried alive. Left unchecked, they can have distressing consequences.

Grieving is a significant part of the recovery process. It is unavoidable and normal. It is a powerful step towards closure and understanding. It's not a one-time event, but a process of remembering, feeling, and expressing. For some, the grief process may last several years. If we want to feel joy again, we must deal with grief. Some people say to just "get over" grief. Healthy people don't get over it—they *go through* it.

Robert Frost wrote, "The best way out is always through." There are many stages of grief and up to 20 different emotions a person may experience. Most often when we talk about "the grief cycle" we speak of certain stages most people go through:

- A trauma event happened which creates emotion. →

Common emotional responses:

98 | The Perfect Counselor

- Shock/ Fear/ Numbness (→ Coping Mechanism) →
- Fear /Denial → Guilt/Shame → Anger/Bitterness →
- Depression/Anxiety → Loneliness/Isolation →
- "Hitting rock bottom" → Desire to move forward→
- Forgiveness → Letting go →
- Forgiveness → Letting go →
- Accepting the event happened and taking responsibility for personal growth and new healthy relationships. →
- Helping and comforting others.

Every person grieves differently. Emotional ups and downs and outbursts are normal. Successful grieving doesn't shut out the emotions and pain; it accepts the suffering and moves forward.

Reflect: Today, where do you see yourself in the grief cycle?

Tears and Waterfalls

"A Jesus who never wept could never wipe away my tears."–Charles Spurgeon

Tears are medicine. Recognize that tears, groaning, waves of grief, nightmares, and withdrawal are not uncommon. The Bible tells us to weep. Jesus wept. Ann Voskamp wrote, "Tears are never a sign of weakness. Tears are always the sign of an open heart." Give yourself permission to feel and mourn. God gave us tears to soften our hearts and cleanse our minds.

Most people say they feel better after a good cry. When you cry, it appears, stress hormones are flushed out of your system. You begin to feel calmer, maybe even refreshed.[48] The Bible says, God collects each tear we cry and will lead us to springs of living water (Isaiah 25:8; Rev. 7:17).

When grieving, expect a waterfall fluctuating emotions. You may battle at any time with an outburst of despair. These emotions will come and go— sometimes in a flood, other times in a trickle. Realize change of moods is normal. *Things will get better. Eventually you'll leave behind the hopelessness and will feel a sense of restored energy and focus!*

Reflect: How does it make you feel to know that God grieves too (Psalm 78:40; Genesis 6:5-6); that He takes every tear, every mistake, and works them into a new vibrant plan; that God *will* make up for the lost years—the years that sin and chaos devoured (Joel 2:25-26)?

Complicated Grief

Some grief therapists refer to the process of normal open and active grief as "good" or "uncomplicated" grief. Grief, over time, with the reliance on God and support of others, leads to positive mental and physical health. On the other hand, "Complicated Grief" (CG) is grief that has gotten stuck or off-track for some reason. In the case of PTS, certain parts of the grief experience can become so protruding that it takes over the griever's life.

Who is at risk for Complicated Grief (CG)?

- People who deny, stuff, or attempt to manage their emotions, as in, "I don't need to cry and get all emotional," or "I need to get over this and move on."

- "Loss overload" can hinder a person's resilience and emotional intelligence so they're no longer able to process their feelings using their former coping skills. Other stressors such as depression or anxiety, financial challenges, or compromised health, often worsen symptoms of good grief. If there is a change in personality and/or emotional resiliency, this is a sign of CG.

- People who have unreconciled conflict or fluctuating feelings toward a person who dies suddenly.

- People who don't have a relationship with Jesus Christ.

- Those who are alone without an adequate support system.

- If we grew up in a culture and/or family that treats grief and loss as abnormal or "something we don't talk about."

- Certain losses tend to be stigmatized, such as suicide, homicide, death by certain illnesses such as AIDS and PTSD. Since social support is often lacking, the griever often takes on a sense of shame, which can lead to CG.

Delayed Grief

Tawney's dad divorced her mother when she was 12-years-old so he could marry his younger girlfriend. She chose not to have any contact with Dad; even though she had a huge daddy hole.

When Dad died from cancer, Tawney didn't see any reason to go to the funeral or mourn his death. Within the year, she began experiencing symptoms of grief.

In many situations, the person experiences "absent or delayed" grief. When someone is *not* given the opportunity to grieve properly, or doesn't think they need to mourn, or is stuck in shock or denial, grief may be "absent or delayed." For example, in the military, if one soldier in the soldiers' presence is killed, they don't put down their guns and mourn. They are trained to keep fighting. First Responders are routinely exposed to traumatic events. They too keep doing their jobs. As such, these people are at increased risk for long-term problems from traumatic stress. The same thing can happen to us if we've lived in an environment where abuse was ongoing and we existed in "survival mode."

Reflect: Can you think of a time when you experienced complicated or delayed grief?

Mourning is Treatment

"We cannot skirt the outside edges of our grief. Instead, we must journey all through it, sometimes meandering the side roads, sometimes plowing directly into its raw center. We must experience it, and then we must express it." –Dr. Alan Wolfelt

Grief is the total of everything we think and feel inside after a significant loss. *Mourning* is the outward expression of that grief; it is our medicine. Mourning is the active part of the PTS healing journey, much like taking care of a wound after the skin has been injured. This can be hard to do, but if we don't we can expect to experience symptoms of CG.

Mental health experts say the rule is: if *you feel* a significant loss, regardless of the world's definition, it is a loss. The goal is not to get life back on track the way it used to be.

How long you spend in each stage will vary depending on the extent of your isolation, depression, family support, belief in God, support from church and friends, etc. *The goal is to find and accept a new normal.*

If we choose to prolong or bypass mourning our losses (termed "carried grief") we can expect to struggle with one or more of these symptoms:[49]

- Difficulties with trust and intimacy.
- Depression and toxic self-talk.
- Anxiety and panic attacks.
- Numbing and disconnection.
- Irritability and agitation.
- Substance abuse, addictions, self-harm, eating disorders.

Connection and Support

Pain and isolation hurts our relationships because connecting is life. Healing means we can't go it alone. No question, intimacy is risky. I'd think, *If I reach out to another woman there's a chance she'll reject me. If I trust my deepest, darkest secrets to another, she may pull back in shock, or even worse, tell others.* Yet, God's plan is we connect with others. Love comes with community.

The New Testament reveals the answer lies in the ordinary church, which is comprised of ordinary people. Jesus said, "*Realize that I am in my Father, and you are in me, and I am in you*" *(John 14:20).* We are the arms, hands, and feet of Jesus— "Jesus with skin on," as some say. This is biblical. Consider how the Bible is written: God Almighty dominates the Old Testment. The Gospels follow, recounting Jesus's life on earth. Jesus said,

"*And I will ask the Father, and He will give you another Advocate to be with you forever. But the Advocate, the Holy Spirit, whom the Father will send in My name, will teach you all things and will remind you of everything I have told you*" *(John 14:16; 26).*

Then Jesus leaves earth, and ascends into heaven to be with the Father. The book of Acts reveals that the doctrine of the Holy Spirit is the doctrine of the Church—of *God living in us.* After the book of Acts, the Bible reveals a series of personal letters addressed to a diverse group of Christians. The overarching theme is they are all "in Christ."

Scripture says, *"Do you not know that your bodies are temples of the Holy Spirit, who is in you, whom you have received from God? You are not your own"* (1 Corinthians 6:19). Dietrich Bonhoeffer wrote, "The Church is nothing but a section of humanity in which Christ has really taken form."

In the Bible, God revealed Himself first as Father, then as Son, and finally as Holy Spirit. God took a huge risk, and today He has fashioned Himself out of individual human beings. Christians represent God's holiness

on earth. Through the power of the Holy Spirit, we are to do God's work on earth. So, if we ask the questions, "Where is God? Why can't I see Him? Why doesn't He show up and meet my needs?" we need to look to the New Testament.

Proceeding the Gospels, there is a different pattern at work. Acts 2:44 reads, *"All the believers met together in one place and shared everything they had"* (NLT). We also see Paul receiving God's comfort in the form of a visit from his brothers. Paul himself led fund-raising efforts to meet the needs of the church.

Just as God Himself met the needs of the Israelites; just as Jesus fed the 5,000 with a few loaves and fishes; God met the needs of the young church just as He met the needs of the Israelites—but He did so *indirectly*. The church is the body of Jesus Christ. Therefore, if the church did it, or does it, then God did it—God showed up.

Our take away: If we want to see God, then we must look at the people who belong to Him. They are His "bodies." God's name may be Linda, or Jeanette, or Joseph, or Pastor. They are the body of Christ.

* * *

We need at least one person we can count on. One study said if a woman has just one trustworthy friend, then she's protected from depression when she experiences a significant life stress. Yet Ecclesiastes 4:8-12 advises,

"One standing alone can be attacked and defeated, but two can stand back-to-back and conquer; three is even better, for a triple-braided cord is not easily broken" (TLB).

We stand strong when we don't stand alone. Look for people who will accept you for who you are; bring out the best in you; will pray for you and keep confidences; point you to Christ. Look for them and walk with them. Also, call for prayer, including prayer lines, when in crisis. And give it time!

As we learn to reach out to other sisters and brothers in Christ, they'll meet us, and new friendships and alliances will take root and grow. Once we embrace friendship then we become that much needed genuine friend to someone else, helping her walk out of the dark valley into the light.

Fulfilling Our Six Mourning Needs

Mourning Need #1: *We need to confront the reality of the traumatic event, and acknowledge that it created several primary and secondary losses.*

Mourning Need #2: *Allow yourself to feel the pain of the losses.* "Bereaved" literally means "to be torn apart." When we are torn apart by traumatic loss, mourning requires embracing the pain of the losses. We cannot deny our feelings or make them disappear, so we might as well express them. Multiple Bible characters experienced deep loss and sadness. Jesus mourned (John 11:35; Matt. 23:37-39).

We can embrace, befriend, even wallow in the painful losses. The message of the Bible is that we can throw our grief, and other emotions, at God. He can absorb them. In the end, this brings refreshment. Remember, *"The LORD is near to the brokenhearted and saves the crushed in spirit" (Psalm 34:18).*

This can be a challenge, for example, if you work all day and have a family. What some counselors suggest, and I am one of them, is that we "schedule" processing our emotions into our daily lives. For a working mom, it may be running a hot bath at 9 PM, locking the door, lighting some candles, telling the family that no one is to disturb her for one hour, soaking in the warm bathtub, talking to God about the painful losses, and allowing herself to weep or scream or yell out at God.

Grief and Loss Table

This is an exercise I do with my clients to help them express mourning need #1 and #2. Putting our experiences and losses in this table format affirms the emotional and physical trauma we have experienced. We can see reality. Then we can name it and begin grieving the primary and secondary losses.

This exercise can answer the question, "Why do I have these symptoms and/or act out this way? For example, grief, anxiety, depression, anger, rage, numbness, addictions, or physical symptoms. The first place to start is to seek safety and comfort. Unless we feel safe and can bring any anxiety and fear down to a functional level, we won't effectively be able to work on mourning.

If you don't want to do a table format, you can get a blank piece of lined paper, title it "My personal loss inventory," then list your losses line by line. Consider creating a table like the one Felicia created. Felicia has been traumatized by abusive people:

Person	Abuse | Event	Loss
Felicia	*Trauma events: 10 years-old —16 years old.*	Childhood
Step-father	Sexual	Virginity; inability to bear children; self-worth | image; sense of security & trust
Felicia	*Told mother. Mom called her a liar & punished her.*	*Secondary Wounding / Compounded Trauma*
Mother	Verbal; physical; abandonment	Voice; love; self-worth sense of safety & trust
Sister	Verbal; abandonment	Love, friend
Felicia	*Coping mechanism: Drugs*	Time; brain function; reality; money
Boyfriend #1	Emotional; physical	Healthy romantic love, self-worth, friend, trust
Boyfriend #2	Emotional (pressures Felicia to get an abortion)	Her child
Felicia	*Stops drug use & loses coping mechanism*	→ Feels flat & indifferent; life has no meaning
God (*passive*)	Abandonment	Love, self-worth

It would not be unusual for you to say, "I'm not doing this! It's too painful to go there." Or, you may think it's a waste of time, which is because your feelings of loss have been denied, stuffed, or inhibited. The wisest man, Solomon, said, *"It is better to go to a house of mourning than to go to a house of feasting"* (Eccl. 7:2). Psychotherapist Tim Clinton said, "The past isn't your past if it is still affecting or infecting your present."

105 | The Perfect Counselor

Suggestion: you may want to do this exercise with another member of your family who has also experienced what you've experienced.

Just as mourning the loss of a loved one takes time, so does mourning the loss of our parts of lives. don't cut short or block the mourning process because of denial or feelings of guilt, shame, or anger. courageously allow the process to proceed.

Unfortunately, we can't lump all our losses into one neat package and grieve it. We must process through each one or each stage. Here are the areas Felicia needed to grieve:

1—*The loss of her past.* Felicia lost her adolescence, years she could never get back. The truth surfaced: She'd been gravely deceived, lost her virginity and ability to have her own children. She submitted to shameful and humiliating behaviors, and never experienced healthy, dating relationships. She threw a college education away. She always wondered: "Who would I have been? How would my life have been different if I'd followed God's original plan and purpose?"

2—*Her family of origin* because there was a high level of abuse, pain, and chaos within it. Like Felicia, we may have to come to terms with the fact we'll never have the loving parent or family we desired; that we never received nurture, safety, love, and/or comfort.

3—*Her own sinful choices.* Felicia stole money from friends and family, and shoplifted to support her drug habit. When other people's lives have been affected negatively because of our actions, we must mourn.

Trauma to the soul is involuntary. Sin is voluntary. Jesus said, *"Blessed are those who mourn, for they will be comforted"* (Matthew 5:4). He is speaking of grieving over our personal sin. "To mourn" means "to show on the *outside* what is going on *inside.*"[50] Notice He said that if we did this we'd be blessed. We acknowledge and confess what we've done and grieve over the loss appropriately.

To "confess" means to talk about; to bring out into the open; to tell the entire truth about our thoughts and actions; agreeing with God that our behavior is wrong. It begins the process of mending and purifying the soul. Other times our anguish comes out of anger at ourselves.

Most women I minister to have a very hard time loving and forgiving themselves for certain things they've done, particularly the damage to their children. Part of coming to love and forgive themselves is learning to talk about and grieve their losses, and renew their minds with the truth.

Part 2: The Things You Did Right

After you finish your table and absorb and ponder over the losses, create a new list. Write down everything you did right. What you are doing is *updating the grieving memories by adding something positive*. This was Felicia's list:

- Broke the secret and told the truth! *The truth shall set you free! (John 8:32)*
- Moved out of an extremely toxic and dangerous environment.
- Adopted another family and church family as her own.
- Recognized the destruction her coping mechanism (drugs) was causing and stopped.
- Participated in a post-abortion Bible study.

All these steps are HUGE!

Mourning Need #3: *Convert the relationship and memory from one of present tense to one of past tense.* We will cover this in the upcoming chapter.

Mourning Need #4: *Develop a new self-identity.* A person changes after a traumatic event; their lives change. Loss tends to force dramatic and painful changes in self-identity. For example, the woman who was raped must slowly, over time and with the compassionate support of God and her husband, reconstruct her sexuality. The mom whose teenager ran away from home, must re-conceive what it means to be a mother. Chapter 9 will cover this.

Mourning Need #5: *Discover new meaning and purpose in life.* After a significant loss, we naturally tend to question the meaning and purpose of life. "Why" and "How" questions are common. This is addressed in chapter 16.

Mourning Need #6: *Receive and accept support from other caring people.* Lloyd Alexander wrote, "Neither refuse to give help when it is, nor refuse to accept it when it is offered." People need people; it's how we're wired!

Reflect: Choose to take a small step forward by committing to one particular action, and then take the next step. Work to focus on God, and the good and hopeful parts of your life that He's divinely ordained. And recognize that God doesn't want us to live a lifetime of mourning. How do you feel about mourning? One woman expressed her commitment in a prayer to God:

Dear God, You gave me the emotion of pain and grief for a reason. I've decided to pay attention to my inner pain, to feel the feelings I've tried to hide inside. I don't want to keep living the way I have been. I know you have a better plan for me. I choose the truth. free my inner heart, give me the strength to explore my losses in more depth and to mourn them with You so I can be free and live with new meaning and purpose. I trust You! In Jesus's name.

7

Insatiable Cravings and Addiction

You're addicted to thrills? What an empty life! The pursuit of pleasure is never satisfied. —*Proverbs 21:17* (MSG)

We all love something too much. We've all got them: Insatiable cravings. Nasty habits. Vices. Addictions. We've *all* got them. We *all* love something too much. We *all* want more. More pleasure. More love. More chocolate. More affirmation. More money.

Most of us know that an unquenchable desire for drugs, alcohol, nicotine, food, shoplifting, and gambling can destroy lives. However, multitudes of people are hooked on things that don't fit the addiction stereotype like love, work, sports, people-pleasing, shopping, exercising, dieting, watching television, even pain and chaos. Add to the list: technology, religious activities, risk taking, celebrity worship, gaming, tattooing, tanning, even love for pets and children.

It's been said that to be alive is to be addicted; that life in America is so stressful that it is impossible NOT to become addicted to some object. We are a nation of materialistic consumers, and the more we consume, the more we want to consume. One Christian psychiatrist stated that "we are all addicts in every sense of the word."[51]

We live in the great age of excess which breeds an unsatisfied yearning for more and more. *You need. You deserve. You must have.* Misplaced affections and insatiable cravings often become addictions. Completely unaware, we harbor an infestation of hidden dependencies because they have silently invaded our lives. And they don't have to be grandiose or visibly evil to do great damage.

Behind every craving is a compelling urge to pursue pleasure—to feel terrific while avoiding pain, physically and emotionally. From the brain's perspective, whatever we do to produce feelings of euphoria is worth repeating. Ultimately, we end up mastered by those things.

Today we're restless, stressed, irritable, discontent, and obsessed. We distract ourselves and medicate our anxiety with activity, mood-altering substances, entertainment, and relationships, because we're unable to simply be present with ourselves. We may love God, but deeply rooted habits take control. Our focus rests on our objects of attachment instead of on Him.

The church culture is not immune either. Christians, as well, hide and deny their behaviors. Many believe the church propagates addiction. The church, however, is in the unique position of becoming its own recovery center. I have a message of hope: *We are not confined to or defined by our insatiable cravings and compulsive behaviors.*

If we're going to be addicted, *let's be addicted to the power of the Gospel*, which not only heals and frees, but empowers; *let's be addicted to the Word of God.*

Reflect: Are you ready to begin a quest to find pleasure in Him, and Him alone? God is calling, "Come back to me and live!" (Amos 5:4)

The Counterfeit Light

For two decades, I lived a secret double life. No, I wasn't a stripper by night or committing crimes or having an affair. By day I worked hard at making my outside sparkle, assuming others would think I had it completely together.

I had the right job, wore the right clothes, and associated with the right people. Yet, behind the scenes I'd retreat into a dark, depressing dungeon where I fought the battles with my demons—with my hidden addictions. My specialty: trashing my own life. I held many secrets no one could know about. The humiliating behavior and degrading consequences I wore as my identity.

Skilled at walking in a counterfeit light to cover my insecurities, I donned a fresh new cover girl mask each day. I used people as objects rather than human beings with whom I could have healthy relationships. I only cared about myself. I lost close friendships. I continued to substitute more objects and actions in their place.

My "favorite things" gave me a *temporary* euphoria. Little did I know that every time I engaged in a destructive or toxic act, I buried feelings of guilt and shame in my unconscious, which surfaced through my drugs of choice. There was a consequence: I lost touch with humanity.

The day came when I couldn't take living with these monsters any longer. Then something happened on my way to hell … I got saved. I said yes to Jesus Christ and stopped fighting God. And I know there is help for anyone who seeks it out.

Jesus saved me from destruction—both present and future. To "save" in the Greek ("sozo") means deliverance from danger and suffering; to heal, to deliver, and to make whole.[52] God knew everything, horrible things, about me; yet, He still sought, loved, and accepted me as His very own. How could I not say, "Yes, Lord, yes!"

A Parable: The Rich Young Ruler

A certain ruler asked him, "Good teacher, what must I do to inherit eternal life?"

"Why do you call me good?" Jesus answered. "No one is good—except God alone. You know the commandments: 'You shall not commit adultery, you shall not murder, you shall not steal, you shall not give false testimony, honor your father and mother.'"

"All these I have kept since I was a boy," he said.

When Jesus heard this, he said to him, "You still lack one thing. Sell everything you have and give to the poor, and you will have treasure in heaven. Then come, follow me."

When he heard this, he became very sad, because he was very wealthy. Jesus looked at him and said, "How hard it is for the rich to enter the kingdom of God! Indeed, it is easier for a camel to go through the eye of a needle than for someone who is rich to enter the kingdom of God."

Those who heard this asked, "Who then can be saved?"

Jesus replied, "What is impossible with man is possible with God."

Peter said to him, "We have left all we had to follow you!"

"Truly I tell you," Jesus said to them, "no one who has left home or wife or brothers or sisters or parents or children for the sake of the kingdom of God will fail to receive many times as much in this age, and in the age to come eternal life." (Luke 18:18-30)

Most often, this passage is used to challenge us. Are we willing to give it all to Jesus? Are we holding anything back? Are we willing to give up the comforts of the American dream to meet the needs of the poor and oppressed? Or, are we saying no to Jesus, like the rich young ruler?

The first thing we must recognize is the issue wasn't the man's wealth; it was his pride; his self-sufficiency. He was self-righteous claiming he'd kept *all* the commandments since his youth. So, Jesus asked him to do something he never asked anyone else to do. It went right to his heart of self-sufficiency. He asked him to take a vow of instant poverty.

Self-Sufficiency

"If you build upon yourself your edifice will be a mere ruin."—St. Augustine

Jesus criticized the self-righteous because He believed that dependence upon God, not self-sufficiency, was the key to wholeness. It takes humility, particularly in this culture, to recognize we're not God and need a relationship with Him to be whole.

We live in a "me" and "looking out for number one" world. Yet what Jesus is telling us (and those in the field of psychology) is humans have a fundamental need to relate to other humans outside of themselves. We are not islands unto ourselves, but interconnected relational beings. Healthy dependent relationships (notice the word "healthy") start with connecting with God. He will enable us to find and develop healthy people connections.

What this culture doesn't teach us is that we need others because they make us stronger. It's like these sayings, "There's strength in numbers" and "It takes a village." Jesus taught His followers never to think of themselves as better than other people (Luke 18:9-14) because they needed those very people to help them be whole persons.

Thinking of ourselves as superior to others and to be dismissive of what they can offer only results in damage to ourselves. Someone said, "The arrogance to believe you are more than others comes from the fear you are less." Interesting viewpoint.

When one's grandiose view of themselves is used to defend against any imperfections, it then becomes an impairment to relationships with others. Those who are humble enough to admit they can learn from others without looking down at them are on the path of whole wellness.

Reflect on psychologist Larry Crabb's words: "I must surrender my fascination with myself to a more worthy preoccupation with the character and purposes of God. I am not the point. He is. I exist for him. He does not exist for me."[53]

Life's Hidden Addictions

"Lust means literally— "I must have it at once, and I don't care what the consequences are."–Oswald Chambers

The sneezing, coughing, watery eyes, nasal congestion, sore throat; we all experience this nuisance—the common cold. This particular year I worked at a medical clinic which stocked sample drugs for anything that ailed you. Desiring a decongestant, I searched the drug closet. I hit the jackpot—several trays of mini Dristan bottles. *Snort…snort. Ah…instant relief! I can finally breathe again.* As soon as it became hard to breathe, *snort, snort.*

I concluded I had one of those long-lasting colds. Ten days passed and I needed more samples, but there were no more Dristan bottles. I asked a doctor what else I could use. He questioned me, "How long have you been inhaling Dristan?" I replied "About 10 days."

He firmly stated, "Stop now! Did you read the label?"

"No," I answered. He said my poor little nose had become addicted to Dristan.

This is an example of a chemical addiction. It taught me a great deal about the characteristics of the addiction process. What I didn't realize is by drying up my nose the artificial chemicals disturbed the natural balance. Trying to restore the balance, my nose adjusted by producing more congesting chemicals and less of its own decongestants. When the effect of the drops wore off, there were more natural congesting chemicals and less natural decongestants than there were to begin with. Therefore, I was stuffier and used more nose drops. Labels today still read, "Do not exceed recommended dosage."

This is a simplistic example of how our body can become addicted to substances. The substance alters a balance of natural body chemicals. The body then adjusts to the change by trying to reestablish the proper balance. In doing so, the body becomes dependent upon the outside supply of the substance. This is how I became addicted to caffeine, nicotine, laxatives, and alcohol. The problem with chemical dependency is it's not dependency per se; it's the dependency upon a *chemical* or a *thing*.

If you don't drink, over eat, gamble or abuse drugs, you may mistakenly assume addiction doesn't apply to you. The same dynamics apply to non-substance addictions. If you spend hours on activities to the exclusion of everything else; even if it is a healthy activity, like bike riding or cleaning the house, it may be a sign of addiction. Everything in life can easily become an object of attachment. As one of my clients said, "Our objects are either a good poison or a bad poison."

Substance and Behavioral Addictions

"In each of us there is something growing, which will be hell unless it is nipped in the bud."[54] – C. S. Lewis

In the world of addiction, there are two major categories: *addiction to substances*, which involves abuse of and dependency upon chemicals; and *addiction to patterns of behavior*. Many compulsive behaviors are hidden addictions. They are overlooked because they cause no harm and appear to be a positive influence on the person's life. They are celebrated—the super-woman, super-mom, super-athlete, and super-sheep. We are more apt to label them as obsessive or compulsive behaviors, not addictions. They may increase one's self-esteem versus tear it down. These compulsive "good" behaviors can wreak as much havoc on families, careers, and lives, as drug and alcohol addiction.

Behavioral addictions, often called *process addictions*, involve problematic repetitive behavior patterns, such as watching television marathons, Internet social networking, working, shopping, eating, reading, risk taking, engaging in sex, jogging, and religiosity. We can also become addicted to pain, worry, chaos, and stress. Many people struggle with both types of addiction simultaneously.

The following are socially sanctioned and usually perceived as healthy, essential activities with which most of the population has little concern or personal struggle. Yet, each of these activities has the potential to become an addiction:

- *Religion:* starting charities, helping, martyrdom, seeking a high from a worship service.

- *Health*: exercising, dieting, bodybuilding, heavy consumption of vitamins and supplements.
- *Beauty*: ongoing cosmetic treatments, plastic surgery, tanning (*tanorexia*), tattooing, apparel and accessory shopping.
- *Therapy*: needing regular fixes from a therapist or pastor to make it through the day.
- *Professional*: over-achieving, over-working, pursuing multiple academic degrees. For a stay at home mom it may be cleaning, cooking, or homeschooling.
- *Investments:* stock market risk taking, hoarding money, collecting, couponing.
- *Recreation*: thrill-seeking activities, Internet social networking, watching sports, TV, gaming, listening to music, reading, gardening, cooking, writing.
- *Family*: worshiping children, a spouse, parents, or pets.
- *Relationships*: celebrity and hero (including pastors) worship, people pleasing, codependency.

Founder of analytical psychology, Carl Jung, said, "Every form of addiction is bad, no matter whether the narcotic be alcohol, morphine or idealism."[55]

Recognizing and Controlling Addiction

My desire is for you to become aware of your behaviors and acknowledge you may have an issue with addiction and control. If you're not able to manage or stop an activity or behavior, there's a good chance you're addicted to it. What I've learned is the difference between having a passionate desire towards something and an addiction is *freedom*.

You can have all the willpower in the world, be working like crazy to stop, but you find you can't stop the behavior.

- If you have been unsuccessful in your attempts to cut out or cut down on your favorite thing, it may be an addiction.
- If your favorite thing interferes with your relationships, your work and family responsibilities, or your worship of god, it may be an addiction.

- If it dulls your awareness of your true feelings, it may be an addiction.
- If you continue to use it or do it despite negative consequences, it may be an addiction.

Addiction is a form of emotional anesthesia; an escape from responsibilities. Addicted people deceive themselves and others. They lie, deny, justify, or cover up their behavior; and rely on confused perceptions and misbeliefs. Life issues which need to be acknowledged and dealt with are not, thereby, enabling them to remain addicted. Like other compulsive behaviors, addiction is driven by deeper emotional factors such as, overwhelming helplessness, failure, rejection, anger, depression, abandonment, criticism, anxiety, even boredom.

Take exercise for example. Physical exercise is important because it enhances fitness and overall health and wellness. True. But if you *must* exercise daily, for extensive periods of time, then you're likely out of balance. Doctors warn there is a fine line between a healthy exercise regimen and addictive behavior that can harm the body. No amount of justification will change the fact that an addiction exists.

As a compulsive runner, my knees took an intense pounding day in day out. Consequently, I had two arthroscopic surgeries on both knees. As my thinking began to change, my rigid regimen began to relax. I could see how compulsive my routine was. It's important to exercise, but it's also important to listen to our bodies and not take exercise to extremes. I still exercise daily, but I've learned balance—when to work out and when to rest.

Reflect: You can have all the willpower in the world, be working like crazy to stop, but you find you can't stop the behavior. Secrets can be poison and lying can become a practice. If you hide it, deny it, justify it, or lie about your "favorite thing" when someone asks, that implies you probably feel bad or shameful. Your habit may be an addiction.

Not sure? Ask people you trust. Approach friends, family and/or a professional, and ask their honest and discreet opinion. "Do you think [issue] is a problem?" Remain silent. Listen carefully to their answer. Don't defend yourself. If they express concern, chances are this issue should be addressed.

The Workaholic

"We are not built for ourselves, but for God. Not for service for God, but for God." [56]
—Oswald Chambers

Tamara was addicted to success. She is what we'd call a "workaholic." She needed to be the best, accumulating accomplishments and always in pursuit of a "better" career. She even believed God wanted her to strive for this kind of success. If she ever started feeling anxious from her work load or like a failure she'd go shopping and buy a bunch of stuff. That temporarily made her feel better. These were her gods; gods that truth be told, didn't produce happiness for Tamara.

We live in a society which defines a person's value and worth by productivity and appearance. How much we get done, how well we do it, and how it looks are the benchmarks of a successful day. We are a people obsessed with meeting and surpassing goals, staying ahead of the pack, and working on weekends.

Maintaining a frantic schedule, being consistently preoccupied with work and performance, and being unable to relax, are symptoms of work addiction, called "workaholism." Workaholism in America has become an all-consuming obsession. Mental health professionals say it needs to be treated as an addiction.

This is a challenge because the Bible tells us we were created to work (Genesis 1:26). Work is part of our divine image, for God Himself is a worker (Genesis 2:2). Yet, for many people work is a curse. In the beginning, work was not a curse or a mountain to be conquered or an obsession. It was a calling. People worked for the glory of God.

What we learn from the creation account is the various activities of human life were never intended to be ends in themselves. We were made to work, but not become enslaved by it. When this balance is broken, work can become an idol … and a source of agony. God created the seventh day for rest for a reason. Our work must be managed within the context of a healthy relationship with God, marriage and family life, church, and community.

Given my personality type and history, it isn't too hard for me to take the work God gives me to do and focus on it excessively. After all, it gives me great pleasure. Doesn't Scripture say what I reap, I sow? Often, that didn't happen.

117 | The Perfect Counselor

Many days I've whined to God, "Where is the fruit of all my hard and laborious work? What did I do wrong?" What did God want from me? The answer: to have Him, not success, be my source of joy. To break the culture's definition of achievement. To live by faith and not sight. To learn to be content with the blessings He'd already given me.

God tells us, *"For my thoughts are not your thoughts, neither are your ways my ways" (Isaiah 55:8).* In other words, our definition of work is quite different from his. I have had to learn to find a balance between contentment and ambition. Anytime we take our focus off Christ and put it on ourselves to dazzle others with our accomplishments, the enemy wins. I constantly remind myself that numbers and success are not that important to God.

Success was not Jesus's ambition. Submission to His Father was. As Pastor Paul Scherer said, "You are not likely to be sent out under the will of God to do startling, impossible things. You are likely to be sent out to do the quiet, unspectacular things that matter, precisely where you are and with what you have."[57]

Reflect: Answer these questions with more than a yes or no. Talk to God about your answers.

- Do you believe God loves you based on what you do?
- Do you feel like you disappoint Him if you're not busy?
- Do you feel He wants you to work harder to be better?
- Do you find it hard to believe God loves you just the way you are?

The Solution

"The heart lusts, the mind lusts, the eyes lust, everything in oneself lusts until one is related to God."–Oswald Chambers

The consequences of addiction are: estrangement from God, habitual sin, health and relational problems. Unbeknown to us, the heart of any addiction is the longing for the holy. The only way to heal completely, I believe, is to first fill the hole in our soul with God Almighty's healing grace made available through Jesus Christ.

If there's any good in any of these addictions, it is that they lead us into the arms of Jesus, the Perfect Counselor. it also helps to remember that the destructiveness of addiction does not lie in the things we're attached to. they are simply part of creation and god made them essentially good. the destruction lies in our bondage to them. Temptation is everywhere, and we all too frequently get sucked into its trap.

Learning to break free of a multitude of negative and unhealthy coping styles has been a major challenge for me. The second step of the 12 Steps of AA states: "We came to believe that a power greater than ourselves could restore us to sanity." That power is Jesus Christ.

Jesus didn't talk about the "kingdom of God" as a physical location. He spoke of it as if it were a direction of the heart—something that we enter with our hearts through a trusting relationship with God. We can't use reason or head knowledge to enter a relationship with Him, only by the faith we carry in our hearts.

Jesus taught that only through our dependency upon God, and other healthy people, are we able to grow to be who He created us to be. Then the kingdom of God can spread—through the power of Jesus in our hearts.

Jesus asked us to trust Him, not because we are weak and needy so much, as it is the only way we can become who He created us to be. Addiction is a bad thing because it usurps and obscures our desire for the truest and deepest form of love and goodness—Jesus Himself. And no matter how religious or spiritual we think we are, our behaviors are always capable of sidetracking our love for Jesus. The more we can understand how enslavement happens, the more we'll be able turn the opposite way—back towards God, the creator of freedom.

Not until I asked Jesus to come and invade my life more deeply and I became hooked on the Word of God did I grasp God's healing grace. My life began to change positively, a direct result of God changing my desires and my mind as I developed a relationship with him and studied the Bible. I have learned to cultivate contentment, stop harmful practices, and challenge inaccurate beliefs. I'm dependent on Him every day because I know Christ in me is the only hope of ongoing positive change.

Identify Insatiable Cravings Exercise

Our objective is to examine everything in our lives that has taken on significant meaning—things we believe give us purpose, meaning and value; things we sense are "a chasing of the wind." I suggest you start to create a list of your habits. Putting your thoughts to paper will help you see the big picture.

1. Write down what you perceive to be the most frequent negative things you do. Think about the things that have become distractions from God. Note the obvious ones. Discovering the less obvious ones will require time.

2. Observe your habits closely. As you go about your day ask yourself these questions: "What activities take up most of my time?" "What do I think about most of the day?" How do I feel emotionally most of my day?

3. Answer this question: When it comes to "your favorite thing," does your behavior involve secrets, lies, deceptions?

This is a good start. If possible, ask your spouse, significant other, close friends, and/or family to share their observations. This requires honesty. They may not want to hurt your feelings. Tell them you desire an honest answer and won't get upset, then remain calm.

Make a commitment to regularly examine those things in your life that tend to take on enormous meaning. Then ask yourself, "Where is God in this?"

For a deeper study on this subject, check out my book, *Something Happened On My Way to Hell: Break Free From the Insatiable Pursuit of Pleasure.*

120 | **The Perfect Counselor**

8

Healing Painful Memories

You have turned my mourning into joyful dancing.
—David, speaking in Psalm 30:11 (NLT)

When the Japanese mend broken objects, *they magnify the damage* by filling the cracks with gold. They believe when something's suffered damage and has a history it becomes more exquisite and beautiful. What a beautiful picture of Jesus's restoration of our lives! When Jesus reunites the broken fragments with seams of gold, He heals the wounds which gives rise to empowerment, self-compassion, and restored dignity.

Freedom finally comes when we confront our past and put it in its proper perspective. *It happened to you but it is not you.* Restoration involves taking time to assess the fullness of the emotional damage, the false beliefs, the anger and bitterness, and poor choices which have developed. It cannot be rushed. We need to honor the feelings surrounding these past events. This means we allow ourselves to feel the anger, rage, sadness, hurt, abandonment, and loneliness of the situation. We simply allow ourselves to experience the feelings—no matter how big or small, scary or painful, uncomfortable, or traumatic. Then we begin to move on to living in today.

God created in us a defense mechanism. Our minds won't allow more pain to surface than we're able to handle. Some people won't recall painful childhood memories until they're adults. We can trust that God will bring the bad memories one by one to the surface when we're ready. When He does, we must see them for what they are: *not today's reality.* God doesn't want the hurts to keep us in bondage. One by one He touches each painful memory. And with His touch comes healing.

121 | The Perfect Counselor

God said, *"Now choose life, so that you and your children may live"* (Deut. 30:19). We were created to really "live." Start by letting God love you. Remember, He'll never force Himself on you. Evil forces itself—not Love. The problems before us are *never* bigger than the Power behind us. Regardless of how dark it seems right now, there is an end in sight! *"When the earth and all its people quake, it is I [God] who hold its pillars firm"* (Psalm 75:3).

Memory Work

In his book, *The Art of Understanding Yourself*, Dr. Cecil Osborne stated that everyone spends at least 50 percent of their energy keeping repressed memories below the level of consciousness trying to avoid anxiety.[58] Anxiety disorders are common. When we begin to recognize the losses, depression can be brought on. If not dealt with, it can quickly turn into despair, then despondency. This is when we stop responding to life.

What we believe about the toxic situation is sitting in our minds. And our brains and our bodies obey our minds. Therefore, if we have toxic emotions and thoughts (unconscious and conscious), we will have sickness. *Therefore, memory work is important.*

Dr. Peter Levine stated in his book *Trauma and Memory*, that *changing our current feeling state* is a prerequisite for effectively working with traumatic memories.[59] It is my objective through the material in this book, and of course through the power of the Holy Spirit, to help you gain control over your present mood, emotions, and bodily sensations (sensation from skin, muscles, bones, tendons and joints)—so you can sort through the memories and let the information shape your present and future in a healthy way.

The objective of memory work is to build new good memories (images) and reshape old toxic memories. Transformation involves altering brain neurology. *Until we can change the automatic triggered images and sensations that define our reality, we will not be transformed.* We can gather a lot of information, use willpower, and pray all we want. But until our internal world is transformed, we won't change. Therefore, the Bible tells us to "take every thought captive to Christ" (2 Cor. 10:5). To be transformed we must "renew" our minds (Romans 12:2; Eph. 4:22-23).

The goal is to work *with* rather than *against* these images and memories so we can break their strongholds. We want to restore continuity between the past and the future.

122 | The Perfect Counselor

Understand Your Brain
–Understand Yourself

"I used drugs and drank alcohol, and had sex with a lot of guys, all between the ages of 11 and 16. Getting a DUI scared me coz I almost killed someone. Right then I quit the drinking and drugs. I've done a pretty good job at straightening out my life. Yet I find that my past is still defining me. I find that old toxic thoughts and memories pop up out of nowhere. I get anxious and stomach aches. What's going on?" –Kesha

Scientists state *every* experience is stored in our brain's visual center. Neurological pathways are created and entrenched. Those images, and sensory data from the experiences, can arise anytime. Each time we recall one of those images we strengthen the neurological pathway, making it stronger.[60] The result is: We can get flooded and blindsided with toxic responses.

Do you desire to be healed from painful experiences? Yes. Then it is important to learn to distinguish between: one, the toxic experience, and two, your emotional response to it. For example, Brenda was verbally attacked by her gym teacher for several minutes in front of her classmates in the 6th grade. Ever since, whenever she sees a large athletic man, fear grips her. She experiences symptoms of anxiety (chest pain and stomach upset).

When we experience an emotion, instructions are sent out to other parts of the brain and then passed on to the rest of the body, leading to physical changes. For Brenda, male athletes and fear have become fused together in her brain. This can happen to any of us.

Our brains process and serve up information with whatever seems relevant for the task it's performing. We automatically assume the information our brains give us is the reality we experienced. We assume it's truth. Our brains don't tell us the information is false, which is why we stay enslaved to lies about ourselves.

The adult Brenda knows intellectually that all male athletes are not bad. But once activated, the image that was created when Brenda was in 6th grade, had the power to override this information. When she comes upon a large male athlete, Brenda enters a reality in which she feels fearful. She has made her 12-year-old experience a present-day reality. As an adult, Brenda doesn't know this is happening because it occurs in a fraction of a second, and she *immediately* feels its impact.

Brenda's brain was effectually doing its job, just the way God created it—but it was being used against her. Her brain was trying to protect her by responding to triggers and immediately recalling past experiences that might help her in a present situation. In a fallen world, the brain often installs lies instead of truth. The past is made present again, and the result is significant bondage to a lie that all male athletes are verbally abusive.

Reflect: What do you conclude from this?

Healing Painful Experiences

"Bring up the past only if you are going to build from it."
—Domenico Cieri Estrada

We can't live like this anymore. We're daughters of King Jesus and must hold ourselves to a different standard than our culture. Christ has called us to be women who know and speak truth, who live in the light, who openly settle our conflicts rather than withdraw, or become embittered, or fight back. More importantly, we need to answer this question: Do we believe that no matter what our past, and what appears to be happening all around us, God is in control and has our best interests at heart? If we don't believe this, then we allow the enemy to take control, and we go crazy!

Our heart's desire is to heal from painful past experiences. To do this means we must learn to examine and investigate the images, memories, and feelings that comprise our inner world (our psyche or soul). We will need to learn to step outside of our thoughts and observe them (dissociate). As long as we remain attached to them, we identify with them. Then we cannot control them—they control us.

Scripture tells us to *"take captive every thought" to Christ"* (2 Cor. 10:5) and to *"be transformed by the renewing of your mind"* (Romans 12:2). Yet, it's very difficult to capture and renew something that's already captured us, and we're not even aware of it. We can wish and pray all we want. But if we keep seeing, hearing, and sensing in our minds the reality that is associated with a negative emotion or memory, it *cannot* change.

Positive Experiences

Have you ever wondered why it feels good to express pain to someone who empathizes with you? For one, we tend to feel calmer, better, and less fearful. People for centuries have touted the benefits of talking about a painful experience with another person.

Neuropsychologist, Rick Hanson, addresses this from the standpoint of what's going on in the brain. Positive experiences can be used to soothe, balance, and even replace negative ones. When two things are held in the mind at the same time they start to connect with each other. That's one reason why talking about hard things with someone who's supportive can be so healing: *The painful feelings and memories get infused with the comfort, encouragement, and closeness you experience with the other person.*

What this means to us is: We can work to update toxic memories by bringing in new, positive relevant information, thereby enabling us to survive and thrive in future challenges.

A neuroscientist at Rutgers University found if other things are in your mind while you call up a memory—and if they're strongly pleasant or unpleasant—the brain automatically puts them together—like two puzzle pieces. When this memory leaves the conscious, it is stored along with those other associations. The next time the memory is activated, it will tend to bring those associations with it. Therefore, if we repeatedly bring to our minds negative feelings and thoughts while a memory is active, then that memory will be saved and focused in a negative direction.

For example, I was fired from a job. I never saw it coming. When bringing up this memorable experience I automatically began attacking myself: *If only I had ... I should have ... then I wouldn't have lost my job.* Recalling an experience while at the same time attacking myself makes this experience and failure appear increasingly worse.

If, instead, I follow up this memory with a positive response, such as,

Truth be told, this job wasn't the right fit. And I didn't put in the proper amount of time learning my tasks. I understand why they fired me. With God's help, my next job will be the perfect fit for me. God promised me in Jeremiah 29:1: "I have it all planned out— plans to take care of you, not abandon you, plans to give you the future you hope for" (MSG).

125 | The Perfect Counselor

I may also choose to add a positive image, such as, "When my sister got fired, it ended up being the best thing that ever happened to her."

This truthful influence will be *slowly woven* into the memory of being fired, and emotionally and physically I will be better off.

Memories are being rewritten repeatedly in one's life. They can be rewritten to move us toward greater empowerment and peace![61] Every time we add positive information and feelings into negative and painful states of mind, *over time*, the accumulation of positive material will literally change our brains. This is *taking captive every thought to make it obedient to Christ.*

Martina said, "I learned one way to take my bad memories and thoughts captive was by doing something good to help other women in pain." Good advice Martina! We need to realize: *We are not what we think, and not what we feel.*

Reflect: We all make the best decisions we can. We get the best information we can find at the time and we just move on it. Sometimes we don't have enough good and truthful information—especially about ourselves. Give an example of when this has happened to you.

Updating A Memory
(Add Something Better to It)

"We may strive, with good reason, to escape our past, or to escape what's bad in it, but we will escape it only by adding something better to it." –Wendell Berry

Seven-year-old Sara recalls her 13-year-old step-brother, Allan, beating her up on a regular basis. She told her mom but Mom never to said a word to Alan. Her response was, "That's what boys do." Today Sara is an adult and is still angry at her mom because she didn't protect her from Allan.

We can't change what happened to us, but we can change the meaning of what happened. We can be taught to neutralize the haunting sense of fear and hopelessness. When something triggers an abusive memory, or feeling, or bodily sensation, instead of shoving it back down, we can choose to introduce a new, positive experience.

Through counseling and choosing to confront her mother about the situation, Sara learned that because her mom was the only girl in her family (she had four brothers) she believed this is what boys do—beat each other up. Her mom's parents never interfered when the boys got into any type of conflicts, physical or verbal. Adding this knowledge to the memory softened it. The process goes like this:

- A traumatizing experience occurred (past). →
- Creates a bad memory. →
- Bad memory gets triggered by some sort of stimulus (from what our senses tell us.) →
- *Signals body:* Causes a physical response we cannot control (part of the automatic threat mechanism God built into our bodies). →
- Increased heart rate and blood pressure; secretion of cortisol and adrenaline; facial muscles form expression of fear and sadness; body muscles tense and posture is slumped. →
- *Feel:* Experience a feeling directly connected to what our body is doing. I.e. fear, sadness, pain. →
- We *think* about what's happening and search for solutions as to why we're feeling this way. →
- *Update the memory* → two possible choices.

Choice #1: Update the memory by adding something negative (Unconscious Driven).

- *Mind develops an action plan to deal with the problem/memory:* Ruminates (means mulls over repeatedly) on the negative experience →
- *Thinks:* "I need these bad feelings to go away. I know shopping for shoes will do this." →
- *Action:* Gets a high from purchasing three new pairs of shoes and temporarily forgets. → Feels guilt and shame for spending money she didn't have to spend. →
- Creates new negative image. → Attaches to the old memory →
- Compounds past negative memory. →
- *Result:* Increased toxic thinking and acting out.

Choice #2: Update the memory by adding something positive (Conscious Driven).

- *Mind develops an action plan:* Chooses *not* to ruminate on the negative experience →
- *Thinks:* "I need to be with someone who can console me," or "I need more information." →
- *Action:* Calls a friend or pastor; and/or gathers truthful and helpful information; and/or recalls a positive image. →
- Creates new positive image. → Attaches to old image/memory. →
- Minimizes toxic body and mind effects; changes present-day images.
- *Result:* The ability to "look back" at a traumatic memory from an empowered position.

This insight gives us hope! By altering a memory, we can find peace. While we don't have the power to directly change our emotions, we can change the image with which our emotions are associated. We can't change fear, shame, jealousy by willing it away. But we can permanently alter the image to which these emotions are associated. *Yet,* we must have the "want to" to do the work and be patient. Re-programming takes time.

Reflect: Think of a time when you intentionally re-focused a thought surrounding a negative situation. What was the outcome?

Intentional Focused Thinking

We can learn to *reframe* negative memories and transform the way we feel about them. We can also create positive events in our minds by experiencing something as though it were real. God tells us how. The Living Bible version of Philippians 4:8 reads:

"Fix your thoughts on what is true and good and right. Think about things that are pure and lovely, and dwell on the fine, good things in others."

Filling our minds with all the good things that God has created, and *experiencing* those good things in our minds, will evoke positive emotions. If we dwell on things that are "the worst," we'll always feel down. If we redirect our thoughts onto things that are "the best," we can feel at our best.

This means what we're able to do, with the power of the Holy Spirit at work in us, is soften, reshape, and reweave the experience. This process will take time, but it is possible. Jeannie was sexually abused by her stepfather. Whenever she visited their home, she'd get extremely nauseated.

Although her stepdad had confessed, asked for forgiveness, and repented, every time Jennie was in his presence, his personal odor triggered the past abuse. In time, through "Intentional Focused Thinking"—*the process of pulling up, visualizing, and practicing "intentional" thoughts in our minds*—she learned to:

- Focus her awareness on the presence of God in that moment.
- Tell God how she was feeling, and reassure herself God was in control and would take care of her.
- Pull up a comforting Scripture she had memorized.
- Become aware of her posture and muscles. She'd work to consciously relax her muscles and sit up straight.
- Told her mind, "I will not let this triggered past memory get in the way of having a positive visit with my mom and step-dad."

What Jennie did was remain centered and focused on a positive experience— the goodness and care of God. She brought the past negative experience into the picture, but not as a dominant focus. She brought her concerns to God, never taking her attention off Him.

Let me be clear: *Updating our memories in no way takes away from the truth that a harmful event occurred, and that grief and outrage may be significant components. And it certainly doesn't negate that an offender must be accountable for the offense.*

Get into the habit of pulling up memorized life-giving and comforting "go to" Bible verses. Begin by choosing one of these Scriptures and read it slowly five times.

- *"Now we can come fearlessly right into God's presence, assured of his glad welcome when we come with Christ and trust in him"* (Ephesians 3:12, TLB).
- *"He who began a good work in you will carry it on to completion until the day of Christ Jesus"* (Philippians 1:6).

- *"I can do all this through him who gives me strength"* (Philippians 4:13).

Hope

"And will not God bring about justice for his chosen ones, who cry out to him day and night? Will he keep putting them off? I tell you, He'll see that they get justice, and quickly." –Jesus, speaking in Luke 18:7-8

God has built into each one of us the instinct to persevere and to heal in the aftermath of overwhelming events and loss. As we've just seen, we are capable of surviving, adapting to, and eventually transforming distressing experiences. God's built into us an innate drive for resolution and triumph!

Your Will + God's Power = Transformation

There is no area in your life so painful, no offense so heinous, that God's grace cannot heal it. When you begin to bring up a memory you may experience a variety of not so great physical symptoms, like anxiety. This is your body telling you that something is wrong; something needs to be fixed.

Our goal is to allow the memories to take their rightful place—to remain in the past where they belong—not in the present or future. God promises to make all things new (Rev. 21:5; 2 Cor. 5:17). I suggest working through these three significant exercises in a quiet, safe environment.

Exercise #1: Telling Our Story

In the Old Testament, we meet Esther (see the book of Esther). She's a young Jewish woman living in exile in Persia, who through her youth and beauty becomes queen of the Persian Empire. Through her wits and courage, she saves the Jewish people from destruction. How? She chose to speak up.

Esther spoke to the king at great risk. Even though she was his wife, it was considered inappropriate to approach the king. Esther had a choice: Speak up and save her people, or remain silent and see them killed. She chose to speak and the Jews were saved. You too can make a difference in someone else's life by speaking up and telling your story.

Telling our stories can be empowering and healing. Developing a narrative can help us regain ownership of our lives. Right now, you may feel stuck, unable to develop the narrative.

Yet, looking at each experience will likely entail lamenting and coming to terms with the suffering—past and present. It is a process of learning to reinterpret it all as a story where God's glory can be manifested. God has an amazing way of helping us call up the past without becoming overwhelmed by what's lurking inside. Everyone has a story.

We've been washed by the blood of Jesus; therefore, we can tell ours without the fear and shame; the grief and rage. In telling your story you can begin to find self-forgiveness, and shift the blame onto the shoulders of the offender. It's a powerful way to validate your experiences. You're the expert when it comes to your story. It must be heard, believed, and respected. If you've been abused, the abusers and perpetrators must be named. In cases where minors are involved it must be reported to authorities.

Speaking out is to open the door and let God's light in. *"The truth will set you free!"* (John 8:32) Jesus will meet you where you're at. He is *the* Redeemer. He'll show you the way out!

Preparing Your Story

"We need to speak as God gives us utterance and boldness and then leave the results to Him."—Dr. David Jeremiah

When you begin to talk about it you don't have to tell the entire story or divulge any uncomfortable or painful points. I suggest beginning by writing your story in small pieces. Writing from the third person perspective (writing it as if someone else is telling your story) may help you move forward and see all sides of your story, while still achieving emotional growth.

Share a portion you feel is significant to your healing. Please remember: Facing the past and feeling the emotions associated with it does not require reliving the past or purposely creating flashbacks. But leaving the past untouched will only negate healing—and empower the enemy, and add to shame and self-hatred. It may help you to write it out first.

Reflect: Finish these sentences:
- The thought of opening my darkest secrets to another person makes me feel …
- Some risks of sharing might be …

- Some benefits of sharing might be …

Telling your story may create a waterfall of emotions, but the feelings will eventually balance out.

Exercise #2: Creating a Safe Memory

What we want to learn to do is pull up the negative visual image, and the feelings and physical sensations of the event, and then create a new positive image to attach to the old toxic image. As you go through the process of feeling and observing everything you are seeing and feeling, you may want to write it down. This can be scary. Therefore, before you begin, pray for clarity, wisdom, and truth. Remind yourself of God's promises to you:

- Isaiah 41:10: *Do not fear, for I am with you; do not be dismayed, for I am your God. I will strengthen you and help you; I will uphold you with my righteous right hand.*
- Psalm 28:7: *The LORD is my strength and my shield [protector]; my heart trusts in him, and he helps me.*
- Deuteronomy 31:6: *Be strong and courageous. Do not be afraid or terrified because of them, for the LORD your God goes with you; He'll never leave you nor forsake you.*

Part 1: Ask God to help you focus your memory on *one* event in your past—a time when you were hurt, where your needs for love, or acceptance, or worthiness, or spirituality, were not met; or where you were left feeling abandoned, unloved, and/or ashamed.

Sit quietly. Relax all your muscles. Close your eyes. Take three deep breaths. Now go there with God. Hold onto this memory. Observe, explore, and feel every bodily sensation and movement in detail.

- What do you see? Is your memory in color or black and white?
- What can you hear?
- Are you "associated" or "disassociated" to your memory?
- How does this memory make you feel? Be specific. Speak to your present mood, emotions, and bodily sensations.
- How intense is the pain in this memory?

- Can you verbalize what the enemy stole from you during your times of suffering?
- Do you experience anything else in your memory?
- When you feel this memory, how and where does it hurt? (For example, in your heart, head, or part of your body?)

Part 2: Now that this memory is active, create a new image that says, "I'm no longer in danger. I'm safe." For many people, this greatly minimizes negative body and mind effects. If we can feel safety in the present moment with God at our side, there can be resolution. God's own words:

"They will live in safety, and no one will make them afraid. I will provide for them ... and they will no longer be victims ... Then they will know that I, the LORD their God, am with them" (Ezekiel 34:28-30).

Our goal is to stay in the present and track our various troubling sensations, emotions, and images—and meet them head on without feeling overwhelmed, yet feeling *I'm no longer in danger! I'm safe!*

Exercise #3: Visualization

We are learning that by adding new experiences, we can become empowered survivors. We can use the power of our imagination, called "visualization." Through *intentional focused thinking,* our thoughts and what we see in our minds alters the brain's neuron and nerve cells, changing the way our brain works.[62]

Practicing Visualization

This is how Jamie used "visualization" to prepare for a meeting with her husband (whom she's separated from). Jamie said, "I felt it was important to really imagine myself strong—a powerful successful business woman. I saw myself walking into that meeting with my head high, shoulders back; projecting tremendous confidence! Everything about me communicated I was strong, in control, and stable. I could feel my arms and legs and shoulder muscles—they were solid. Then I saw myself interacting with him competently. I was in complete control!"

This new experience of empowerment, added to the old experience of being victimized, updated Jamie's memory of feeling overwhelmed and helpless in the face of her abusive husband with a new empowered version.

When you think about future events, envision yourself talking and acting in ways that help you feel confident about yourself. Envision God at your side, and putting a hedge of protection around you.

After visualizing the situation, feel the *strength* and *power* in every part of your body that is responding. Spiritual power will help you mobilize and stand up for yourself, getting what you need, thereby opening new possibilities.

The good news is: God has designed us as beings who are capable of surviving, adapting to, and eventually transforming traumatic experiences. He's built into us an innate drive for perseverance and triumph! Now when the devil brings to your mind any toxic thought or memory of the trauma, tell him—*I am no longer in danger! I am safe! God's got me!*

Reflect on Eleanor Roosevelt's words: "You gain strength, courage, and confidence by every experience in which you really stop to look fear in the face. You are able to say to yourself, "I have lived through this horror. I can take the next thing that comes along. You must do the thing you think you cannot do."

Self-Soothers

These exercises are tough. It's important we care for ourselves as we go through each one. The Bible says, *"Slow down. Take a breath. What's the hurry? Why wear yourself out?" (Jer. 2:25, MSG)* Here are three self-soothing suggestions:

Breathing. Place one hand on your chest and the other on your stomach. Breathe normally. Focus on feeling your chest rise. Now breathe deep from your belly so you can feel your other hand rise. Practice three deep breaths. When people are stressed, they tend to breathe shallowly from their chests rather than from their stomachs. Deep breathing from our stomachs activates a different brain pathway which causes the brain and body to calm down.

134 | **The Perfect Counselor**

Relaxation. Sit comfortably or lie on the floor. Close your eyes. Flex and tighten your feet for two seconds while inhaling deeply. Hold your breath and then exhale deeply. Relax your tightened muscles after each deep exhale. Do this with all your muscle groups: the calves, buttocks, stomach, hands, shoulders, face, scalp, and ears. *"Be still and know I am God" (Psalm 46:10).*

Focus on God's character and/or on Scripture. We all need to discipline ourselves to have a constant internal dialogue with God. An amazing thing happens when we slow down, relax, and begin focusing on God—certain parts of the brain are activated, which result in peace, order, and calm—health to the mind and body. For this benefit to happen, we must willfully, persistently, and determinedly choose to listen and focus on God.

9

You Mean I'm Not Stupid or Crazy?

Your eyes light up your inward being. A pure eye lets sunshine into your soul. *—Jesus, speaking in Luke 11:34* (TLB)

Mirror, mirror on the wall, who's the fairest of them all?

What does your mirror answer? *Not you—you're stupid, crazy, ugly, unlovable, bad, unacceptable, weak, a failure, and hopelessly damaged!*

If you're like many women, the "you" that you experience is not the real "you." The "real you" is trapped inside the "you" who has been conformed to this world; the "you" who's been largely defined by your upbringing, past experiences, labels, and the culture in which you live. The result is you start believing lies about yourself. If you believe the lies long enough, it becomes truth—at least, truth as you perceive it.

Imagine you're a brand-new tube of *Arm & Hammer Truly Radiant* toothpaste. What happens over time to a tube of toothpaste when the paste is forced out? It changes shape. And the more the paste is squeezed and forced out, the tube changes shape until it is unrecognizable. It's no longer "truly radiant." God made us like the brand-new tube—*Truly Radiant!* Yet, what we feel like and see in our mirrors is a damaged, flattened, and empty tube.

One challenge we have in dealing with falsely wired feelings and beliefs, and complicated grief, is that *we identify ourselves with those beliefs*. Our brains have hardwired our conclusions about "the real me"—which is out of sync with the "true me." Our identity—our image of ourselves—is wrapped up so tightly with our feelings that we can't imagine who we are without them, which only keeps us in bondage.

136 | **The Perfect Counselor**

Moving forward, when we stare at our mirrors we must envision and believe in a new identity for ourselves—the identity God created for us. We must *doubt our belief—even though it feels real.* Then we can bring any false belief about ourselves into alignment with the truth.

Who Am I?

When I was a kid, several times a year I'd put together a play for my parents, grandparents, and the neighborhood. I was the screenwriter, director, and of course—the star. And direct I did: "I'll be the fairy princess. Philip (brother) you be the tree. Jeff (brother), you can be the frog." A few neighbor kids were always hanging around, and they'd ask: "Who am I going to be?"

Like my brothers and the neighborhood kids, we look to others to tell us who we are. "Who am I?" is a difficult question to answer on our own. We can only answer "Who am I?" when we're in relationships. Tamara said, "When I got divorced my title of wife vanished. I had a new label: unwanted, rejected, and loser. Every day, I hated myself. I continually battle feeling like a worthless nobody, like I have no identity."

Have you noticed we tend to label people … and ourselves? If we believe the label that's been given to us, then we think and behave like it. *We become what we believe.* Tamara, like so many of us, has no genuine self-esteem apart from her role (label) of wife and mother.

Lies we believe about ourselves *feel* more real than the truth does. If we've been told repeatedly we're stupid, ugly, incapable, fat, unlovable, or worthless by those we thought cared about us, it's extremely difficult to *not* believe these lies. Thus, we hustle for our worthiness by constantly performing, perfecting, pleasing, and proving.

If you've seen the movie *The Wizard of Oz,* then you remember the wizard. His booming voice and larger than life presence came alive on screen. He wanted everyone to think he was big and powerful. When Dorothy approached him, he frightened her. One day when he was ranting about how powerful he was, Dorothy's little dog, Toto, found the wizard hiding and exposed him. The truth was out. This assuming powerful man wasn't a wizard, nor was he very big. He was rather small and ordinary.

When we believe the lie that others are big and we're small and unimportant, we feel helpless and powerless. It's spiritual identity theft. It is critical to our overall health that we learn to detect the lies and then demolish them. We must come to see ourselves the way God sees us. *Nothing outside of God will ever give us what we're looking for.*

Reflect: What lies and/or labels do you wear as your identity? How is your identity attacked because of pain in your life?

Our Stories

"Memory is the selection of images; some elusive, others printed indelibly on the brain, each image is like a thread, each thread woven together to make a Tapestry of intricate texture, and the Tapestry tells a story, and the story is our past."
– Eve's Bayou, Screenplay by Kasi Lemmons

A magnificent characteristic of the mind is it weaves what we encounter through our five senses into a "story." We are storytelling creatures. To think, feel, and act, we must construct a story that fits all the bits of information we take in every second of the day. We need to put it together in a way that makes sense. These stories make up our belief systems. From these stories, we develop a particular way of seeing ourselves and God—which directs the way we think and act. Every belief we have operates under our radar, on the unconscious level, influencing us. Just as our bodies are built from the foods we eat; our minds are built from our experiences.

Every person is born with a brain that is split into two parts—right and left. The left side is more *rational*. The right side, more *relational*. This is how it works: the feeling beliefs from our right brain are formed in the first 2 to 3 years of life. They establish our feelings about ourselves. We ask unspoken unconscious questions such as:

- *What am I like? Am I lovable or unlovable; valuable or worthless?*

- *What are other significant people in my life like? Are they understanding, compassionate, caring. Or, are they controlling, unloving, critical, or abusive?*

- *Is this world a safe and secure place? How do I fit and connect into the world?*

Our beliefs are based on the answers to these questions, which continue to change through ongoing life experiences. *We believe what we feed into our minds.* For example, if I *experience*, versus if I'm told, that I'm lovable and my home is a safe place, I'll likely grow up happy and well-adjusted. On the other hand, if I've never *experienced* real love and proper care, and I *experience* that power and control are what makes a functional family, this is what I'll believe; it's my reality.

It is a fact: If a little girl has never seen a goat; never seen a picture or had one described to her, and you show her a cow and tell her it is a goat, she'll believe you. The point is: We accept what we are taught without questioning. Once a belief or thought about ourselves goes into our minds, it becomes true as far as we're concerned. We don't question its validity. What's the problem here? Failure to see truth.

This is interesting: Even if we can't remember (recall) specific events from our baby-toddler years, scientists state the memories nevertheless leave lasting traces that effect our behavior.

Once we learn something it becomes an automatic and unconscious belief which we carry into adolescence, then into adulthood. These beliefs become responses, and are triggered automatically whenever we meet or think, or even smell, another person or situation that reminds us of an earlier, perhaps even painful, experience.

Our emotional right brain nearly always wins the battles because it developed earlier than the left rational brain. Yet, it is the left brain that convinces us that our thoughts are correct and we're in full control. For example, we think we're being rational in a certain situation, but others would disagree. We put our own spin on our thoughts!

We experience this in our relationship with God too. Our logical left brain believes, "God loves and forgives me" because this is biblically true. But our emotional right brain automatically disagrees. It says, "Look at what I did! God won't forgive me for this. It's unforgivable." Or, "God isn't trustable, because all men are not trustable."

Reflect: How can you use this knowledge to help you heal?

139 | **The Perfect Counselor**

Our Selfies and Beliefs

"Our mental health is largely dependent on our understanding of the world and our thoughts about ourselves, other people, the future, and the world." –Dr. Peter Kinderman

We live in a culture of "selfies." If you own a smartphone you probably take selfies to share via social media. Some people can't stop taking them. Over our lifetime, it's like we've created a book of selfies starting at about 2-years-old. Each selfie is made up of interpretations, evaluations of situations, and words spoken to us. Then each one was carefully placed and glued into our minds, like a photo album. From all these experiences, we construct in our minds who we are—our selfie. This is called our "self-image."

Once a belief about ourselves goes into this picture it becomes true as far as we're concerned. We don't question its validity. *Feelings of inferiority don't originate so much from facts or experiences, but rather from conclusions we make about those facts or experiences.*

As a kid and young adult I suffered from a poor self-image. You could say I was self-centered: Low self-esteem kept me focused on my weaknesses. I believed no one could love me. I chose to socialize in bars because it lowered my inhibitions when I drank significant amounts of alcohol. This of course, created other problems.

Most often, we feel inferior because we judge, compare, and measure ourselves against some other person's or society's standard. We conclude we must measure up to that standard. If we believe we can't, we *feel* unworthy. If I feel unworthy, then I *feel* I don't deserve to be loved or happy.

Dr. Maxwell Maltz wrote, "You'll act like the sort of person you conceive yourself to be … you literally cannot act otherwise, despite all your conscious efforts." Proverbs 23:7 says, *"For as he thinks in his heart, so he is."*

Reflect: Someone once said, "I am what I am today because of what I believed about myself yesterday. And I'll be tomorrow what I believe about myself today—unless new positive experiences change how I think." Who are you today because of what you believed about yourself yesterday?

Love and Worth

"No one can make you feel inferior without your consent." –Eleanor Roosevelt

What amazes me is no matter the culture, we all struggle with self-image, beauty, and belonging. To understand why, we need to grasp the difference between *unconditional* and *conditional* love.

As a recovering passive people-pleaser, I can tell you I'm this way because I was raised in a home where I was made to feel acceptable only if I behaved in ways that won my parents approval. I made choices based on the rewards promised me. So, I learned it was safer to be and do what others wanted me to, rather than make my own choices. Consequently, I had no sense of my true self.

Conditional love means there are conditions attached to love. It teaches us we are what we do, or have, or look like. So, we're driven to see our value and worth by conditions around us. We feel the need to prove ourselves, become over-achievers, perfectionists, and people-pleasers to validate our worth. It's a punishing way to live because we're all fatally flawed.

Unconditional love instead says, "No matter what I do or say or look like, I'm loved—period." The Greeks called this "agape" (pronounced *ah-gop-ee*) love. It is an unselfish, thoughtful, sacrificial love that voluntarily suffers inconvenience, discomfort, and even death for another person *without expecting anything in return*. Unconditional love delights in giving, and keeps on loving and giving, regardless of the other person's response. It says, "I've seen the ugly parts of you and I don't think any less of you. I'm staying!" This is how God loves us. "God is love" (1 John 4:8). Because God *is* love—He is unable to otherwise.

Victor Hugo wrote, "The greatest happiness of life is the conviction that we are loved—loved for ourselves." Jesus loves us with agape love. Want proof? While we were sinners and rebelling against God, He died for us—*without expecting anything in return*. The only thing He desires is that we place our faith and future in Him.

Reflect: Make a list of people who've given you different names, or labels, or diagnoses in your life. Write beside their name the label you heard.

- Answer, "Did this label help or hinder you in your personal growth?"
- Then go back through the list and put an X through the labels you wish to leave behind.
- Repeat this exercise, this time write down the labels you gave yourself. For example, *Mother:* Lazy; *Doctor:* ADD; *Teacher:* Bad girl; *Me:* stupid, bad, incapable.

We Become What We Believe

It's true: *We become what we believe.* Personally, because I despised myself, I lowered my standards in the men I got into relationships with. I felt unworthy, therefore, I gave them what they wanted sexually. The way I *behaved* was based on what I *believed* about myself. When we're told *we are* "something," then we'll act it out. Sexual abuse survivors, for example, often reason, "*I'm* a dirty slut, so I *will act* like one." Sadly, they have no idea that in God's eyes they're *exceptionally* beautiful, valuable, worthy, and lovable.

It makes no difference whether our beliefs are true or false. What really matters is how often we are exposed to the messages behind the beliefs. Research from UCSB showed that a weak message repeated twice becomes more binding than a strong message heard only once.

One single person's message, repeated only one time, has the power to unconsciously change our beliefs! This explains why the advertising industry does what it does. When we're not conscious of what we're exposing ourselves to, repetitive messages will always have their way.

Visualize God saying to you, "Look at the way you view yourself. You've been labeled and deceived. You don't feel worthy, pretty, or accomplished. You don't feel valuable, or loved, and accepted. Those were horrible lies you believed about yourself. Your labels are not who you are. Resolve that your feelings are not always a credible source of your worth. I created you to be free! Free your mind to experience real life under my Lordship."

What is your reaction to these words—how do you feel spiritually, emotionally, and physically?

The Truth Is …

So often our life experiences, which are deeply entrenched in our unconscious right brains, force us to believe things that conflict with what we know the Bible teaches—and what we so badly want to experience in our relationships with God and others. *Therefore, we find some of our behaviors and beliefs so difficult to change.* It is like that image of the devil on one side of your shoulder and an angel on the other side, arguing back and forth.

The solution: We investigate and become detectives our thoughts. And when we discover the truth, we can argue back, "This is my emotional right brain speaking the lie I've believed for decades. The truth is, God loves me and truly forgives me—now and forever. I won't listen to my lying thoughts anymore!"

Pain comes from believing you are someone other than who God says you are. There will always be conflict between who you are being and who God created you to be. Anxiety, depression, fear, and pain are alarms that say, *"Look at what you're thinking right now. Your self-talk is not true. You're living a story which isn't true."* Therefore, we must acknowledge and learn to interrogate deeply embedded lies and misbeliefs. (The upcoming chapters will move you through the process.)

Reflect: Today, how do you act like the person you imagine yourself to be (who does your mirror tell you who you are)?

Discover the Beauty You've Always Had

God creates. Our real story begins in Genesis, which means "beginning." Genesis 1 is the first part of the creation drama—God sets the stage for "life." After God filled the earth with every kind of creature, the Bible reads,

"Let us ["us" is the triune God: God the Father; Christ the Son; Holy Spirit] make human beings in our image, to be like ourselves… God created man in his own image, in the image of God he created him; male and female he created them" (Genesis 1:26-27). … "And the LORD God formed man [human beings] of the dust of the ground, and breathed into his nostrils the breath of life; and man became a living soul" (Genesis 2:7).

This is an image of intimacy. Like a master sculptor and artist, God "formed" us, just as a potter forms a beautiful pot out of a lump of clay. Man is the only creature upon whom God "breathes" the breath of life. Picture it: God spoke. He took some of the new earth and made an image into which He imparted some of Himself. He sent His Spirit, an invisible beam of light and divinity, into mankind; and man's soul came to life. This is our "spiritual nature."

Image of God simply means "made like God." We were made to resemble Him and to reflect His characteristics. Only man is described in this way. Genesis 5:1 says, *"When God created mankind, he made them in the likeness of God."* God skillfully created us as an intricate masterpiece! We're not called to be God, but be "like God." The reason becomes clear in the first few chapters of Genesis 2: Man is a creature with whom the Creator, God Himself, has a personal connection and relationship with. He created us with an innate desire or "drive" for relationship, with Himself first, then others.

"In His image" means, we've been designed like God to love and be loved; to share and be shared with. And, when we're connected to God, through prayer, meditation, and Bible study, all the networks of our brains function at their best.[63] This is how we've been designed!

Wonderfully Made!

In Psalm 139, David acknowledges how God created us,

"For you created my inmost being; you knit me together in my mother's womb. I praise you because I am fearfully and wonderfully made; your works are wonderful" (13-14).

Mankind was not made from some "cookie cutter" mold, but as a rich tapestry of features, appearances, talents, gifts, and personalities. God used the "dust of the ground" to create our entire being. We were created from dirt. Many people take offense to this. I don't. Being made from the dust of the earth's ground means *I'm a star.* We are made of the same material as stars—those heavenly celestial twinkling points of light.

The theory that every person and everything on Earth contains minuscule star particles dates to the early 1980s when the late astronomer Carl Sagan stated, "We are star stuff." There's solid science behind this. Almost every element on Earth, including mankind, was formed from the heart of a star.

144 | The Perfect Counselor

It is ironic: I hate a dusty house and work to keep my home dirt free. Yet this was the artistic medium God chose to display His glory! We may be formed from the star-dust of the earth but we are not some galactic accident as most astrology experts claim.

Made Like God

"God "set his seal of ownership on us, and put his Spirit in our hearts ..." (2 Cor. 1:22). Each of us wears a label, "Handmade by the Lord."" –Kimberly

God breathes into every human being the very breath of life—the very breath of Himself. Despite the fact we're all broken, flawed, and sinful, God created us with inherent majesty and dignity, making us "a little lower" than Himself, crowning mankind with glory and majesty (Psalm 8:5).

You are God's masterpiece (Ephesians 2:10); have the highest possible value (Psalm 8:5); are brilliantly made (Psalm 139:14); like a pearl of great value and an abundance of sparkling jewels (Matthew 13:45; Isaiah 54:11-12).

Scripture also tells us we are whole human beings. Think of yourself as a star made up of five radiating and connecting star points: *Soul; Spirit; Body; Mind (includes brain); and Heart.* Scripture says, we are "complete" because God lives in us (Colossians 2:9-10). When all five parts are in balance we can shine like stars. When we're out of balance, it is difficult to do.

Colossians 1:17 *By Him* (Yeshua) *all things are held together.* Laminin protein holds us together

We are complicated and complex beings which could only have been designed and formed through the power of God Almighty. He is the choreographer and author and of our genetic code, DNA, language, and every cell in each organ. One amazing example is "laminin." Laminin is a cell in our bodies with significant characteristics that stump and awe most of us. It is a *glycoprotein* that holds us together. The mystifying thing about laminin is this protein looks like a crucifix. Thus, laminin's physical properties are also symbolic. Isn't that awesome!

Reflect: What is your reaction to this material? What stuck out to you the most?

Our Brains and Bodies

The control center of the human body is the human brain. It is by far the most complex information-management system in the entire universe. Unlike any man-made computer, the brain is made of living cells that constantly change as we acquire new skills and information.

The physical architecture of the brain itself changes in response to experiences, which makes it possible for us to grow and adapt to our changing environment. *This means human transformation—real change—is possible.* It means that none of us must be stuck in old toxic patterns, thinking, and lifestyles.

What we *do* with our *bodies* and what we *think* with our *minds* literally changes the structure of our brains. *No matter our age, we can change!* People who regularly focus on God's love through prayer and meditation experience less stress and a reduction in blood pressure.

What happens is, the part of the brain associated with focus and attention (*prefrontal cortex*) becomes more active over time, helping them avoid distraction and be more intentional. Focusing on God's love makes us more loving and less angry, and easier to forgive ourselves and others.[64] This is how you've been designed. Give God a "halleluiah!"

A New Beginning

God comes to the doors of our hearts and knocks. When we open the door and trust His Son Jesus Christ as our Lord and Savior, God responds, *"I will give you a new heart and put a new spirit in you ..."* (Ezekiel 36:26). Even though we're all born with the DNA from our family tree, when Christ comes into our lives He basically says, "Through *my power,* now you can have a new life and a new relationship with me." A new dynamic happens—we get God's spiritual DNA and we come to life. Jesus said, *"... you are in me, and I am in you"* (John 14:20). Jesus said to two disciples, "Come and see" (John 1:39). In other words, "Come and see with my eyes, listen with my ears, and feel with my heart."

God's spiritual DNA, living in me, gives me the ability to create a whole new life, to think and act more like Jesus. When we believe that He is loving and trustworthy then our physiology and spirituality unite. Our brains become permeated with love and truth from the Holy Spirit which restores God's balance. Then we have a greater capacity for love, compassion, empathy, forgiveness, understanding, and wisdom, which corresponds with the development of higher brain circuits!

Jesus's Spirit in us gives us a desire to want to be better and clean up our lives—but our baggage must be opened, looked at, then dumped at His feet. Your past can be put to death and you can live a holy life! *Who you are hasn't changed despite your history. You're not defined by the things you suffer, or the labels which have been put on you.* You have every right to love yourself—you're made in God's likeness!

Reflect: How do you think of yourself and judge yourself differently than how your Creator does?

I Know Who I Am!

Unlike us, the Bible doesn't record Jesus asking "Who am I?" I'm sure as a human, there were times in His life when His sense of value and self-worth was questioned. But for the most part, Jesus wasn't one who needed to go out and find Himself. Nor did He feel the need to prove Himself.

"As soon as Jesus was baptized, he went up out of the water. At that moment heaven was opened, and he saw the Spirit of God descending like a dove and alighting on him. And a voice from heaven said, "This is my Son, whom I love; with him I am well pleased"" (Matthew 3:16-17).

Jesus found the answer to "Who am I?" He found His answer in the voice of God. Jesus understood Himself to be loved unconditionally by His Father— and that was enough. After He was baptized a voice from heaven told Him who He is. He heard God's voice, not at the end of His earthly life, but at the beginning—before He healed anyone; before He did any miracles. He didn't do great things so He'd be loved and accepted and pleasing to man— He did them because He understood He was loved.

I want you to see yourself as Jesus. You say, "That's absurd! He's God." Just listen. Jesus prayed,

"I am in them and you are in me. May they experience such perfect unity that the world will know that you sent me and that you love them as much as you love me" (John 17:23, NLT).

"Them" and "they" refer to all believers. This means all of Scripture belongs not just to Jesus, but to all of us Christians. When God says to Jesus, *"This is my Son, whom I love; with him I am well pleased,"* He is saying to you: "This is my daughter, whom I love; with her I am well pleased." When Jesus said, *"you love them as much as you love me,"* He is demonstrating to us that God loves us with agape love.

Drs. Martha and Wes Fehr wrote, "Often, we are our own worst enemy, feeling that unless we are perfect, we have no right to feel good about ourselves. God's evaluation of us is "very good" (Genesis 1:31)."

Show me in the Bible where it says you're a loser, ugly, unlovable, insignificant, stupid, fat, or a whore? It doesn't say that. God says, *"You'll be called Sought After, the City No Longer Deserted"* (Isaiah 62:12).

Reflect: How does it make you feel to know God is pleased with you; seeks you out to bring you to Himself?

Your Adoption

Did you know your birth was not a mistake? Your parents may not have planned to have you, but God planned and welcomed your birth. Long before your parents conceived you, God conceived you. He thought of you first. *You are alive because God wanted to create you!* Scripture confirms this,

"For he [God] chose us in him before the creation of the world ... In love he predestined us to be adopted as his sons [daughters] through Jesus Christ, in accordance with his pleasure and will" (Ephesians 1:4-5).

Fact: *God adopts you because He chooses to.* To be adopted by God is to enter a parent/child relationship that is different than any other. *The Message* paraphrase of Psalm 1:1 says, *"How well God must like you!"* One pastor said, "God loves you so much He cannot keep His eyes off you. If He had a wallet He'd carry your picture in it."

The bottom line is: If we can't see ourselves as loved as Jesus, we can't let go of, "Who am I?" Jesus found in God a love that gave Him great value. He sees Himself as adored and cherished. After claiming that value for Himself, He offers it to others—to us. (And we're to do the same.)

Never forget: *another person's opinion of you is not your reality unless you believe it.* Their words make them polluted and are *powerless* against you. God's Word about you is your true identity. But it's up to you *–you are free to believe it or not.*

Reflect: Right now, what do you think God believes about you? Can you grasp that you've been specifically chosen and are unconditionally loved? Do you feel special and honored? Why or why not? Explain.

G.R.O.W. [God Restores Our Worth]

"The curious paradox is that when I accept myself just as I am, then I can change."
–Carl Rogers

We all carry "mind baggage," and it's hard to get rid of. It's hard for us to grasp that what we've done is not who we are; the pain inflicted to our souls has made us who we've become. We replay old toxic tapes that are programmed into us so deeply that it takes a lot more than "mind over matter" to change our thinking and actions. The more a negative message in our mind is activated and replayed, the more potent it becomes—which is why we need to do the work to overcome them with *truth*.

Lies versus Truth

"Right is right even if no one is doing it; wrong is wrong even if everyone is doing it."
—St. Augustine

Second Peter 2:19 states, *"For you are a slave to whatever controls you."* It is important to realize that our feelings about ourselves cannot always be trusted. Feelings need to be measured against facts. If we don't feel we're acceptable, lovable, capable, or special, we need to examine the facts of our acceptance—the truth, as explained to us in the Bible. Before moving forward, we must define "truth."

What exactly is truth? Truth usually means "factual, genuine, that which corresponds to reality." It's the opposite of a *lie*, which is the denial, repression, perversion, or distortion of the truth; deliberate or not. *The thing about truth is that it is possible the things we experience as truth and reality are rooted in untruths* (particularly when we consider this world is governed by the cosmic deceiver).

Satan does everything in his power to prevent God's truth from reaching our understanding. He uses people to give us a twisted version of the truth: a false statement presented as truth; something often meant to deceive or give a wrong impression. *We have no way to distinguish what is in fact really true.* We are ignorantly held captive by illusions. We automatically assume our experiences reflect truth, when in fact it doesn't. *Bondage always begins with a lie, even a half-truth.*

The other thing Satan does is tempt us to feel like a fool. When we figure out we've believed a lie, or series of lies, we feel stupid, even moronic. This can lead to feelings of shame and self-condemnation. I think it's easier to define what truth is *not*. Truth is not:

- *What's merely rational or understandable.* A group of people can form a set of beliefs based on a set of falsehoods. They all agree to tell the same false story, but it doesn't make their story true.
- *What makes people feel good.* Bad news can be true. Good intentions can be wrong. Truth is like surgery—it may hurt, but it heals.
- *What's necessarily our reality.* For example, thoughts around "should" or "shouldn't" statements are thoughts *we impose* onto our reality.
- *What the majority says is true.* We think, "So many people can't be wrong!" 51 percent of a group can reach a wrong conclusion.
- *Repeated assertions.* If a statement or belief is repeated long enough, people start to believe it, regardless if it is false.
- *Blind faith.* Faith rests on *evidence* and doesn't take the position we avoid searching for further evidence. Faith accepts God's Word as evidence (Hebrews 11:1).

As Christians, we believe truthful thinking is based on the solid foundation of God's Word. Hebrews 4:12 compares the Word of God to a sword. It is powerful because it's sharp and able to pierce the inner man with truth. If you're a believer, then you have immediate access to truth. If we don't believe what God says about us in His Word, then in essence we're calling Him a liar! Jesus said,

"I will ask the Father, and He'll give you another Advocate, who will never leave you. He is the Holy Spirit, who leads into all truth. The world cannot receive him, because it isn't looking for him and doesn't recognize him. But you know him, because he lives with you now ... and the truth will set you free!" (John 14:16-17; 8:32, NLT)

Reflect: How does Jesus's promise of giving you the gift of the powerful Holy Spirit help you move closer to the truth and to freedom?

Experience the True You

Researchers state that toxic thoughts build toxic memories. The brain grows heavy with memories that release a toxic load, interfering with the brain and body's function.[65] But when we hear positive messages about ourselves and practice healthy self-talk we build new healthy memories.

If we fill our minds with what God says about us—the truth, then when the devil hits "replay," we pull up Jesus's words such as, *"you are more valuable"* (Matthew 10:31). The God of all creation has chosen to speak *truth to you* through His Word. Today He speaks into your soul that you are *really* a new creation in Christ (2 Cor. 5:17). There's no need any more to struggle in vain to change external behaviors. Grow accustomed to the fact *you are a new creation in Christ!*

What does "in Christ" mean? It means our suffering becomes Jesus's suffering; our actions become His actions. What happens to us, happens to Him. The two worlds, the seen and unseen, merge in Christ. Our ordinary human bodies become vessels of goodness—nothing less than the incarnation of God on earth.

This is important: If our knowledge of who we are in Christ remains immaterial, it will *never* be adequate to deprogram our brains of false information and accusations. Our true identity will never permeate our mind and become part of our lives. *For real transformation to occur, we need to experience who we are as defined by God.* We must believe that God wasn't an inept workman when it came to creating us. We must *experience* what He says about us concretely and vividly.

Our brains have installed every event we experienced—the good, bad, and ugly. If we desire to experience our true self, we must create and install new experiences that confirm our God-given identities. When we start to input the truth about ourselves, the brain will produce positive feelings versus negative ones.

Remember what I said before: All of Scripture belongs not just to Jesus, but to all of us. Before we can experience God's Word, we must have faith. *Experiencing our real identities is all about the size and scope of our faith.* If we don't have faith in the author of the Word and our Creator, then we won't experience much change. It's been said, "We tend to experience what *we expect* to experience."

Reflect: How would claiming your true self-worth as a gift from God empower you to go forward in your own life?

Talking to Our Souls Exercise

What is true of the brain's programming process is also true of its reprogramming process: it requires an event.

We need to work with God to create events in our minds that communicate truth intensely. Our goal is to align our minds with the truth, and then benefit from the experience of our real identity in Christ.

To experience the "true you" I suggest putting this exercise, *Talking to Our Souls,* into practice. Look up each one of these biblical truths. Choose one or two each day, and then concentrate on it several times a day:

Deuteronomy 32:9-10	Psalm 8:5; 34:9; 139:14	Isaiah 54:11-12	Matthew 5:13-14; 13:45
John 15:16	Romans 3:23-24; 8:1-2, 17, 37-39;	1 Corinthians 1:2; 6:17, 20; 30; 3:16; 12:27	2 Corinthians 1:21-22; 5:17
Galatians 3:28	Ephesians 1:1,4-7, 13; 2:10; 5:1	Philippians 1:6; 4:13	Colossians 2:9-11
2 Timothy 1:7	1 John 5:18		

Look up the verse and translate it into a sentence: "I am …" The goal is to experience the thoughts, attitudes, feelings, and behaviors of the real you. Say to your soul, "Listen soul, because of Jesus Christ—*then insert the biblical truth.* This is the true me!" Speak each truth to yourself *slowly.*

I suggest this table format:

Biblical Truth	See	Hear	Emotion	Physical
I am God's beloved child (John 1:12; Ephesians 1:5)				

153 | **The Perfect Counselor**

Take the time to reflect on each truth. Close your eyes and relax. Record what you see, hear, feel emotionally and feel physically. Create in your mind a new experience by visualizing it as reality. Don't just recite the Scripture, *get a picture of yourself and note how you're different from the way you presently feel about yourself.* Observe how you think and feel about the truth.

Don't be discouraged if creating an image of the real you is initially difficult. If you are persistent, you'll find it gets easier. The more we meditate on scriptural truths like these, the more we'll believe them.

Old beliefs will begin to lose their power and in time will disappear. When we find our mind grabbing a toxic thought from the past, we must consciously reject the thought, then bring into our minds our newly created experience.

When you've completed the study, create a personal affirmation like: "I'm a truly spiritually radiant and loving person; valuable, worthy, and lovable. I have genuine warmth and creative talents and intelligence." Or, "God, the creator of this universe, has chosen me as His beautifully loved daughter. Therefore, I can take rejection in stride."

Our thoughts can work either for us or against us. The next time a toxic memory or image pops up and replays an old tape that says you're bad, etcetera, *create a new image.* Don't be surprised if you hear, "These words aren't for you—not with all of the things that you've done in your life." Simply reply, "Soul, you're wrong! God doesn't make junk. I'm incredible and amazing because I'm made in the image of God Almighty. *I'm His beloved and free to be me!*"

Reflect: Finish this prayer: "Dear God, I'm just discovering that I'm beautiful and loved because you made me this way. Sometimes it's hard for me to believe that because ... I have a hard time thinking of my . . . as beautiful. I think this is because ..."

Love Yourself the Right Way

How many times have you tuned someone out who said, "You just need to love yourself!" Truth: Loving yourself is the beginning of making your life better, all the way around. Have you ever done any of these things:

- Spent money on yourself because you "deserve it."
- You do things for others so they'll like and accept you.
- You keep searching for the "perfect" relationship.

If you said yes to any of these, I can tell you that you're going about loving yourself the wrong way. When we've experienced hurt and fear; when our heart and needs have been ignored, it is normal that we'd choose to do these things. We naturally seek comfort and love to soothe those uncomforted wounds.

God didn't wire us to live chaotic lives. He wired us for love and order. He has given us three amazing gifts: *power, love,* and a *sound mind* (2 Timothy 1:7, KJV). When we take back control using the power and sound mind God gave us, we can love like God loves. And it begins with loving ourselves. This can be particularly questionable when all we've known is unhealthy love; love which is conditional and ever changing. Matthew 22:37-39 says:

"One day a Pharisee asked Jesus what was the most important commandment in the law of Moses. Jesus replied, "You must love the LORD your God with all your heart, all your soul, and all your mind. This is the first and greatest commandment. A second is equally important: 'Love your neighbor as yourself'" (NLT).

Every Christian is called to love God, others, even our enemies. We are even to love ourselves. When Jesus says, "as yourself," self-love is assumed. Why? Because He made us in His image! This means we respect and accept ourselves because we're made in the amazing likeness of God. Here is the catch: We can only love ourselves if we're in a relationship with God, allowing Him to love us first. Then we can separate our worth from our behaviors.

When Jesus said, *"Love your neighbor as yourself,"* He was saying that the love of self could not be separated out from the love of others; one is dependent upon the other. This means when we devalue ourselves it hurts those around us. Biblical self-love implies I see myself through God's eyes. I respect myself. I believe I'm an important, lovable person, created like God in His image, for a specific purpose—to further God's mission here on earth. There's a saying that goes, "Broken crayons still color."

There are people who take Jesus's words, *love yourself,* as a reason to focus solely on themselves. God counter-balances any notion that our focus in life ought to be on ourselves (Philippians 2:3).

1 Corinthians 13 ~ God's Love Chapter

One of the most puzzling paradoxes of Christians is the intense dislike many of them have for themselves. They're more frustrated, impatient, unforgiving, bitter, and irritated with their own deficiencies than they are with other people! Bernard Bush says it this way, "If you love yourself intensely and freely, then your feelings about yourself correspond perfectly to the sentiments of Jesus."[66]

1 Corinthians 13:4-9 illustrates how we can agape love ourselves. (We will revisit this passage again in Chapter 14 as it relates to love relationships.)

"Love is patient, love is kind. It does not envy, it does not boast, it is not proud. It does not dishonor others, it is not self-seeking, it is not easily angered, and it keeps no record of wrongs. Love does not delight in evil but rejoices with the truth. It always protects, always trusts, always hopes, always perseveres. Love never fails."

When Paul wrote this, he had in mind a character sketch of Christ. He is thinking of a Jesus-kind-of-patience; a Jesus-kind-of-kindness; etc. which Jesus imparts into our souls, making living out these qualities possible.

- *Love is patient.* Often, we're more patient with other people, even bad people, than we are with ourselves. Be less hard on yourself.

- *Love is kind.* Treating ourselves kindly is to protect and take proper care of our bodies, minds, and spirits; and whatever else God has given us charge over (such as children, a job, education, ministry). Give yourself permission to be kind and caring to yourself.

- *Love does not envy or boast; is not proud.* An insecure person tends to compare and covet what someone else has. On the other hand, this isn't usually an issue for the woman with low self-esteem. How are you at accepting compliments? Can you accept a compliment and merely answer, "Thank you" without feeling like you don't deserve it, or feel you must explain or justify what you're being complimented for?

- *Love keeps no records of wrongs.* Forgive yourself when you mess up. Because you've been forgiven by God this means getting rid of guilty and shame-based feelings; all records of wrongs.

156 | **The Perfect Counselor**

- *Love rejoices in the truth.* You may have been told you're a looser, or fat and ugly; that you're unwanted and insignificant. God never said these things. He said you are a saint, and holy, and precious!

- *Love trusts.* We can rest assure that if we're in God's will and following His instructions, then our choices will be trustworthy.

- *Love always hopes.* Oswald Chambers wrote, "Every hope and dream of the human mind will be fulfilled if it is noble and of God."[67] Focus continually on God. Believe in a bright future.

- *Love protects.* We're responsible to stay safe, protect ourselves and our children. We don't have control over another person's violence, but we can control how we prepare and respond to it.

- *Love perseveres.* If you love yourself you don't give up on yourself, even when you fall or fail. *Believe* yourself the image of God, and *you'll* receive a new source of strength and power!

- *Love never fails.* We must believe and move forward knowing God will always be there and has a great plan for our lives (Jeremiah 29:11) … and always completes what He begins (Romans 8:29).

Reflect: Which of these love characteristics are you strongest on? Which are you weak on? Why do you think so?

Finish these sentences: "What I now know about myself is …" "What I still want to know is …"

10

The Power of the Mind

For God hath not given us the spirit of fear; but of power, and of love, and of a sound mind. —*Paul, speaking in 2 Timothy 1:7 (KJV)*

A tale goes: A patient was told by his doctor he had a gigantic brain tumor and needed a brain transplant. The doctor said, "I have good news and bad news." Sadly, a couple was just killed in an auto accident. The good news is you can have one of the brains transplanted. The man's brain costs $300,000; the woman's brain costs $60,000." Naturally he asked, "Why such a difference in cost?" The doctor replied, "The woman's brain is used."

Apparently, women speak between 20 to 25,000 words a day; a man speaks 7 to 10,000. One man said, "My wife and I had words, but I didn't get to use mine." Seriously, experts believe human beings have anywhere between 50,000 to 80,000 thoughts per day. That's an average of 2500 to 3500 thoughts per hour! Apparently, 98 percent of those thoughts are the same thoughts from the day before; and 80 percent of them are negative!

Is your mind your friend or foe? No doubt, our minds are a battleground, not a playground. For two decades, I battled with food. It started when I put on weight my senior year in high school. My dad called me fat and ridiculed me (called *fat shaming*). Therefore, I *believed* I was fat.

Suffering is often a warning that we're attached to a toxic thought. When we experience a stressful feeling—anything from mild discomfort to intense sorrow, rage, or despair—*there is a specific thought causing our reaction, whether we're conscious of it or not.*

Toxic thoughts are generated from one of two seeds: the seed of *sin*, which is *voluntary* (we make a bad choice); or the seed of *trauma*, which is *involuntary* (we had no choice). Since our brains are not wired for disorder,

158 | **The Perfect Counselor**

these lethal thoughts produce toxic byproducts. Science states that *75 to 98 percent of physical and behavioral illnesses come from a negative thought life.*

Thoughts associated with a painful experience release negative chemicals that travel through the body changing the shape of the receptors on cells lining our hearts; thereby increasing susceptibility to illness. Toxic experiences cause brain cells to shrivel and die compared to positive experiences which make brain cells expand.[68] If we haven't dealt with a toxic memory, when it hits you it can come as anxiety or some other symptom.

This also means that 75 to 98 percent of physical and behavioral healings come from a positive thought life.[69]

Healthy, truth-based thinking today has become an integral aspect of treatment for everything from allergies to liver transplants. When we think positively instead of negatively, our tolerance for pain is higher, our recovery from illness or surgery is quicker, and our blood pressure drops. We have the power to stop the stress of a disordered mind by investigating the thinking that lies behind it, and then changing it.

Rumination

"I am convinced that life is 10 percent what happens to me and 90 percent how I react to it. And so it is with you. We are in charge of our attitudes." –Unknown

Have you ever noticed when we women get together that so often the stories we tell focus on what went wrong and what we did wrong? Women have a high tendency to "ruminate." This means we reflect on something *repeatedly* in our minds; we over-analyze; worry about a past stressful event; we chew on a thought or a situation just like a dog chews on a bone. *I should have; I could have; If only; Never; I can't.*

Valerie's son became ill and she took him to the doctor, who diagnosed him with an ear infection. He got worse. Valerie took him to the Emergency Room. The doctor shared the same diagnosis. However, her son only got worse. She took him back to the ER where they diagnosed him with meningitis. Because his condition was so advanced, he died that day.

Riddled with guilt, for months Valerie ruminated, "if only I …" She judged herself as failing her child, and began drinking to diminish the pain.

The truth was that she had no medical training. She took her son each time to physicians, who missed the diagnosis. She had fallen into the trap of judging herself on the outcome—rather than on her good actions and intentions. Dr. Clifford Nass at Stanford University explains,

"The brain handles positive and negative information in different hemispheres. Negative emotions generally involve more thinking, and the information is processed more thoroughly than positive ones. Thus, we tend to ruminate more about unpleasant events."[70]

Researchers have found that rumination is associated with chronic inflammation in the body; depression; and other mental and physical disorders. Worry, for example, turns into anxiety, which turns into depression, which is trauma to the brain.[71] These "strongholds of the mind" take our minds captive if we continue to feed the thoughts, give power to the thoughts, and then act on them.

Pain and traumatic thinking is not permanent; it's temporary. Our automatic reaction to pain in this culture is to "medicate" in some way. What happens when we do this is we take away the medicine Jesus longs to give us—Him. He longs for us to turn to Him so He can help us work through our pain and issues in order to grow and mature. The transformation process He desires us to experience requires we push through and investigate, and in time change our thoughts—not medicate ourselves.

Reflect: What is your reaction to this information?

Become Aware of Your Thoughts

"Reality is merely an illusion, albeit a very persistent one." –Albert Einstein

Answer this question: *Given all the pain you've experienced; can you really trust your thoughts?* Think on this for a couple of minutes.

Thoughts are based on information we receive, and then processed by the brain, and then stored over our lifetime. This makes up what we call "thinking." By "thoughts" we usually mean *all the ways in which we are conscious of things.* This includes memories, perceptions, and beliefs.

Ruminating words that fall into this category are: *"could," "would," "ought"* and *"If only you/I …"* or *"I wish I/you had …"* Wouldn't you agree women are pros at worrying about some future event which hasn't even taken place. In these cases, we must ask ourselves this very important question, "How can it be helpful and healthy to argue with or ruminate on something which has already happened or has not happened?"

Take the word "should." How many times a day do you say or think, "I should …" or "My husband/boyfriend should …" or "That person should …" or "This organization should …" When we create "should-thoughts," we are wanting reality to be different than it is.

These two phrases are popular: *"You need to …"* or *"I want you to …"* Much of our anxiety comes from living outside of our own business. When I start ruminating on the *"You need to …"* or *"I want you to …"* I am in your business … and I need to get out. Your business is between you and God. When I'm in your business, then I'm not in my own, and I wonder why my life isn't working so well (a technique called *deflection*). I think there's only one exception: if you're a parent and are teaching your child responsibility.

Peter said to Jesus, *"Lord, and what about this man?"* Jesus said to him, *"… what's that to you? You follow Me!"* (John 21:21-22). Ask, "Whose business is it?" If it's not yours, then you have no reason to feel hurt. Simply put, to think that I know better than God what's best for someone is arrogance. And it results in anxiety and fear.

Reflect: Think about this: *Much of the stress we feel is usually caused by arguing with something that is NOT reality!*

- Ask yourself, "How do I know that what "should be" is really true?
- What do you conclude from this?

Moving Toward Something Good

All ruminating is good for is muddling our brain circuitry and stressing us out, which leads to feelings of guilt, condemnation, and depression. We know this isn't what God desires because research has shown that when we think negative, stressful thoughts, and make bad choices, over time this changes the brain's structure, creating damage, and then making our bodies vulnerable to disease.

In a Stanford University study, people who focused on negative aspects of themselves, or of life, generated waves of fear which released a flood of destructive neurochemicals into the brain.[72]

For example, our bodies release the hormone *cortisol* which weakens the immune system, and causes weight gain! We've been designed by God to build good thoughts which lead to a healthy soul, mind, heart, and body, thereby, enabling us to love God and receive His love and good things for our lives. When we feel love, and think positive thoughts, then our bodies release the hormone *DHEA*, and our brains release positive healthy chemicals.

If we want overall wellness we must give all *the "should's" "could's," "would's," "ought to's"* and *"need to's"* to God to handle. We can trust He'll act justly and objectively. *We need to accept "what is" and leave the rest to God.* We've got to look at where we are—not where we wanted to be, or thought we should be, or wishing something hadn't been. *Acceptance is the point at which we start moving toward something good.*

Reflect: Think back to a recent situation that made you feel frustrated or despairing; where you found yourself ruminating and using a *I should have … I could have … If only I had … I can't do … You need to …* statements.

- Write down the experience.
- Then answer: "This thought made me feel…"
- Write down your perception of what triggered the thought.
- Name three ways you can work to avoid this type of toxic thinking in the future.

The Power of Your Mind

"Kimberly, you are fat!" For two decades, my life revolved around dieting. It became an obsession because I believed "I was fat." I *believed* my significance was directly tied to having a perfectly thin body. Each day I'd begin a diet. Inevitably I'd be tempted to eat something loaded with fat or sugar, like *Fritos* and Chinese almond cookies—total comfort food! Simple psychology says: *actions = identity.*

Then my mind would go down this path of all or nothing thinking, "You blew your diet! You might as well just pig out and start all over again tomorrow." That's what I did. Then I'd feel fat and miserable. So, I'd throw the food up and feel worse. Inevitably I'd compare myself to someone who I admired—a woman who was skinny and popular and successful. I'd say to myself, "I know she's not sitting at home by herself pigging out. She's got a real life. The kind of life I want!"

Toxic self-talk alleged, "Kimberly, you're bad, weak, a loser." Then optimistic self-talk would reply, "Tomorrow I'll be good and strong and stick to my diet—then I'll be a winner!" It didn't happen.

Proverbs 14:12 says, *"There is a way that seems right to a man, but in the end it leads to death."* It was a never ending miserable destructive cycle because the deceiver in my life had *power over* me.

Reflect: Describe a time when your mind took you through a destructive cycle.

The Power of the Unconscious Mind

Jesus said, *"This is why I speak to them in parables: "Though seeing, they do not see; though hearing, they do not hear or understand.""* *(Matthew 13:13)*. Jesus knew forces outside of our conscious awareness operate in our minds—often preventing us from seeing and dealing with things that are right in front of us.

An understanding of how our minds operate unconsciously can keep us from becoming one of those who do not see or hear. Unless we learn to become aware of the beliefs we hold in our unconscious, we'll continue to battle with ourselves and never win. So, let's dig deeper!

The *unconscious mind* is the part responsible for all our involuntary actions, and describes how our minds filter what we are experiencing. The *conscious mind* makes us aware of the present moment. It only works when we're awake. The unconscious works 24 hours a day, and makes up 90 to 95 percent of who we are. Compared to our conscious mind which makes up 5 to 10 percent of who we are. We don't have easy access to the information stored in the unconscious.

E. Stanley Jones states it well, "The conscious mind determines the actions, the unconscious mind determines the reactions; and the reactions are just as important as the actions."

For example, during childhood, we acquired countless memories and experiences that formed who we are today. However, we cannot recall most of those memories. They are unconscious forces, beliefs and personal experiences that drive our behaviors. The *unconscious* decides where and how your memories are stored. It may hide certain memories, such as traumas, that have strong negative emotions until you are mature enough to process them consciously. When it senses you're ready, whether you consciously think you are or not, it will bring them up so you can deal with them.

Tanya's husband Colton believed in corporal punishment and frequently spanked their children with his belt. This is because his father did the same thing. Colton developed an unconscious belief about a father's authority: *for a man to be respected in his home, he must be feared by all who live there.* He learned this from his father which made him believe that if he didn't dominate the members of his family, then he'd be a failure as a man and a father. Colton needed to become aware of these unconscious beliefs. When he began to see that these unconscious beliefs caused him to act this way, things began to change in his home.

The unconscious is our mind's way of keeping us from thinking and feeling everything at once. That would be overwhelming. Since we aren't designed to deal with everything all at once, we can't be fully aware of *all* that is going on inside our minds at any given point in time. We work on unfinished business in the unconscious.

Troublesome or unfinished things are often revisited in the unconscious. Psychologists say we will go over them again and again until something changes. Without realizing it, we keep repeating the past to get it right. This is Albert Einstein's definition of insanity—to continue the same behavior while expecting different results.

The good news is that we can take advantage of the power of both the unconscious and conscious. We can use our conscious mind to "redesign" a thought or memory (see "Updating a Memory," page 126). It is the work of the Holy Spirit to bring back to our conscious minds the things that are stored in the unconscious. Just as He will bring to our minds a particular

Scripture or word from God to help and guide us in the moment, He will bring up a certain memory at the right time. Be patient. Change doesn't happen overnight, but it can happen and become a new habit in a couple months!

Reflect: Find a quiet place and relax. Close your eyes. Imagine you're looking into your mind; into your thought life. Focus on whatever is coming into your mind. Now open your eyes and write down some things you heard or saw, even if they're illogical.

What you've just written down are thoughts which have moved from your unconscious to your conscious mind. This is an exercise in developing awareness of what's coming into your mind. Practice this regularly. If the thoughts that pop up are negative, take them to Jesus and talk to Him about them immediately. *"Jesus, what should I do with this information? Is this something that I must change or modify or control?"*

Thinking Our Way to Healing

The body has an amazing ability to heal itself, which has been documented through research on the mind. No doubt you've heard of the *placebo effect*. It is a counterfeit treatment which produces powerful results in the body's chemistry—the effect of suggestion. It highlights the strong relationship between mind and body. Our minds are so powerful. They can even be our enemy. The *nocebo effect* refers to the power of *negative* suggestion that can lead to bad health, even death.

One woman sought a physician who could tell her why she'd been feeling weak and bloated. Her doctor ran numerous tests. When she came back for her follow-up visit he declared, "You have TS," then promptly left the room. Suddenly she began breathing rapidly and hyperventilating. An intern, who was also in the room, examined her and found fluid accumulating rapidly in her lungs.

The intern questioned her about her sudden upset. Her response was that the doctor said she had TS—"Terminal Situation." This poor woman misinterpreted the medical acronym for "tricuspid stenosis" (low-grade congestive heart failure).

Shortly after, she was in massive pulmonary edema and continued to worsen. Within the hour, she died of congestive heart failure. She misunderstood the information she received and interpreted it as a death sentence. Her brain processed the information as truth and triggered a shutdown in her body. I guess we could say this woman was killed by her own thoughts.

This story also reminded me to *not* go to the Internet for medical advice!

The placebo effect demonstrates that our thoughts influence our health and well-being. The mind is powerful—but also easy to manipulate and deceive. That is what the advertising industry banks on … and why Satan targets our minds. The good news is: It is possible to identify thoughts and habits in our lives and either change them or strengthen them—if we choose to work with Jesus and let Him renew our minds. *Creating new hopeful and Bible-based beliefs has the power to change us positively!*

Distinctive Beliefs

One day on a subway train, a woman stood up, slapped the face of the man next to her, and then ran to the exit. Each of the passengers who saw what happened reacted in a personal way. A middle-aged man felt sadness for the man who was slapped. A younger woman was frightened. A teenage boy was angry. Another woman felt excitement. How could the same event trigger such a range of varying emotions? The answer is found in our mind's unconscious belief system.

- The sad middle-aged man thought, "He'll never get her back."
- The fearful woman thought, "She is going to really pay a price for that tonight at home."
- The angry teenager thought, "She humiliated him; like most women, she must be a real jerk."
- The excited woman thought, "Serves him right. What a strong woman!"

The point: Our versions of an experience are never identical to another person's, nor identical to what truly happened. In each case, the event was interpreted, judged, and labeled, instantly. The person's unique belief resulted in a distinctive, personal emotional experience.

Reflect: What do you conclude from this as it applies to your thinking?

Why We React the Way We Do
A: Automatic—B: Belief—C: Consequence

James 1:24 states, *"For if you listen to the word and don't obey, it is like glancing at your face in a mirror. You see yourself, walk away, and forget what you look like"* (NLT).

James is telling us is that if we read God's Word but don't apply it, we immediately forget it. For example, you may hear a great sermon and come out feeling like an empowered "new creation." Yet, if you don't keep feeding yourself the Word of God, then you'll easily forget you're a new creation. This happens all the time. *We see ourselves, walk away, and forget what we look like.* Even confronting people who cling to their unconscious beliefs with facts, even Scripture, don't change their minds because they've come to their own conclusions. Why doesn't God's Word immediately transform our lives? There's a reason.

Our minds have been pre-programmed through life events. This is the lens we see the world through. Everything stored in our unconscious mind is real and truthful for us. Our beliefs are our "reality"—our measure of truth. Those beliefs translate into behaviors. To understand our own behavior (and the behavior of others) we must discover the underlying beliefs behind our choices and actions. When we are put in any new situation, this is what goes on in our minds—the *A B C's of behavior:*

- An event occurs today. →
- My mind *automatically* and *unconsciously* evaluates the situation based on what I already know and feel from previous life events (comes from my unconscious belief system).→
- The mind generates an image. →
- A feeling (positive or negative) attaches to the image →
- The image creates a *belief* (or story) about the situation to make sense of it. →
- My body *automatically* responds (chemicals are shot into the bloodstream and distributed throughout the body; electrochemical signals are sent to muscles, organs, and limbs). →

167 | The Perfect Counselor

- Creates a *motive.* → I decide to act based on unconscious beliefs and emotions, called the *consequence.* For example, if I'm verbally abused, I hurt and re-experience feelings of shame. To cope I choose to get high and to isolate. This is done automatically and unconsciously.

A belief that we carry is just that—*a belief.* It doesn't become *reality* until we act on it—*the consequence.* We all transfer our unconscious beliefs, based on past experiences, onto our present worlds. We don't know we're doing this because we do it *automatically.* This can create conflict. Our present-day reality tells us one thing, but our unconscious beliefs tell us something else. The unconscious usually wins out. Just because we can't consciously see something, that doesn't mean it can't hurt us. *What we don't know can hurt us.*

Reflect: Byron Katie wrote, "Behind every uncomfortable feeling, there's a thought that isn't true for us." What do you think she is saying, and how does this apply to you?

ATEs and PMSs (Thinking Errors)

"Heart at peace gives life to the body." –Proverbs 14:30

Fact: Toxic thoughts don't go away because we believe them. We all have a choice as to how we'll handle our thought life. We can *repress it* and leave it in the unconscious (the most dangerous), or bring it into our conscious mind and *express it, interrogate it,* and then *release it,* which is the healthy solution.

Many Christian women live by "Automatic Thinking Errors" (ATE) and have fatal PMS of the mind: "Powerful Mental Strongholds." Like a computer virus, it's not always easy to detect an ATE or PMS in our belief system. False and infected beliefs are so engrained we don't even realize we have them. We don't know that a cow is really a goat (see page 140). Consequently, there will be a cost. David asked God, *"Guide me in your truth and teach me"* (Psalm 25:5). God desires to help us. He will respond.

Freedom from Unconscious ATEs and PMSs

"Traumatic and toxic thinking is not who you are—it's what you have become."

The brain functions according to how it's been programmed, like a computer. And God wants to load a brand-new software program into our minds, one that He's designed specifically for each one of us. Toxic thinking is not permanent. These thoughts are alterable. God designed us to constantly change. We may not be able to control every single ATE|PMS from popping up, but with God's supernatural presence in our lives we can make good conscious choices.

We can stop undesirable and ineffective behavior by controlling our reactions to our thoughts.

We don't have to do what our mind says! The Bible says, *"We demolish arguments and every pretension that sets itself up against the knowledge of God, and we take captive every thought to make it obedient to Christ"* (2 Corinthians 10:5).

Notice *we* are the ones responsible to do something—we destroy, we capture, and we obey Christ. It's not an easy task, but if He tells us to do something, He'll give us His power to do it! *What thoughts do we have to capture?* Anything that goes against the truth of God—in other words, lies. Our mission is to become aware of and then quickly capture our deceptive thoughts; investigate and then reframe them with truth.

The word "captive" has the meaning of confining or caging up. It's like we take that ugly deceptive thought and isolate and quarantine it. It is our spiritual union with Jesus where our power—to demolish—to take captive—to submit and obey—comes from. Talk with Jesus daily about which thoughts you need to capture.

The Behavior and Customs of this World

A disordered mind can be turned into an ordered mind! Negative thought patterns can be broken! We now know the brain is not as rigid as once believed, but is pliable and changeable. Brain scientists have found that our brains can rewire and heal themselves, called brain *plasticity* or *neuroplasticity* (*neuro* = brain; *plastic* = change). The University College of London stated it takes, on the average, 66 days to redesign our brains and form a new habitual thought pattern; and 60 days to break the old pattern.[73]

The Bible says God has given us a *sound mind* (2 Timothy 1:7, KJV). God designed us with the ability to have full control over our thoughts; to create new pathways; to be free from negative self-talk; to perform functions that allow us to walk in His ways, while expressing a free will. Romans 12:2 states:

"Don't copy the behavior and customs of this world, but let God transform you into a new person by changing the way you think. Then you will learn to know God's will for you, which is good and pleasing and perfect" (NLT).

What stands out to you in this verse?

God is the one who does the transforming. How? By changing the way we think. No other method or person or place changes us into a new person. We only change when we let God work in our minds. Yet, it's a partnership. We must do our part.

Scientists state: *Our thought life doesn't control us; we control our thought life.* If our desire is to change a negative thinking pattern, we can do that through intentional focused thinking. How? The Word of God can heal our minds, bodies, and our relationships, as we intentionally expose our minds to Scripture, personal and group Bible study, and church. Then we begin changing our brains. Our thinking is re-shaped, and our trust in God deepens. Are you ready to make a commitment to do this work?

What is God's good, pleasing, and perfect will? That we be transformed into the likeness of Jesus. Then God can use us to bring transformation to this world!

* * *

Recognize that all the untruths that have infiltrated our brains over our lifetimes are "the behavior and customs of this world." Every message, every mental image, and every internal voice that tells us we're something other than who God says we are; anything meant to steal, kill, and destroy a part of our lives is, "the behavior and customs of this world."

When my own father called me "fat" and routinely scolded me about my appetite and weight, he was really saying, "Let me help you see what's wrong with you." He didn't help. Instead, I created a picture of my ideal self— possessing a body shape that would be impossible to attain. The media was also responsible.

I ended up in a life-and death physical struggle driven by the "behavior and customs of this world." When I saw another skinny person or model, I "knew" I was fat. You could have told me I wasn't fat, but it wouldn't have done any good to help me out of this false belief system I'd already created.

I held onto conscious information which didn't translate into transformation. My brain suppressed the truth about healthy body image, and instead I experienced unhealthy body image. We all automatically suppress thousands of truths, and instead experience reality that is a flat-out untruth. *"You see yourself [hear the truth] and forget what you look like"* (James 1:24). This is how we're conformed to the "behaviors and customs of this world."

Reflect: Why might we be afraid to allow our thinking to be changed? Why do we resist letting God transform our minds?

To Renew

It is a fact: *We have power over what we believe and what we believe holds power over us—the power to thrive or be defeated.*

When God says "renew," He means our minds are readjusted or altered to what He's got in mind—which is transformation into the likeness of Jesus, God's perfect will. Scripture says believers, *"have the mind of Christ"* (1 Cor. 2:16). *We have a sound mind* (2 Timothy 2:7) The word "have" is a verb that means to "to possess," "to own." *This is the result of God renewing our minds!*

No matter what years of pain, chaos, and negative self-talk have done to your brain, it's possible to exchange your old way of thinking for a new way of thinking—thinking like Christ.

Reflect: What has stuck out in your mind as you've read this information? What "good news" points are you processing right now?

Transforming Encounters

The stories of our lives are not complete. *The Gospel has the power*—not us or any positive thinking book—to lead to changes in the brain which transform us from the inside outside, changing our thinking and personalities.

Remember, mind transformation isn't about mastering Bible facts. The devil knows the Bible better than any of us, and look at his existence! We need life-transforming encounters with God through the Scriptures, which means making a commitment to:

- *Prepare & Pray.* Before reading our Bibles, we ask God to eliminate distractions and help us remain focused so we can spend enough time in the text. Get into the habit of consistent reading so it becomes part of your daily routine.
- *Have a positive experience.* We want to experience what God is saying to us so it becomes a real encounter with Him.
- *Absorb it.* Our desire is to remain in this emotionally rewarding experience for as long as we can.
- *Apply* what He teaches to our everyday lives.

11

I Changed My Mind!

If the Son sets you free, you'll be free indeed.
—Jesus, speaking in John 8:36

Shala, in her group session, described her husband as incredibly "powerful" and "intimidating." She felt she couldn't talk to him about things which bothered her. One day the group had a chance to meet her husband. He appeared small and squirrelly. The group described him as "mousy." Turns out, this is how his co-workers and friends also described him.

Shala's belief is, "My husband is powerful and intimidating." Yet, the group believed, "Shala's husband is quiet and mousy." Granted, many abusive men wear a mask in public, but her husband didn't. Shala needed to see where her distorted view of her husband as powerful and intimidating came from. We discovered this was a description of Shala's father. Consequently, Shala saw all men she needed the same way. She had no idea she had this tendency to distort.

It *wasn't true* that Shala's husband was powerful and intimidating. She needed help to begin investigating, questioning, and changing the way she thought. Most of our *personal worlds are made up of unexamined and untested beliefs.* Therefore, we must examine, test, and change what isn't biblically true. Ephesians 4:22-24 tells us.

"You were taught, with regard to your former way of life, to put off your old self, which is being corrupted by its deceitful desires; to be made new in the attitude of your minds; and to put on the new self, created to be like God in true righteousness and holiness"

What action words stick out to you in this passage?

173 | The Perfect Counselor

The words "put off" and "put on" require us to do something. We partner with the Holy Spirit, letting Him take the lead in renewing our thoughts and attitudes. Our desire is to "put on" or exhibit the characteristics of Christ, and "put away" thoughts and actions which dishonor Him.

Think of your mind like a large, clear vase filled with dirty, murky water. Your job is to fill the vase with clear, fresh water until it is no longer dirty and cloudy. The clincher is—you only have an eyedropper to do it. After adding the first few drops, you don't see any change. This is when you may be tempted to give up. But don't give up! Eventually the water is less dingy. The more drops of water we add, and the more lies that are replaced by truth, the cleaner the water, our mind, becomes. Let's begin!

Change Your Self-Talk— Change Your Reality

Our self-talk is composed of thoughts—the past, present, or future; about what should be, could be, needs to be, etc. The thing about our self-talk is these judgements are usually untested and uninvestigated theories. Small incriminating thoughts breed bigger ones; the bigger ones' breed "theories" about who we are and how life should be.

Remember: *An overwhelmingly negative situation is only one part of your life.* The reasoning and logic skills given you by God can help you detect deceit. The solution: Reframe the situation; step back and look at the bigger picture. Put on your detective gear. Let's begin to inquire and investigate our thoughts!

The Five Steps to Mind Freedom

"Dear friends … I have written these letters as reminders to stimulate you to wholesome thinking." –Peter, speaking in 2 Peter 3:1

Growing up, we accept what we are taught without questioning. The left brain convinces us that our thoughts and beliefs are true. We then rely on feelings generated from these lies. This has been the basis for our decision-making.

Low self-worth, insecurity, and fear, are most often rooted in untruths. Therefore, we must use the reasoning powers God gave us to determine if the belief is in fact true or false. God wants us to believe based on evidence. We can choose how we will react to self-talk and life situations. Therefore, we need to *look for proof and inquire deeper.* To believe something without sufficient evidence is unreasonable. In this process, we will need to learn how to separate our feelings from fact; our emotions from biblical evidence.

We must ask, "Is there biblical truth to support this belief?"

People mistakenly believe that if it *feels* right, it must be right. *Feelings can lie!* Our actions should not be made solely on feelings themselves, but on the facts, evidence, and truth associated with the circumstance.

After Christ's resurrection, two disciples were walking on the road to Emmaus. They were joined by a stranger, who unbeknownst to them was Jesus. Jesus could have performed a miracle to prove it was Him, but *instead He took them to the Word.* He opened biblical evidence to them, and their hearts "burned within them" (see Luke 24:13-32). Biblical evidence resulted in a change of emotion for the disciples, and not the other way around.

Put Your Mind to Paper

Our goal is to work on identifying and questioning the thoughts that cause emotional, physical, spiritual, and relational toxicity. These investigative exercises will enable you to take your toxic thoughts captive to Jesus Christ (2 Cor. 10:5). Think of completing these five steps like doing brain surgery on yourself—but without the scalpel and blood! Remember, *your thought life doesn't control you; you control your thought life.*

Write everything down. Writing is an emotional outlet, and form of prayer, that does something no other form of expression can do: It makes the invisible visible. Naming our beliefs, and writing about distressing events in detail, is the only kind of writing that clinically has been associated with improved health. When we can clearly see our thoughts and issues on paper, we can hand them over to God who heals and comforts and counsels.

The first thing we need to do is *identify the predominant negative thought or belief we want to conquer.* You say, "I have so many!" Pray and ask the Holy Spirit to reveal the biggest one you struggle with today. Take several days to work through one thought. I suggest doing one step per day.

175 | The Perfect Counselor

> **Step 1—State your belief (about yourself, another person, or situation).**

We all have in our minds judgements about ourselves, about others, or situations which cause stress in our lives. Be detailed. Examples are:

- "Rick is never home anymore. I know he's going to leave me."
- "I'm a failure."
- "Dad doesn't deserve to be forgiven."
- "My daughter's addiction is killing her."
- "My mother doesn't love me."
- "My best friend betrayed me."

Notice that each statement is a variation of a single theme: *I shouldn't have to experience this. Life isn't fair. God doesn't care.* Write your thought/belief out just the way your mind is saying it, and any images you see that are attached to this belief. *This is your reality!*

> **Step 2— When I believe this thought, how do I react?**

Write down how you react, feel physically, and how you treat yourself and others when you believe this thought. *Get honest and claim your true feelings.* If you're sad, say so. If you hate someone right now, say so. If you feel defeated, admit it. Talk about the suffering, frustration, anxiety, rage, sadness, discomfort; whatever you are feeling. Make it a conversation with Jesus. He'll help you see on paper what's whirling around in your mind—*your reality!* These questions may help you:

- What *emotions* arise when you believe that thought? Do you feel: angry, confused, helpless, anxious, indifferent, afraid, hurt, sad, judgmental, disgusted, distrustful, shamed, guilty, pitiable, envious, disrespected, contempt, or other.
- What *physical* sensations arise as you think that thought and witness those images? For example, your blood pressure rises, experience insomnia, hands start to shake.
- Do any obsessions or addictions surface when you believe this thought? (An *addiction* is repetitive a pattern of thought we set up in our minds; something we have a powerful relationship with.) Do you

act out by using or over-using: alcohol, drugs, shopping, food, sex, television, or social media, for example?

- How do you treat yourself when you believe this thought? Others?

Step 3—Who would I be and how might I feel if I didn't keep this thought?

Often this thought has become our identity, and it can be very difficult to visualize who we would be without it. As you write what's coming to your mind, make it a conversation with Jesus. He'll help you see who He created you to be without the thought. Remember, *it's the thought that's painful—not your life, not you!*

Step 4— Question and investigate the truth of the thought.

What we believe are facts are unconscious beliefs we've convinced ourselves are truth. For every negative thought and belief, we want to answer, to the best of our abilities, these two powerful questions:

1. *Is it true?* "Yes." Then answer:
2. *Can I be absolutely certain it's true? Is there biblical truth to support this belief?*

To answer #2 truthfully, we must inquire, look for proof, and dig deeper.

Step 5—Create a new thought: Experience the truth and turn around the thought. Also, ask: **Can this situation be changed?**

Once we recognize the toxic thought is false, then we must replace it with something. We create a new thought. The Bible gives us precise instructions:

"Whatever is true, whatever is noble, honorable, whatever is right, whatever is pure, whatever is lovely, whatever is admirable—if anything is excellent or praiseworthy—think about such things" (Philippians 4:8).

The phrase "think about such things" is critical. In other words, "focus and keep your thoughts on," "concentrate your attention on," and "let your mind dwell on."

---

177 | **The Perfect Counselor**

The challenge we have as Christians is to lay down a new set of thought patterns that lead us naturally to think on that which is good, right, pure, and lovely. Notice the first quality mentioned to think on is truth. *Is there biblical truth to support this belief?*

In the next verse, Paul says,

"Whatever you have learned or received or heard from me, or seen in me—put it into practice. And the God of peace will be with you" (4:9).

Practicing this verse is essential if we want to live a healthy life with God, one another, and ourselves. Satan *will* deceive the mind that chooses not to think on truth and the qualities in Philippians 4:8. How? Let me suggest:

Experience the Truth:

- *Visualize yourself living out the biblical truth:* Take the biblical truth and ask the Holy Spirit to create a vivid picture or movie of what this truth looks like for you personally. For example, after creating your new thought, such as "I am made in the amazing image of God!" *picture* who you'd be without this negative thought—*visualize yourself the image of God Almighty!* What does that look like to you, and mean to you personally?

- *Experience the biblical truth:* Once you see yourself living in the truth, ask the Holy Spirit to help you associate and experience it through your own mind and five senses.

- We can visualize specific ways we can overcome a fear. For example: David prayed, *"With your help I can advance against a troop; with my God I can scale a wall"* (2 Samuel 22:30). You respond (complete the sentence): *"With your help I can … with my God I can …"*

- Another example: We can visualize being conformed to the image and likeness of Jesus. We can see ourselves being compassionate and loving to people we have a hard time with. Say to your soul, "Listen soul, because of Jesus Christ, I'm made in the amazing image of God. All these things I visualize are the true me!"

Turn the Thought Around:

178 | **The Perfect Counselor**

Second, we ask the Holy Spirit if we can turn around the thought. This is particularly applicable when the belief is about another person. It is a fact: We dislike, even hate, in others what we often dislike or hate in ourselves.

Turned around thoughts can be powerful when we discover that what we see on the outside; or see in another person, is really a projection of our own minds. It is easy to see the wrongs in others that we are equally guilty of (Matthew 7:5; Romans 2:1).

If your judgment about another person feels uneasy, ask yourself if you've hit on a belief *about yourself* that you haven't investigated yet. For example, "He should love me," turns around to "I should love myself."

Try this exercise: Think of a couple of people you dislike. Make a list of the top five things you dislike about them. It is likely you'll have the same five things buried deep in your unconscious. Often, we react most strongly to the things in other people that we have issues with ourselves. When we recognize this, then we can create a brand-new thought based on our knowledge.

Changing a Belief about a Situation:

Third, we must ask ourselves, "Is the situation changeable?" Not all are. You may choose to: *List all the ways you can change the situation.*

A good exercise is to make two lists: *Givens* and *Not Givens*.

- The *Givens* lists what cannot be changed. For example, Betsy has been trying to "fix" her sister Darlene. She had to admit, "Darlene is never going to change without God's supernatural intervention. I can't fix her."

- The *Not Givens* are situations which can be changed. For example, you are very angry and believe your dad doesn't deserve forgiveness for sexually assaulting your daughter. It won't be easy, but if you choose to draw on God's power, you can process through your anger and in time forgive your dad, thereby freeing yourself.

- The objective with the *Not Givens* list is to come to think differently about the situation.

Givens	Makes me Feel	Not Givens
Dad's controlling ways.	*I feel like I don't have a voice or a choice.*	I can set boundaries, speak up, move forward following God's lead and not dad's lead.
Ex-husband believes I'll always be an addict and a loser.	*I feel like a loser.*	I can get clean; choose my destiny: go back to school, get training, find new friends, etc.
5-year prison sentence.	*I feel like my life is over; I feel shamed, even suicidal.*	I can choose to condemn myself and be miserable; or look at the sentence as an opportunity to grow, get clean, and take advantage of free programs.

We can fix, reframe, or change *Not Givens*, and let go of the *Given* list. And we can remember this popular quote, "Sometimes our plans don't work out because god has better ones."

You have just learned five ways to take a toxic thought or core belief captive and change it, thereby changing your reaction; thereby changing an outcome. This is mind freedom!

Change a Thought about Yourself

"Why are you thinking these things?" –Jesus, speaking in Mark 2:8

A false belief about yourself cannot be changed until it is honestly dug up and faced. To help yourself, review this list of the most common thinking errors. Pray as David did, *"Search me, O God, and know my heart; test my thoughts"* (Psalm 139:23, TLB). Ask a friend, family member, or counselor to help you.

Most Common ATEs and PMSs (Thinking Errors)

These are the most common ATEs and PMSs, and suggested investigative questions to help you uncover truth, thereby, changing your reality.

All or Nothing Thinking ("black and white" thinking). This person automatically thinks in absolute terms, like "always" or "every" or "never." "I *always* mess this up. I'll *never* be a success." *Ask yourself (and God)*: "Am I looking at the negatives, while ignoring the positives? Is there a more balanced way to look at this situation?"

People Pleaser. One way *fear of man* reveals itself is we become people pleasers. This person thinks, "I must be loved or approved by every significant person in my life. I depend on others for my value." *Ask yourself (and God)*: "Who am I doing this for—me, others, God?"

Exaggerates/Overgeneralization. This person takes isolated cases and automatically makes wide amplifications or generalizations (often to avoid taking responsibility or deflecting blame).

For example, she sees a single negative event, like not getting a promotion, or getting a C on a test, as a never-ending pattern of defeat. Put the situation in perspective: *Ask yourself (and God)*: "What are the good things about the situation? What can I do to change it and see it in its proper perspective—the way God sees it?"

Evasive/Deflects/Vague. An evasive person uses the phrase "I don't know" to avoid difficult, stressful, or embarrassing questions or issues. "Deflecting" is automatically changing the subject or shifting the focus off yourself and onto someone or something else. "Vagueness" is avoiding concrete, truthful answers to questions. *Ask yourself (and God)*: "Why don't I want to talk about the details of my life? What fears are keeping me defeated? What are the facts and Truth, versus my own interpretations?"

"I Can't." Some people say this to express their refusal to take responsibility and accountability, which is really saying, "I don't want to" or "I won't." Others say it because they have very low self-esteem. Someone important may have told her she could never do anything worthwhile. To say "I can't" is to say we're too dependent on ourselves to depend on God—and not believe God's Word which says, *"I can do all this through him who gives me strength"* (Philippians 4:13). *Ask yourself (and God)*: "Am I saying this because I don't want to; or because I don't believe I can actually do it; or I don't want to rely on God?"

Mind-reader. This person jumps to conclusions and assumes the intentions of others. She is convinced that her prediction is a fact, therefore, will have set consequences. *Ask yourself (and God)*: "What's the evidence to prove it will turn out this way? How do I know what other people are thinking? Just because I assume something, does that mean I'm right?"

Catastrophizes/Worries. This person is consumed by fear and automatically assumes something negative is going to happen when there's no evidence to support it. They go ahead of God and make their own assumptions and plans, showing a lack of trust in God. They lose sleep and put their health at risk. Psalm 37:8 says, *"Fretting only causes harm and leads to evil." Ask yourself (and God)*: "What are the facts and Truth versus my interpretations, and how might they be false?"

Exercise: A reputable study stated *only 8 percent* of what we worry about in the future ever comes true. List numerically on a piece of paper every situation you are presently worried about. When finished, take 8% of that number. For example, if you list 15 worries; 15 X 8% = 1.2 of your worries will come true. Faith counteracts by remembering that if something troublesome does happen, God will use it for good (Romans 8:28; Genesis 50:20).

Personalizes. This person holds herself personally responsible for an event that is out of her control, like Valerie did when her son died (page 162). *Ask yourself (and God)*: "Am I really to blame and why? Am I making this all about me? What other explanations might there be?"

Jealous/Envious. This person compares and covets what someone else has, such as material things, a person (like a boyfriend), or physical traits.
Making one-sided comparisons leaves her feeling inadequate; or she does it to make herself come out on top (pride). She compares *her inside* to the other person's *outside*. *Ask yourself (and God)*: "Why am I comparing myself with someone who is created totally different than me, with a different purpose? Am I making fair comparisons?"

Victim/Blames. A victim thinks, "My past determines my present behavior because something once strongly affected my life and continues to do so (blame). I can't help the way I am."

The good experiences don't count because in her mind only bad things happen to her, which is usually someone else's fault. This is the opposite of accountability. The victim often believes she gets what she expects. *Ask yourself (and God):* "What's the best that can happen in this situation? How can I amend it? Do I believe the truth*: "You, dear child, are from God and have overcome them, because the one who is in you is greater than the one who is in the world" (1 John 4:4)?"*

Prideful. This person seeks to satisfy an inner longing for value or esteem. Pride has been called the sin from which all others arise, such as selfishness, criticism, insensitivity, self-justification, narcissism, and vanity. *Ask yourself (and God):* "What do I fear by having my prideful nature exposed *and* removed? Do I want to live on self-will, or submitted to and powered by God?"

Judgmental/Critical. This person finds fault with everyone else. She "labels." This makes her feel good about herself: *I'm thinner|prettier|smarter| a classier dresser than her!* In other words, *I'm better than her.* Wayne Dyer said, "When you judge another, you don't define them, you define yourself." *Ask yourself (and God)*: "Am I judging the situation or the person (her outside)?"

* * *

1—Write down your judgement statement about yourself. For example, *"I am a failure at everything I do."* (Sadly, too many women believe they are failures, and have similar beliefs of unworthiness. I want women to uncover the evidence they are not a failure through this example.)

2—When I believe this thought, how do I react? What do I do when I feel this feeling? How do I behave? *"Feeling like a failure makes me feel like if I do anything it will be wrong. I feel depressed, like I'm the only one who struggles with this."*

3— Who would I be and how might I feel if I didn't keep this thought? *"Without this thought I'd be a more peaceful and confident person. I'd feel free, like a huge weight has been lifted off my back."*

4—Question and investigate the truth of the thought. *Is it true?* Naturally your statement appears true because it is based on a lifetime of uninvestigated unconscious beliefs. It's what makes you feel good. If you answer yes, then ponder the answer to:

Can I be absolutely certain that it's true—that I'm a failure? Your parents may have said so, therefore, you say so. But *can you be absolutely certain it's true that you're a failure? Or did you draw a wrong conclusion about yourself based on your parent's opinion, and not truthful reality?*

Remember, things we believe may be *old truth* about us from our "BC" (before Christ) days. However, the *new truth* about us is we have a new identity that brings with it new truths about ourselves. We must choose to live in this reality, "IC" (in Christ), by believing new truths.

Look for the proof and inquire deeper. *Is there biblical truth to support this belief? Did His Word say you're a failure?* No!

- You're fearfully ("awesome") and brilliantly made (Psalm 139:14).
- You've been created for a specific purpose (Psalm 139:13-16).
- There's a special, divine blueprint for your life (Jeremiah 29:11).
- You're a conqueror (Romans 8:37); God will complete through you what He's called you to do (Philippians 1:6).
- You have a spirit of power, love, and sound mind (2 Timothy 1:7).
- God will use your weaknesses and strengths to conform you to the image of Christ—to be a difference-maker (Romans 8:29).

Never forget, your calling and gifts are special and unique. You can't be a circle if God created you to be a triangle. You will feel like a failure. Think of all the great heroes in the Bible who redirected the course of human events when they followed God's plan for their lives. *You can change history!*

To prove you're not a failure, work with God to discover your unique blueprint. Write out the answers to these questions:

- How can your past "survival skills" become a great strength and ministry? What differences could you make tomorrow?
- Do you feel empathy for a certain type of person or cause?
- What talents and gifts do you believe God has given you?

184 | The Perfect Counselor

- What do you enjoy doing; care about deeply; have a passion for?
- What sorts of projects motivate you to action?
- Should you seek career and/or financial counseling to get ahead?

Look at everything you wrote down. Then ask yourself if it's true that you're a failure; that you'll never amount to anything. The answer is NO! The evidence is clear and reveals your real worth.

5—Create a new thought and experience the truth. Ask: *Can this thought be turned around? Can this situation be changed?* This thought can be turned around.
- I have special gifts and talents!
- I'm not a failure. I am a success!
- I have been chosen and appointed to bear fruit (John 15:16).

Now picture who you'd be without this negative thought. Picture yourself a successful missionary for God and a conqueror. Tell your soul the different ways you are a success and conqueror.

We must choose to soak our minds in God's teachings, so they will slip into our unconscious minds. The day will come when one of those teachings will emerge to the conscious mind. We will instantly decide whether we'll accept His Word or not. If we accept it, then we'll choose to make ourselves do what's right, even despite our feelings. Then we're using our transformed minds of Christ. The Bible says the result is the peace of God!

Change a Thought about Another Person

1—Write down your judgement statement about this person. Who in your life angers, confuses, saddens, shames, or disappoints you? What is it about them that you don't like or approve of?

"I'm (i.e. angry at; or saddened | frightened | hurt | disappointed) with NAME.

Now, expand on this statement: *"I'm angry at Bill because …"* Go further and write out *all* your feelings. Why do you want him or need him to change? What do you believe Bill should or shouldn't do, or be, or think, or feel? What do you need from Bill to feel peace and joy? What is it you don't want to experience with him again? *"I don't ever want to or I refuse to …"*

Katie's Experience

Katie wrote, "When Jared gets mad at me, I feel so victimized that I want to break up with him."

2—When I believe this thought, how do I react? What's the consequence? Katie pictured herself the suffering victim when Jared gets angry at her. She reacts by tensing up, and sees everything through fearful and guilt-ridden eyes.

3— Who would I be and how might I feel if I didn't keep this thought? Katie believes she'd be more self-assured and loving without this thought.

4— Question and investigate the truth of the thought. *Is it true?* Yes. Here's the proof: When Jared gets angry his face is red, his neck throbs, and he yells at me. *Can I be absolutely certain Jared is mad at me?*

Find the proof. Inquire deeper. *Is there biblical truth to support this belief?* In this case, no. Here are questions Katie can answer to get a step closer:

- Do you know for certain it is *you* Jared is mad at?
- Do you know for certain what's going on inside his head?
- Can you know for certain what any person is really thinking and feeling by their facial expressions and body language?
- Is he being clear about his own thoughts and emotions?
- Have you ever been angry and found yourself pointing the finger or blaming someone else?
- Do you know for certain you feel hurt because Jared is angry? Is it really Jared's anger that is causing your hurt? Might it be possible, there is something else which is hurting you, that you're angry about? If yes, ask: What am I angry about? Is my anger justified?

Let's say it *is not true.* On this occasion when Jared got angry it was because his employee didn't meet an important deadline. *The truth is Jared is projecting his anger onto Katie,* and he needs to be made aware of this. By believing Jared is angry with Katie, and then reacting in an unhealthy manner, this technically means Katie is stepping into Jared's business. She's taking onto herself an issue that's between Jared and his employee.

Let's say the thought *is true:* Katie failed to do something she promised Jared she'd do. Jared is indeed mad at Katie. We go to step 5.

5—Create a new thought and experience the truth. Ask: *Can this thought be turned around? Can this situation be changed?*

Katie can ask herself if she's hit on a belief *about herself* that she hasn't investigated yet. A negative reaction to others is often a symptom of an inner wound in yourself. Might Katie's thought really be saying, "I'm hurt and acting out in healthy ways because I let my husband down. I feel guilty."
If this is the truth, Katie needs to create a new thought: "I'm a fallen human and will make mistakes. God forgives me and I can ask for Jared's forgiveness. He loves me and will forgive me."

Reflect: We are all in control of our choices, no matter how we feel. We can choose to either dwell on a toxic thought, and how unfair life and God are. Or, choose to work with God to renew our minds, and watch our reality and life change dramatically!

Throughout the Scriptures, people are reminded of their choices and asked to take responsibility for them. Like Paul says, if we choose to live by the Spirit, we'll live; if we choose to follow our flesh nature, we'll die (Romans 8:13). Making decisions based on ATEs and PMSs, or others' approval, or on guilt/shame, for example, breeds toxicity. *Today, choose truth!*

187 | **The Perfect Counselor**

12

Shame Off You!

With unfailing love I have drawn you to myself. I will rebuild you ... You'll again be happy and dance merrily ...–*God, speaking in Jeremiah 31:3-4* (NLT)

One night I met up with a guy friend at a bar. As usual I'd begun my journey to getting plastered. He took me to a small party at some dude's apartment where we continued to booze it up. I was led into a bedroom by one of the guys. Wasted and barely conscious, I didn't realize until hours later that four guys raped me.

The word spread like wild fire in the college dorm that I "pulled a train" (when a group of males, one after the other, have sex with a woman). My guy friend didn't stand up for me, and my peers ostracized and ignored me, presuming I "wanted it." To them, and to me, the only difference between me and a prostitute is I didn't exchange money. Instead, I walked out covered inside and out with the vomit of shame—that couldn't be covered with makeup, or wouldn't wash off no matter how many showers I took.

What I've done can never be undone. I'm a very bad person. I'm hideous and worthless. It's no secret. I'm ignored as if I don't exist. I'm naked for everyone to stare at. I have no value to those whose opinions matter most.

I believe shame is the most toxic human emotion. And the shame of sexual abuse is the worst because the abuser invades your internal organs, your very soul. Being used for someone else's sexual gratification is humiliating and demeaning; it kills the soul. A naked body is so intimate that when abused it brings on overwhelming levels of shame. Eventually I just became numb to being used and thrown out. The way I felt was the way I acted. (I'm so glad all this happened before phone cameras!)

188 | The Perfect Counselor

Reflect: To what degree, or in what ways, do you relate to my story?

The Weight of Shame

Imagine I'm holding up a plastic bottle filled with water. I ask, "How heavy is this bottle of water?" One person answers, "16-ounces." Another says, "No, 12-ounces." Another answers, "I think it's less." My reply, "The actual weight doesn't matter. It depends on how long I hold this bottle of water.

If I hold it for one minute, it's not heavy. If I hold it for one hour, my arm will ache. If I hold it all day, my arm will feel numb and paralyzed. In either case, the weight of the bottle doesn't change. It remains 12-ounces. The point is: The longer I hold this bottle, the heavier it becomes." The emotion of shame is like this.

Think on a shame-based thought for a moment and nothing usually happens. Think about it longer and it begins to hurt. And if you think about it all day long, and then again the next day, and the next, you'll feel paralyzed and incapable of doing anything. The weight of shame is cumulative. Year after year, it weighs us down more and more.

The big problem is: Shame corrodes the part of us that believes we're capable of change because *we believe our shameful thoughts are true*. You can see why we find it far easier to just repress and deny those toxic feelings.

Shame is not the same as guilt or embarrassment. Embarrassment doesn't afflict a person's soul. You eventually laugh about it. With shame, you never laugh. Typically, guilt is a result of something *we do*. It's a valuable signal indicating a wrong or bad behavior.

Most often, *shame* is a result of something *done to us* by another person. It is an indictment on us as a person. We see our *identity* as flawed, like we're a mistake. We feel shame when we've done nothing wrong. Shames says, "You're the exception to the saying, *God doesn't' make junk*." On the other hand, with guilt, we see ourselves as having flaws which can be remedied.

Guilt	Shame
Is about what *I do*—my **behavior.** "I screwed up."	Is about *me*—**who** I am. "I'm a screw-up."
A result of an act; of *doing*. *What did I* **do***? Why did I do* **that***?*	A result of *being*. *What did* **I** *do? Why did* **I** *do that?*
Involves a *choice*.	No choice; *involuntary*.
Involves *conviction*.	Involves *condemnation*.
You did a wrong = truthful.	*You are a bad person* = a lie.

Shame is the prime motivator of toxic behavior. The strength of shame most often comes from the combination of shame and guilt. "If I do bad, then I am bad."

The Walk of Shame

Imagine walking down the aisle of the grocery store and you see and hear a man cursing a 5-year-old girl. He's calling her every foul name. Do you think, *What a terrible little girl?* No! You (should) recognize the man is being verbally abusive. What do you think the little girl walks away feeling like? And what if the man is her father?

Too many of us are this 5-year-old girl. Shame most often comes from specific beliefs we were taught about ourselves by family members or other significant people. Today, whenever someone treats us badly, we *automatically* believe there's something wrong with us; we unconsciously pull up our 5-year-old memories.

Shame usually comes out of *a lie someone told you about yourself—a lie that you were 'less than.'* Some people are raised in shame-based families. Feelings of shame, worthlessness, and humiliation are often communicated from one or both parents whose child rearing techniques are based on the idea that a properly shamed child is a properly behaved one. Some parents can instill these killer beliefs, like *"You'll always be a dirty and worthless little ..."* into their children before they've even developed language skills. They don't have any self-esteem or ability to fight back.[74]

If you were this child, take this poet's words to heart, *"We come through our parents, not from them."* Believing this can be life-saving. Think about this: *If we didn't long to be wanted and loved, then we couldn't be shamed by other's rejection or attacks.*

Those whose souls have been damaged know what "the walk of shame" feels like—the feeling that everyone in the room has their eyes on you and knows all your dirty secrets and indiscretions. People who feel shamed feel exposed. Even if other people aren't looking at them, they imagine how awful they seem in the eyes of others. They tend to ruminate endlessly on shameful thoughts. Therefore, many women put up walls to relationships. It's their way to self-protect against being hurt and shamed. They tend to curtail their normal activities.

Shame blackmails: *"If everyone knew the truth about you they'd see you're a fraud."* The accuser's voice scorns: *"You* asked for it and everyone is going to know what a horrible person you are ... *You did this* to yourself so you better keep this secret ... You'll have to live with this alone ... If you need comfort, you can find it in a bottle; even better, why don't you kill yourself."

Reflect: What condemning words has the accuser spoken to you? How have those words shaped your life? Circle any of these words that describe how you feel today: *deficient, rejected, diminished, defeated, alienated, bad, evil, unlovable, unacceptable, [add your own word].*

The Condemnation

"Condemnation" means you've been judged unfit; there is strong disapproval. The result: *You* bring charges against *yourself* and pronounce *yourself* fit for punishment. Therefore, you may choose to self-harm or abuse substances. Condemnation comes from the devil, other people, even ourselves—but never from God—*never!* Shame is different than guilt in that shame attacks our identity in Christ.

What happens is: Following a traumatic act (emotional or physical), toxic thoughts begin to form tracks (or pathways) in the brain. The tracks grow deeper and stronger every time we believe that an outsider has confirmed a shaming thought. We then feel even more inadequate; less loved; less wanted.

For example, Sara's mom constantly tells her she isn't good enough. When her teacher tells her that her homework assignment didn't meet class standards, then Sara repeats to herself *again* that she is not good enough, making that toxic thought track deeper, therefore, harder to get out of.

Sometimes shaming words are not even spoken. Body language experts say *directly pointing* or *rolling your eyes* or *showing disgust through facial expressions* is a way of shaming and bullying that person. Shame can make us feel so devalued that we may find ourselves becoming the "shamer" (a tactic I practiced a lot). If we can shame someone else, that makes us feel better about ourselves, and even feel superior to the person, thereby taking the focus off our own toxic feelings. We use: sarcasm, name-calling, expressing disgust, and eye-rolling to communicate to the person they are not worthy of respect.

Reflect: Name a time when you were the shamer. How did this make you feel?

The Cover Up Shame Cycle

"As a kid, no one was ever there for me. A lot of bad things happened to me. I'd lash out in anger and be sent home from school. I started to drink when I was 12-years-old. That was the only time I felt okay—when I was drunk. A lot of guys wanted to have sex with me. I let them do what they wanted. When I was drunk I didn't care and the pain went away. Then I'd sober up and I'd remember my crappy life. I got into drugs but they cost too much. So, I prostituted myself for money. I didn't know how to stop the destructive cycle." –Janelle

Janelle's story demonstrates the damage created by pain, abuse, abandonment, and the resulting shame that leads to high risk behaviors. What we do know is guilt fuels shame. The cycle typically goes like this:

- Someone hurts you and tells you a lie about yourself: *You deserve this. You're a very bad person.* →
- Believe and internalize it: *Something is wrong with me. I'm a very bad person* (a result of something done or said by another person) →
- The pain is intense. Response: *I don't want to feel like this anymore.* →

- Create a coping mechanism ("medicate" in some way)→ *substance abuse, isolating, eating disorder, self-injury, rage, envy, secretiveness, people-pleasing, codependency, rationalization, projection, controlling, minimize, perfectionism, depression, behaving abusively.* →
- Feel guilty (a result of something caustic you've done). →
- Guilt morphs into another lie and toxic shame, *I'm a wretched horrible person for doing this. So, I am worthless and undeserving of forgiveness.* →
- The lie festers → Creates distortion, even suicidal thoughts. →
- Experience more feelings of shame, compounded by guilt. →
- Re-medicate and/or repeatedly act out in a destructive manner which intensifies the feelings of guilt and shame.→
- The result: a destructive cycle of severe pain and bondage.

Reflect: Think of a time when you couldn't get off the merry-go-round of shame. How did the cycle impact your life?

Sexual Abuse and Shame

I have learned that *sexual those in pain experience the strongest, most toxic and destructive feelings of shame.* Sexual abuse has an exceptional negative effect on a person. Since our sexuality is the most intimate part of a person, when there's inappropriate sexual contact or exposure, the result is *deep shame.* Dr. Stephen Tracy affirms this. He wrote,

"God made our sexuality, particularly our genitals, very sensitive and personal and thus, susceptible to creating great shame. Our genitals are not shameful, but are so intimate that any inappropriate exposure or contact can bring overwhelming levels of shame regardless of whether we chose to expose our bodies or consented to sexual contact."[75]

When a person is sexually abused or assaulted, sometimes she'll feel intensified shame because she may experience some sort of excitement or physical pleasure during the assault. *This doesn't mean she enjoyed the experience or really wanted it.* If this happened to you, recognize that our bodies were designed by God to respond to sexual touch—a response that can happen even when the touch is unwanted.

This creates shame because the woman feels there's something wrong with her for feeling this way. No wonder so many women choose to deaden this pain in a destructive way.

Reflect: If you have experienced sexual abuse, what can you conclude from this information?

Shame and Anger

You may say, "I don't feel shame, it's more like anger." Anger is not a primary emotion. It is a secondary response to feelings such as guilt, shame, trauma, inferiority, grief, and fear. *Anger is often substituted for shame*—anger based on trying to avoid feeling shamed. They often become intertwined. Anger works to temporarily protect us.

For example: Say your husband or boyfriend expresses something, either intentionally or unintentionally, that leads you to feel degraded and humiliated. Rather than sharing your hurt feelings with him, in an act of self-protection, you may automatically and unconsciously react by finding something to attack him for. It may be something petty, or an act of revenge. You're basically attempting to make him feel the same way you feel—demeaned and hurt, "You're the one who is worse!" Now you don't feel shamed and hurt—at least temporarily.

Reflect: Can you think of a personal example of when your shame has turned to anger? What were the results?

Three Steps to Overcoming Shame

Shame's only positive purpose is to lead us into a relationship with the Perfect Counselor. We must ask the Holy Spirit to help us root out these killer thoughts and beliefs, and begin tearing them down. The first step is to figure out who is responsible.

1: Clarify Ownership

Miranda described an incident with her husband, Joe, in which he told her dinner must be ready at 6:00 PM. Miranda served dinner at 6:20 PM. To strike back, he threw his plate into the sink, breaking it. He proceeded to give Miranda the silent treatment for rest the night.

The next morning, Joe stated, "Why do *you* disrespect my wishes? I wouldn't have to punish you if you'd serve dinner when I ask you to."

Miranda responded, "It wasn't his fault. It's mine. I'm a bad wife."

Let's analyze this situation:

When a person submits to the control of another person for a sufficient period of time, it slowly erodes her self-identity, and the ability to think and reason for herself. The submissive person begins to think through the eyes of the controlling person, rather than with her own mind. Miranda had surrendered her identity to her husband and accepted his version of reality as her own. Shame became her identity. It's clear that Joe's actions and words created Miranda's shame. Consider what Jesus said:

"The things that come out of the mouth come from the heart, and these make a man 'unclean.' For out of the heart come evil thoughts, murder, adultery, sexual immorality, theft, false testimony, slander. These are what make a man 'unclean' ..." (Matthew 15:18-20).

Some people can torment us into believing we're dirty, unworthy, and unacceptable to God and to others. In biblical times this condition was called "unclean." Unclean translated means "impure."

Jesus is saying: *It's not what goes in my mouth that defiles me; it's what comes out of my mouth and heart that defiles me.* The mouth reveals most clearly the condition of the heart. Therefore, if another person spews their verbal vomit onto me—calls me a *blah...blah blah*, they cannot destroy my soul with their tongue, or make me feel contaminated because the verbal vomit came out of *their* mouth; it came out of *their* heart.

Jesus said, *"Don't be afraid of those who want to kill your body; they cannot touch your soul"* (Matthew 10:28; NLT). The only thing that can dirty me is what comes from inside of my heart. When we love another person, and that person has power and authority over us, we take the person's "unclean" dirty words and internalize them; believe they are truth.

This is what Miranda did. We believe the lies and convince ourselves we're defiled and condemn ourselves. This is how some people maintain power and control. The fact is: Joe is the unclean person, not Miranda.

Reflect: Explain in your own words what Jesus has taught you. How does His therapeutic words of wisdom make you feel?

Investigate the Truth

"No one and nothing can make you an outcast, dirty, or untouchable. People can't; the sins of your family can't; abusers can't." –Dr. Edward T. Welch

Decades ago when my dad called me a "fat piggy" I internalized and believed it. Healing meant investigating this statement. *Was it true?* I believed it was. I saw fat in the mirror. *Could I be absolutely certain it was true?* Upon further investigation, I recognized I was a little overweight, but I'd never been a "fat piggy." I was "clean." Dad's critical labels made him unclean—not anything I did, or ate. *Other people's evil words only taint themselves and make them filthy.*

The best indicator of our heart's condition is our speech. Even joking and small talk reveals our character. Thus, the Bible has so much to say about our words. Let me wrap this up with Jesus's Word, *"I tell you that every careless word that people speak, they shall give an accounting for it in the day of judgment"* (Matthew 12:36, NASB). Jesus meant that our speech is such an accurate index of our hearts that even idle and careless words reveal who we are, and therefore, evidence on which to judge us. Someday my dad will give an accounting for his words to God.

Reflect: How do you still carry the shameful incident with you? In other words, what thoughts, feelings, motives, and/or actions replay consistently?

Already Clean!

Jesus said, *"You are already clean because of the word I have spoken to you. Remain in me, as I also remain in you. No branch can bear fruit by itself; it must remain in the vine. Neither can you bear fruit unless you remain in me"* (John 15:3-4).

Re-read this passage, but substitute your name for the word "you." This is a beautiful description of our personal relationship with Christ. We connect with Jesus; He connects with us. To "remain" or "abide" in Jesus is to be rooted, and grounded, and filled with Him. The result: We are part of Him.

We are one. What is your response? Do you really believe what Jesus says is truth? If yes, then *you* are "clean." Remain connected to Jesus and you'll continue to be clean—free from any kind of contamination.

In this parable, we are the branch—the branch attached to Jesus, the vine. According to *Vines Complete Expository Dictionary,* the word "fruit" means "the visible expression of Christ's power working inwardly and invisibly" inside of me. So, let's read it again in this context: *To receive the visible expression of Christ's power working inwardly and invisibly in you; you must remain in Jesus Christ.*

In other words, when I connect with Christ, His power will be at work in me. I will produce good stuff, not bad stuff. In biblical terms, I'm a "good tree." Jesus said, *"A good tree cannot bear bad fruit, and a bad tree cannot bear good fruit"* (Matthew 7:18).

- Fact: You are connected to Jesus.
- Fact: You are clean.
- Fact: You are the image of "good fruit" and a "good tree;" of goodness, not sin!

Jesus said, *"No good tree bears bad fruit, nor does a bad tree bear good fruit. … A good man brings good things out of the good stored up in his heart, and an evil man brings evil things out of the evil stored up in his heart. For the mouth speaks what the heart is full of"* (Luke 6:43-45).

Let this sink in: Even if you've had contact with an unclean person, as a believer in Jesus Christ and His Word, *you cannot bear bad or evil things!* Second Corinthians 5:17 confirms that *you are a new creation in Christ.* The old life is gone; a new life has begun! As one commentator put it, "We're not reformed, rehabilitated, or reeducated—we're recreated."

Reflect: A proverb goes, "Just when the caterpillar thought the world was over, it became a butterfly." Envision the miracle of a caterpillar (representing your old life) turning into the most gorgeous butterfly (representing your new life). Only God can perform such a miracle! How do you feel now?

Yes You— Are a New Creation!

What I love about Jesus is He constantly associated with people who were considered "bad" or "unclean" by others, like tax collectors, prostitutes— sinners! But He never thought of them as "bad." He condemned the sinful behavior, but never the sinner.

To Jesus, every person had the ability to repent and have a relationship with the Father. He constantly invited other people into relationship with Him because He knew *connecting with Him* is what gave them the power to be "good" or "clean."

Open your eyes to see the sin in the person who hurt or abused you—not the other way around. They must take ownership of their actions—not you! Never forget that when we accept Christ as Lord, the Bible tells us God dismisses all charges against sinners.

We make an exchange: *our sin for His righteousness; our shame for His purity.* The Bible states,

"Anyone who belongs to Christ has become a new person. The old life is gone; a new life has begun! ... For God made Christ, who never sinned, to be the offering for our sin, so that we could be made right with God through Christ" (2 Corinthians 5:17; 21; NLT).

Jesus said, *"Do not call anything impure that God has made clean"* (Acts 10:15). I believe we hinder God's work in us by not believing that we are clean and whole; a new creation. If we allow shame, unworthiness, and rejection to rule our lives, then, we're rejecting God's Word, which says we are *new, clean, pure, white as snow, and righteous.* (Rejecting God's Word is disobedience.)

Part 2:
Shame Which Comes from Our Actions

Following a gruesome bulimic episode, I grabbed the near empty bottle of *Windex* and ripped off three squares of paper toweling and proceeded to clean up around the toilet bowl. After tossing the residue of a gaping emotional wound into the garbage I sat down on the couch numb. *I feel like garbage.*

In addition to purging food I found pleasure in binge drinking because my shame and insecurities vanished. It changed my reality for a moment. It gave me the confidence to do things I'd never do sober. The promiscuity was a way to fill my deepest need to feel loved—even if it was only for a minute. I believed this is where my worth lay—that I "owed" sex to men. I slept with so many guys that I couldn't count them anymore. And I couldn't stop the cycle. These were the coping mechanisms I chose to cover the pain of shame.

As a coping mechanism, we may:

- Act out the pain in a destructive manner, and thereby, hurt others.
- Become abusive ourselves.
- Turn guilt into unhealthy shame if a shameful thought attaches itself to a guilty thought. Using my previous personal example: I felt guilty for putting myself in that "party" position; I felt shame because I had sex with multiple guys.

If this is you, you must work to forgive yourself, and do everything possible to create a mentally and emotionally healthy life. I suggest these six R's.

"Six R's to Freedom"

Recognize: We must first recognize our wrong and/or destructive behavior. Acknowledge the guilt (the action), but *not the shame.* →

Respond: We take responsibility for what we recognize; we first confess our wrongdoings to God, and then to one other person (called accountability). We ask God to forgive us. David wrote,

"When I refused to confess my sin, my body wasted away, and I groaned all day long. Day and night your hand of discipline was heavy on me. My strength evaporated like water in the summer heat. Finally, I confessed all my sins to you and stopped trying to hide my guilt. I said to myself, "I will confess my rebellion to the LORD." And you forgave me! All my guilt is gone" (Psalm 32:3-5, NLT). →

Repent. God is quick to forgive when we feel a deep sorrow for our actions and resolve not to act in the same way again. God can change the heart *if* there's the willingness to change God's way. →

Reconcile. We take responsibility and make amends with any persons we've hurt, or offended, or avoided (if possible). I heard someone say, "It takes the acceptance of others to deliver us from the shame." →

Resist. When the urge to do or say something destructive arises (called *temptation*), we immediately go to the Perfect Counselor and pray. We ask Him to help us interrogate our thinking, and to remove the toxic thought and feelings. We can also reach into our minds for Scripture to resist the temptation. →

Rest. Jesus chose to die for our sins, which means our guilt and shame has permanently been lifted! Jesus has already turned tragedy into triumph. We can rest in God's mercy and forgiveness, and allow His unconditional love to transform our lives forever.

Reflect: What is your reaction to the *Six R's?* If you have engaged in unhealthy behavior, are you motivated to go through these steps? Why or why not?

Change Your Self-Talk— Change Your Reality

My personal example: I wanted to free myself from the shaming belief that I was garbage because of my promiscuity. I invited Jesus, my therapist, to be part of my *Change My Self-Talk—Change My Reality* exercise.

1—Write down your judgement statement about yourself. *Belief:* I've slept with many men whose only motive was to use me, therefore, I'm an awful person. I'm garbage.

2—When I believe this thought, how do I react? Since I feel dirty and unattractive, this thought makes me try to clean myself up with new clothes, makeup, dieting, and exercise. The shaming thoughts make me feel like an outcast, therefore I drink so I can morph into another person.

3— Who would I be and how might I feel if I didn't keep this thought? Without this thought I'd be free to be myself, the woman God created me to be; to engage in healthy relationships with men and other people.

4—Question and investigate the truth of the thought. Is it true? Yes.
Me: If I weren't garbage these guys wouldn't have taken advantage of me. They would've wanted to pursue me as a girlfriend and not a sex object.

Jesus: Are you absolutely certain this is true? (**Look for the proof and inquire deeper.**)

Me: No. These guys never actually said, "I'm going to use you and don't desire a relationship with you." But, their actions said this.

Jesus: What did their actions say?

Me: "I'm going to coerce you into having sex with me. Then I'm going to leave and never contact you again, unless I can coerce you into having sex with me again."

Jesus: Why did you go along with them?

Me: I wanted to be loved and desired.

Jesus: The truth is these guys coerced and deceived you in a worldly Satan- like act. You were looking for love, which is what I created you to seek because I am love! So, Kimberly, in this scene, who is clean? Who is unclean?

Me: I was clean and they were unclean.

5—Create a new thought. Jesus said, *"you are more valuable"* (Matthew 10:31). The truth is: I'm not dirty, polluted, or contaminated even though I encountered an unclean person. I'm clean and valuable. *He is unclean—not me!* Jesus will deal with him, and all the others who took advantage of me.

* * *

Most of us focus on things *outside of us,* which includes other people's verbal vomit. "One's dignity may be assaulted, vandalized and cruelly mocked, but it cannot be taken away unless it's surrendered" *(Saving Milly).*

When you do your own *Change Your Reality—Change Your Self-talk* exercise, you will come to separate and throw out the shaming labels and voices. Separate them from who you are as a *new creation in Christ. You are not your past, nor are you sin!* We need to let God give us a new set of eyes to see ourselves as we truly are—righteous, pure, and perfect!

Reflect: What obstacles stand in your way of accepting yourself as clean—as righteous, pure, and perfect?

Step 2: Shift Your Emotions

One way to experience real healing is to shift our emotional thinking from guilt and shame to grief and sadness. In other words, replace toxic emotions with healthy emotions. (Review chapter 6: The Grief We Call PTSD).

Step 3: Go to the Perfect Counselor

Imagine the guilt you'd feel if you ran over an innocent pedestrian with your car because you were texting, and he died. It was your fault—*you are guilty.* You deserve to be punished. Now imagine years later that a stranger comes to your door. It's the person you ran over, but now he is alive—not just alive, but alive with heavenly splendor, so beautiful and majestic that it's mind blowing. You automatically think: *Why's he here? For vengeance? Retribution?* You know you deserve whatever punishment he might demand of you. But no … your victim hasn't come to condemn you; instead he's come to offer you forgiveness.

His only desire is to free you of the guilt and shame which has haunted you for decades. All you must do is to believe this truth and accept it.

I do believe! Immediately your guilt evaporates because your victim lives!

In just the same way, because of our sins, each one of us is guilty of crucifying Christ. Because of our sins, He was killed. His blood is on our hands. Yet on Easter Sunday, He rose from the dead. He's not dead at all—the guilt has been lifted!

In the resurrection, God shows not only His mercy, but also His ability to turn tragedy into triumph. From *any* defeat, He can bring victory. Jesus is at our doors saying: *You don't have to feel guilty anymore, or be afraid, or hide the truth any longer. I'm alive! You're forgiven! Now go forth and sin no more.*

The Mysterious Bleeding Woman

In the book of Mark there are two stories of two people who brought their shame to Jesus. The first story is in Mark 5:25–43 and speaks of a mystery woman who had been slowly bleeding for 12 years. Kierkegaard said, "When you label me, you negate me."

Let's not negate this precious lady with the "bleeding woman" label. Pastor and author David W. Jones suggests we treat all unnamed burdened persons as a person, not an illness. Let's call her Amy which means "loved."[76]

Jewish law (Leviticus 15) considered menstruating women "unclean," physically and socially contaminated and dirty. No one would go near her. Even though she hadn't caused the problem, she felt bad about herself, and had no friends. Can you imagine the pain and the shame? (As a counselor, I find it interesting that some people believe that if they avoid contact with a person in emotional pain, that somehow, they'll protect themselves from the same kind of pain. Their avoidance of the hurting person only increases that person's isolation and decreases their self-worth.)

Amy, desperate for pain relief, heard that Jesus—HOPE—was coming. Picture it: As a huge crowd gathered, this desperate woman threw aside her feelings of disgrace and believed, *If I just touch his clothes, I'll be healed.*

Amy went to Jesus; notice she didn't wait for Him to find her. She positioned herself on the ground and touched His robe. *"Immediately her bleeding stopped and she felt in her body that she was freed from her suffering."* Unbeknownst to Jesus, His power physically decontaminated her! Through Jesus, Amy touched the Holy Spirit of God.

Jesus realized at once that healing power had gone out from Him, so He turned around in the crowd and asked, *"Who touched me?"* By touching Jesus, Amy would make Him ritually unclean. (Women didn't reach out and touch a man who wasn't their husband.) Yet, Amy stepped up. No doubt she expected Jesus to be angry with her, and anticipated the crowd would rebuke her for soiling Jesus's ceremonial status.

Trembling with fear, Amy knelt before Him, admitted what she had done, and told her story. No one listened before. Jesus did. (Telling our stories can be empowering and healing.)

Jesus simply responded, *"Daughter, your faith has made you well. Go in peace. Your suffering is over."* No mention of uncleanness. No anger. Just affirmation, validation, and good news. He purified her.

Jesus called Amy "daughter." This is the only time in Scripture when He calls a woman "daughter." Jesus gave her a name when no one else did—a name worthy of a child created in the image of God. If she was unaware of being loved and valued at the beginning of the story, she certainly felt it by the end. Jesus wanted all to know that she was healed and restored as a full member of their community. Jesus cares. He wants to hear you tell Him your story. He wants to heal you.

The Social Leper

In Mark 1:40-42 one leprous man also heard about Jesus's miracle healings. Mark doesn't tell us this guy's name. So, we'll refer to the leper man as Amos— "Amos" means "burdened." In biblical days' leprosy represented a physical, emotional, and spiritual death sentence. It was the equivalent of what it was like in America when AIDS first came to the forefront.

As lepers passed others on the streets they had to call out, "Unclean! Unclean!" (Leviticus 13:45-46.) This was like yelling out to the crowds, "I'm contaminated and polluted. Stay away from me or you'll be infected too." People had to keep at least 6-feet away when they passed because they were contagious. Today herpes and gonorrhea is widespread, yet it still has a shameful stigma attached to it. Imagine walking into your workplace or a mall yelling, *Herpes! Gonorrhea! Herpes! Gonorrhea!*

Little children ran away from lepers in fear. *Mommy, there's a monster over there!* Older kids threw stones and objects. Rejected and treated like garbage, these poor people were forced to live in an isolated leper colony. They were barred from feasts and festivals, weddings and funerals, worship and rituals— anywhere "insiders" congregated. Can you imagine the shame of being shunned by society around-the-clock?

204 | **The Perfect Counselor**

Yet one brave and desperate leper sought Jesus out and begged, *"If you are willing, you can make me clean."* Jesus reached out His hand and touched the man. *"I am willing," He said. "Be clean!" Immediately he was cured."* Jesus is *willing* to heal us—to take all the shaming unclean messages we've believed, and turn them into clean and truthful messages.

* * *

These stories remind us that even when we face pain, and everyone else turns away from us, Jesus is still present. Despite their conditions, these precious people, Amy and Amos, reached out to the Perfect Counselor. Risking His own reputation, Jesus knew exactly what they needed—His divine healing touch. Deemed "unclean" and feeling totally shamed and unworthy, Jesus filled each one with hope and compassion. By doing this, He showed His unity with every outcast.

Psalm 81:6 says, *"I removed the burden from their shoulders; their hands were set free from the basket."* When no one else seems to understand the pain, Jesus does. His healing spirit is ready to touch us, setting us free. He never turns away from us.

Reflect: Are you willing to surrender to Jesus all your pains and shame-filled beliefs, and believe and hope as these two people did? Yes. Now, in your own way, touch Him.

13

Set Yourself Free with Forgiveness

Make allowance for each other's faults, and forgive anyone who offends you.
Remember, the Lord forgave you, so you must forgive others.
—Paul, speaking in Colossians 3:13 (NLT)

"**I**'ll never ever forgive my mother. She put her head down the biggest ostrich hole to cover up my dad's drinking. *He's had a bad day at work.* When, as a 9- year-old, I told her I was kissed and groped by the neighbor boy who babysat me, she chose to put on her satin blinders. She dismissed it, and had the nerve to say that what he did could have been far worse." –Tara

The day came when Tara did something many women have a hard time doing. She forgave her mother. She acknowledged she had a problem and needed help. Do you want to get through to the other side of your pain? There is a way—it is found in forgiveness. Psychologist Gregory Jantz wrote,

"If the child of the past and the adult of the present are to integrate fully into the person of the future, there comes a time when both must release the hurts of the past. This doesn't mean you forget what has been done to you, but that you forgive those responsible, whether they deserve your forgiveness or not. Forgiveness is the final destination on your healing journey. The road that lies beyond is one of health."[77]

Reflect: Think for a moment: What difficulties have you had with forgiving someone who hurt you? Explain what you mean.

Anger

"Anger is just one letter short of danger." –Unknown

"I lost my childhood because of my mother's neglect and denial. She'd take me to the bars with her and then leave me alone with all the other drunks. I hate her." –Dorothy

Sometimes the offenses committed were so horrid it's difficult not to hate the person and desire revenge. It seems natural to want to hurt the person who stole our dignity, trust, innocence, and life. Sometimes we hide the anger and rage because we don't want to meet with rejection and disapproval from others.

Anger is a classic symptom of pain and trauma. Anger is a God-given emotion, and important for survival. It's a natural and appropriate response to abuse, evil, oppression, and wrongdoing; to broken trust and unfaithfulness. It's a normal response when our basic needs aren't met (especially when we're children), or our rights have been violated, and to any perceived threat.

Yet, some people lock into the anger. The situation turns them bitter and their outlook can remain toxic for the rest of their lives. When horrid offenses are committed, they become heavy burdens, filling the person with bitterness, rage, hate, and unforgiveness.

Like cancer, anger feelings contaminate our lives by corroding the soul and disorganizing our thinking. Satan knows betrayal, bitterness, and anger are destructive. It's a popular poison he uses. Somehow, he knows how to exploit these toxic emotions. Therefore, the apostle Paul said to forgive—to keep from being outsmarted by Satan (2 Corinthians 2:10-11).

Anger is God's response too. I knew if I were to grow, I had to release the hurts and anger of my past. This meant I had to ask God to empower me to move forward to release the angry feelings and to forgive those responsible, whether they deserved it or not.

* * *

Let me share with you what a psychologist taught me. I recalled two incidences when I was a teen and my dad yelled at and then kicked me, and gave me the lectures of all lectures, and proceeded to ground me. He was angry!

The first time this happened was when I came home from a day at the beach and was slightly intoxicated. The second time I had sunburned my face and back so badly that I was covered in blisters. Angry and hurt I thought, *How can he treat me this way!*

The psychologist said, "He must have loved you very much."

I replied, "Loved me? That's not love!"

He said, "Sure it is. Why else would he put out all that energy into trying to correct you? I don't think he was fighting *with* you; I think he was fighting *for* you—the best way he knew how."

At that moment, I saw these incidences in an entirely new light. I said, "I'm pretty sure that's how his own dad dealt with him. That's what he knows." Through a new lens, I re-interpreted my father's anger, not as rejection, but as love. I concluded, it was the only way my dad knew how to deal with a situation like this.

Let's not forget: God gets angry too! God is love, but there are things that make Him angry. He gets angry at injustice and *"evil men who push away the truth"* (Romans 1:18, TLB). Jesus Christ became angry when people were victimized by evil of any kind and God's will was thwarted.

Reflect: Can you think of a time you were made to feel guilty or shamed for feeling angry? Can you now accept that it is a normal emotion?

Vengeance

"Nothing causes us to so nearly resemble God as the forgiveness of injuries."
—John Chrysostom

I heard this story (but cannot confirm its truth). One evening a husband said to his wife, "Perhaps you should start washing your clothes in *Slim Fast*. Maybe it would take a few inches off your rear-end." His wife was hurt. She decided she'd had enough of his sarcasm and verbal blows. So, she sought revenge. The next morning the husband took a pair of underwear out of his drawer. A little dust cloud appeared

So, he asked her, "Why did you put baby powder in my underwear?" She snickered, "It's not baby powder ... it's *Miracle Grow.*" Then he got really angry!

208 | The Perfect Counselor

Some authors and clinicians promote the hang-them-high attitude. Other people argue that since Christ forgives us, we should not only forgive others, but fully relinquish them from the consequences of their actions.

In either case, I don't believe this is what God intends. Sometimes our expression of anger takes the form of vengeance. *I'll get even!* In other words, I prefer to avoid any healthy expression of my anger. As Christians are not to be vigilantes. Dr. Mark Baker, author of *Jesus: The Greatest Therapist Who Ever Lived*, wrote,

"We think if we feel bad, someone must have done this to us, and the only way to make things right is for that person to pay. Jesus had a different idea. The sacrifice of his life was all the payment that would ever be needed. Now the way things can be made right when we've broken relationships with other people is by what we *give* to them in the way of forgiveness, not by what we *get* from them in the way of payment."[78]

Anger is healthy when expressed with the intention of informing others about our personal limits, values, rules, and boundaries. We need to ask ourselves if the anger is righteous or selfish. We will come to know what those righteous things are as we study the Bible.

Many of us find it difficult to let go and forgive because we believe the person will get away with their offense, particularly if no penalty exists. No one *ever gets away with sin*. The Bible says one day we'll all be accountable to god for what we did on this earth, known as "judgment day" (or "retribution;" 2 Cor. 5:10). Jesus explains the coming of judgment day in Matthew 25:31-46, using the parable of the sheep and the goats.

When we forgive we're not making excuses for someone else's behavior; we're letting go of the person and letting God deal with them.

- *"Do not take revenge, my dear friends, but leave room for God's wrath, for it is written: "It is mine to avenge; I will repay," says the Lord"* (Romans 12:19; 2: 5-11; 2 Thessalonians 1;6-10).
- *"The LORD will not leave the guilty unpunished"* (Nahum 1:3).
- *"I, the LORD ... give all people their due rewards, according to what their actions deserve"* (Jeremiah 17:10).

Reflect: If you have been feeling the need, or have taken steps to get revenge on someone, how does it make you feel to know God will take care of it, and all you have to do is surrender this situation to Him and walk away? How easy do you think it will be to do so?

Hate or Forgive?

On October 2, 2006, a 32-year-old gunman entered a one room Amish school in Pennsylvania. The killer opened fire and shot 10 girls, killing half and leaving the others critically wounded. Then he killed himself. Before the sun set on that awful October day, members of the Amish community brought words of forgiveness to the family of the man who had slain their precious children. Those in the outside world were skeptical that forgiveness could be offered so quickly for such a heinous crime. For the Amish, their actions revealed the true character of their faith.

It may not seem like it but hate is a choice. Being hurt isn't a choice, but the action we choose to take is. If you decide to hate, you give Satan a place to unpack his bags and camp out. You also outrage every cell in your body and will pay the price physically.

Forgiveness is a choice. In the movie based on this event, *Amish Grace*, Gideon Graber, one of the fathers who lost a daughter said, "Hate is a very big, very hungry thing with lots of sharp teeth. It will eat up your whole heart, and leave no room for love." Gideon tells his wife Ida, who is struggling with hate, "It's not easy to forgive. The Lord does not ask us to walk an easy path ... But this I know, faith when everything is as you want it to be is not true faith. It's only when our lives are falling apart that we have the chance to make our faith real."

The killer of the Amish girls was in pain. He wanted to get back at God for taking his daughter who died at birth. He sought revenge on God. These Amish families paid the price ... so did the killer's wife and children.

Reflect: 1 John 2:9-11 states: *"Anyone who claims to be in the light but hates his brother is still in the darkness. Whoever loves his brother lives in the light, and there is nothing in him to make him stumble. But whoever hates his brother is in the darkness and walks around in the darkness; he does not know where he is going, because the darkness has blinded him."*

According to this passage, if we want to see clearly, we must let go of any hatred. I used to read this passage and feel confident about myself, after all, I didn't hate anyone. Then I discovered the Greek word for "hate" ("miseo") doesn't refer to murderous kind of hatred. It means to "detest" someone or something. Is there anyone I can I despise or loathe to be around? (Hate may feel like we're taking back control from the person who hurt us; that we're finally in the power position, but Scripture says we're not.)

Forgiveness is a Choice

"To love means loving the unlovable. To forgive means pardoning the unpardonable. Faith means believing the unbelievable." –G. K. Chesterton

Forgiveness seems like a great idea until we have something to forgive! When we've been betrayed, hurt, and violated, the thought of forgiving the person who hurt us can make our anxiety level rise quickly. Monique put her feelings to paper as a poem:

"My 15-year-old niece got pregnant by a 40-year-old man. While he says she was just a tease, that baby was born with a disease. He got five years which is too mild. I say give him the chair, poke out his eyes and pull out his hair."[79]

Forgiveness is a choice—a courageous choice. If you're not ready, that's fine, especially if you're beginning to feel re-traumatized. No two those in pain will handle forgiveness quite the same. At some point in time you'll have to address forgiveness if you want to heal fully. Just remember: *Forgiveness is not about the other person—it's about you*—and all the benefits you'll receive spiritually, emotionally, and physically.

Forgiveness Terminology

"Forgiveness does not erase the bitter past. A healing memory is not a deleted memory. Instead, forgiving what we cannot forget creates a new way to remember. We change the memory of our past into a hope for the future." –Lewis Smedes

211 | The Perfect Counselor

Unforgiveness is a deliberate refusal to let go of ill will. It's based on the attitude that somebody must pay for the hurt, a position for which there is no biblical justification.

Forgiveness is to put away our anger so it no longer controls us. The Greek word for "forgive" means to put something away; set it free, to move on. You say, "I'm not built to do that." You're right! Transformation of our hurt and hardened hearts can *only* be brought about by our love and devotion to Jesus.

Completed forgiveness means giving up both resentment toward someone else and the right to get even, no matter what the person has done. It's saying, "I choose not going to hurt anymore because of what you did to me, even if you're not sorry."

Why Forgive?

Jesus said, *"For if you forgive men when they sin against you, your heavenly Father will also forgive you. But if you do not forgive men their sins, your Father will not forgive your sins"* (Matthew 6:14–15).

What is your reaction to Jesus's words? This passage has often been misused to say, "Don't notice the offense," "What's wrong with you that you can't forgive." It's also been used to get people to act as if they forgive an offender before they really do. When this happens, the person struggles with forgiveness repeatedly. Context of Scripture is important. When Jesus said, *"My heavenly Father will also do the same to you, if each of you does not forgive his brother from your heart"* (Matthew 18:35), the emphasis is on integrity and purity of heart.

Jesus's words are *life shattering* because He declares that our forgiveness of others is evidence, or lack of, our spiritual condition. First, we must see how great our offenses against God are. We must understand how great a debt of personal sin He's forgiven. When we realize that Jesus paid off our sin debt with His suffering and blood, how can we possibly *not* forgive the sin debts that others inflict on us?

Jesus's words are *life changing* because as we experience the power of true forgiveness, our hurts, anger, bitterness, and resentments are transformed into peace, joy, contentment, and love. The weight we shouldered is lifted, freeing us to love others the way He loves us.

212 | **The Perfect Counselor**

There are benefits to letting go: healthier relationships, greater spiritual and psychological well-being; less anxiety, stress, and hostility; lower blood pressure; fewer symptoms of depression and cardiovascular disease; a lower risk of: substance abuse, cancer, hormonal changes, immune suppression, arthritis, and possibly impaired neurological function and memory.

Jesus's words are *life giving* because as we forgive those who have hurt us, we enter a deeper understanding of His love and mercy that leads to a more intimate relationship with Christ, and then others.

Let us not forget that we don't have the know-how to be judge and jury. The Bible discourages us from getting even. Instead it gives numerous promises that God will take care of it.[80] We don't have to forgive. God doesn't force forgiveness. Yet, to forgive is to show God we love and want to obey Him.

Reflect: What reasons do you have for *not* wanting to forgive? What reasons do you have for *wanting* to forgive?

What Forgiveness is NOT

"Forgiveness means it finally becomes unimportant that you hit back. You're done. It doesn't necessarily mean that you want to have lunch with the person. If you keep hitting back, you stay trapped in the nightmare." —Anne Lamotte

Understanding what *forgiveness is not* is often the key to successful forgiveness.

Forgiveness is Not Letting the Person off the Hook

Often an offender's actions destroy lives. Some choices produce serious consequences. This doesn't mean you don't hold the person accountable. King David committed adultery, then murdered a man to cover his sin. God judged David's sins and he paid dearly for his deceit for the rest of his lifetime. The consequences were irreversible. *Sin which has been forgiven and forgotten by God may still leave human scars, and often does.*

When God forgives our sin He's not saying our past behavior is disregarded. If somebody has a history of abusing children, although they experience God's forgiveness, the laws of our land demand they be held criminally responsible for their crimes. For example, after they've served their

213 | The Perfect Counselor

sentence, the person shouldn't be allowed to work in children's ministry.

Forgiveness involves mercy and grace, but it also involves accountability. If we let them off the hook too easily, they may conclude the offense wasn't really that serious because the consequences were light. God sets penalties, and He gives us the ability to do so.

Forgiveness Does Not Excuse, Minimize, or Justify

Janna's parents demanded she forgive her brother for making her watch pornographic movies with him. She agreed and said, "He didn't know what he was doing," even though she believed he knew right from wrong.

When someone apologizes, often the other person answers, "That's okay," because she's been told to 'forgive and forget,' or she doesn't want a confrontation. Yet, she still hurts and is distrustful.

Did you know the mind cannot accept a rationalization? When we carefully rationalize some behavior, we may convince ourselves at an intellectual level, but not at the emotional and spiritual level. The inner spirit knows better and will usually feel conflicted.[81]

You may be asked to forgive because your family wants you to. Families have a way of justifying or minimizing what's taken place. Many offenders want you to take responsibility for their behavior. Forgiveness is not saying, "It's not a big deal." If it's no big deal, then there's nothing to forgive. If you find yourself apologizing for how you caused the person to offend you or others, you've been significantly misguided and deceived.

Forgiveness Does Not Forget

There is a word which cannot be associated with forgiveness: "forget" (as in "forgive and forget"). The fact is, we don't forget. Brain studies reveal whatever is significant to us is stashed away in our long-term memory.

Paul said, *"I forget what's behind ..."* (Philippians 3:13). The biblical word "forget" in this context doesn't mean "put out of one's mind." It has the meaning of letting go—not allowing the past experiences to dominate the future. Many have used this verse to prod a person into silence about painful, unresolved issues of the past. What Paul is referring to is his religious performance, which he drew acceptance from.

214 | The Perfect Counselor

Furthermore, if someone is taught to be a "good Christian" and to forgive and forget, the offender, and others involved, may get the message the behavior is acceptable.

There is another scenario: "I can forgive him but I cannot forget." Biologically this is true. Yet, in many cases it's merely another way of saying, "I will *not* forgive."

Forgiveness Does Not Take on the Blame

Many people are very good at getting us to take the blame for their wrong. The mirror must be put up to their face. They must recognize and admit their wrong, then ask for forgiveness. We must understand God's reconciliation process: when we forgive, the offense is forgotten *as far as the relationship is concerned* because it's no longer relevant to the relationship. The memory isn't erased; the facts of the event aren't expunged. This type of forgetting can only safely happen after the person has repented.

Forgiveness Does Not Stay Silent

The healing process for us, and the repentance process for the offender, requires talking about the offense. The healing process evolves when we talk about the pain and have our feelings validated. The offender may ask, "Why do you keep bringing up the past? You said you forgive me. Let's put this aside and move on." These are indicators of lack of repentance. They're often saying they don't want to look at your wound or be accountable for what they did. When the person allows you to express your feelings, and they feel true sorrow, then it's possible to move forward and *"forget what's behind."*

Forgiveness Is Not Contact or a Future Relationship

"I know I'm supposed to forgive and trust, but I can't let myself be hurt again. If I let him back in I know he'll hurt me again." Who said anything about letting him back in and trusting him? People are reluctant to forgive because they don't understand the difference between forgiveness and trust and reconciliation.

Forgiveness has to do with the past. The hurt person makes the choice to let the offense go. Trust and reconciliation have to do with the present and the future. It takes two people to be willing to reconcile. *The offender must prove he/she's changed over time and are trustworthy. Therefore, forgiveness is not an expectation of a future relationship with the person.*

If trust has been violated it can only be rebuilt over time. Sometimes it cannot be restored. If the offender is open to change, they need time to take the steps required for true recovery. This is a good rule of thumb: *Keep the future differentiated from the past.* Forgive the person for the *past;* reconcile in the *present* by discussing what the limits and boundaries of trust will be in the *future.*

Relationships are important to God. Reconciliation is a significant theme in the Bible: *"Make every effort to do what leads to peace and to mutual edification"* (Romans 14:19). God calls us to be active in working to reconcile relationships which have been damaged, but are we mandated by God to reconcile with someone at any cost; on any terms? No. There are times when relationships are broken, stressed, and dangerous due to repetitive and serious sin—and apologetic words aren't enough. Remember: *The person who offended you doesn't have to be present or have any part of your forgiveness. This is between you and God.*

If you believe this person is a psychopath or dangerous, do not meet with him/her. In my opinion, you'll most likely be dragged right back into the same old mind games. You can forgive them, but for your safety you don't have to tell them you forgive them. The only person you must tell is God. Understand you are in this good place now because of your distance away from this person, not because you need closure.

Forgiveness is Not Waiting for an Apology

Some say, "I'll forgive him as soon as he says he's sorry." There are people who will never apologize. They will continue in their destructive, rebellious, and foolish behavior. Others will be stubborn and never confess or admit their sin. Some will move away, and others will die before they ever repent. We choose to forgive them anyway because we know it's God's desire.

We need to remember *forgiveness is not a feeling, but a choice.* It's a process, and dependent upon God's help and intervention.

Reflect: How has this "Forgiveness is Not" list changed your mind about forgiveness? How has it freed you to move forward in the process?

The Process: Decisional & Emotional

"Bear with each other and forgive whatever grievances you may have against one another."
—Paul, speaking in Colossians 3:12–13

Think of a time when you chose to do something important that went contrary to your feelings. How did you do this?

Forgiveness is not a one-time event. It's a process, and may be a long process, particularly if the offense is great. There are two concepts of forgiveness we need to understand: *decisional* and *emotional.* Dr. Neil Anderson sums them both up in this statement, "Don't wait to forgive until you feel like forgiving. You'll never get there. Feelings take time to heal after the choice to forgive is made."[82]

The *decisional forgiveness* process usually comes first. It's not a feeling but *an act of my will* to obey God. I won't necessarily feel love for the person, especially if the offense was great. Yet, I choose not to hold this injustice against the other person or seek revenge. We must put our faith in God's justice and leave it to Him. *"The eyes of the LORD are everywhere, keeping watch on the wicked and the good"* (Proverbs 15:3).

Kate finally realized she would relieve herself of the bitterness, resentment, and pain, if she chose to forgive her husband (even though she had biblical grounds for divorce). She also learned that by making the decision to forgive her husband, this didn't change him; it didn't make him any more trustworthy.

Until he could prove he was, she chose to separate from him. Kate decided move on. She told him, "You hurt and wronged me, but I choose not to hold it against you. I trust God to judge you fairly … but I have to put a safeguard and boundary into place so this event doesn't happen again."

Some people choose to forgive but it's what I'd call *prideful forgiveness.* They do it to "be the better person" which simply is not real forgiveness.

Talk to God in your own words. You may say something like,

"God, as you know, I'm having difficulty forgiving [*name*]. I know I'm not following your command to forgive and I want to. I need your strength to forgive [*name*]. My desire is to take [*name*] off my hook and place [*name*] on your hook. Thank you for forgiving me, and being patient and understanding."

The second type, *emotional forgiveness*, is the process of replacing negative feelings with positive emotions. We cannot change our feelings—only God can. With decisional forgiveness, I choose to forgive you, but I'm unable to manage my negative emotions.

Decisional forgiveness takes place instantly, while emotional forgiveness can be a recovery process—a process of emotionally releasing and forgiving, time and again. Peter asked Jesus, *"Sir, how often should I forgive a brother who sins against me? Seven times?" "No!" Jesus replied, "seventy times seven!"* (Matthew 18:21-22). Jesus wasn't chalking up the scoreboard to 490. He was demolishing it. In other words, forgive time and again.

"They Don't Know What They're Doing!"

Jesus underwent a horrific torture and humiliation for our sins. Sinless, He did nothing to deserve crucifixion. As His beaten, naked, and torn body hung nailed to the cross, He said, *"Father, forgive them. They don't know what they're doing"* (Luke 23:34). He didn't summon His angelic army to rescue Him and then annihilate those who tortured Him. His compassionate response said He understood people, and forgave them unconditionally. They didn't understand, even though what they did made sense to them.

Jenna wrote, "I now realize the person who hurt me is a victim like I once was. He's suffering in his own lusts. He not only hurt me but also God. God has forgiven both of us so I've chosen to forgive him even though I still hurt and wear the scars. And I've set healthy boundaries. God's love covers the hurt and I'm free!"

No healthy and happy person wakes up one day and decides to hurt or abuse another person. *Ask God to give you an understanding of the person who hurt you;* a glimpse into their pain, called empathy. Only God knows the truth about the person. Every person, including the evil ones, have worth in God's eyes, and Jesus paid a huge price for that person's freedom.

To protect ourselves, society locks up the bad guys. But followers of Christ are commanded, and empowered, to pray, have compassion, and love such people. Harper Lee wrote, "You never really understand a person until you consider things from his point of view . . . Until you climb inside of his skin and walk around in it."

Many of my prayers to God have been, "Help me change my mind toward this person and help me to try to see [*name*] as you see her/him." If the person isn't a believer, God sees them as lost, hopeless, and broken. If they are a believer, He sees them as perfect in Christ.

Reframing is a big step in dealing with our anger against a person (including God). We can reframe this situation by changing the way we think about the circumstances. We should ask, "Is the person I'm angry with a victim himself/herself?"

We can choose to broaden and deepen our perspective of what happened. This person may or may not have intended to inflict immeasurable damage on us. But for the fullness of forgiveness to heal the wounds, and possibly the relationship, the offender must still look at and be accountable for their actions.

Reflect: "Pray for those who persecute you" (Matthew 5:44). Want to make the devil mad? Pray for your offender! For those in pain, one of the most appropriate expressions of extending grace is to pray for the offenders healing. It requires asking God for a heart to forgive the person. How does putting these points into action make you feel? Anxious? Fearful? Angry? Or something else?

Express Yourself in Healthy Ways

Someone said, "Getting angry is like leaping into an expensive sports car, gunning the motor, taking off at a high speed, then discovering the brakes don't work." If the idea of forgiveness seems impossible, begin by *expressing your feelings about the offender to God.* God wants you to release your anger and offenders to Him. This is between you and God; not you and the offender.

Tell God *why* you're angry (or other emotion you may feel). The psalmists freely spoke to God; confident He'd sort it all out. The psalmists stated they felt they'd been treated unfairly, and laid out the charges before God.

Pray, "Lord, if I keep this anger pent up in me, Satan will use it to destroy me. Therefore, I'm releasing my thoughts and burdens to you."

Some people begin the process by *writing letters* to express their anger—to either the offender, or to God. Most don't send the letter, some do. If you're angry with more than one person, write a letter to each person. If you write to God you might say something like: "Dear God, I'm angry with [*person's name*] for [*offense against you*] and now I feel [*express your feelings*]." Some write out their feelings and then burn the paper. Others go to the alter at church. Some people put a doll or stuffed animal in a chair representing the person, then speak their mind to it. This type of ventilation can be liberating and bring relief. I urge you to try one of these methods.

Completed Forgiveness

Realize that pain and forgiveness are different yet interrelated. Pain can continue after forgiveness has been granted. But forgiveness, honestly given in due time, can help ease the pain. We often need the help of a trained counselor or pastor, along with the support of friends.

Often, we assume that when our pain resurfaces, it means forgiveness hasn't happened. This isn't true. It may take years to heal depending on the severity of the wound.

Whether we've forgiven the person depends *not* on whether we remember the incident, but rather on our attitude. We know we've truly forgiven when we're no longer controlled by the pain (or no longer wish the person dead). *We remember what happened—but that memory no longer has power over our thinking and actions.* This is *completed forgiveness.*

This is how God forgives. God promises that when we ask for forgiveness He'll remember our sin no more. A seminary professor explained it this way: With God, there is no forgetting the history of our lives. He is omniscient (all-knowing). Yet, when we accept His Son as our Savior, our hearts are in harmony with His. As far as our relationship is concerned, our sins are forgotten. God chooses not to remember; He doesn't bring it up again. It's no longer an issue.

I knew God forgave me for having an abortion. But God also urged me repeatedly to participate in a post-healing abortion study. Today He uses my story and counseling abilities to help post-abortive women. If my abortion had been wiped out completely from His record book, none of this would have happened.

* * *

Forgiveness is the hardest call of a Christian, and our choice alone. Notice the two syllables in the word "for-*give*." Forgiveness is something we give; a gift to God and to the person who doesn't deserve it. It's a gift to ourselves in its healing power—physically, emotionally, and spiritually. Each day you must make the decision to forgive. Every day you must take your emotions to God. Jesus said, *"I'll never let you down, never walk off and leave you"* (Hebrews 13:5, MSG).

Reflect: What do *you* need for your healing *today?*

- Do you need to make the decision to forgive your offender?
- Do you need empathy and understanding towards the offender?
- Do you need to forgive yourself first?
- Do you need to ask someone else for forgiveness?

Forgiving Ourselves

"To forgive others you must forgive yourself first. Be courageous enough to forgive yourself; be compassionate to yourself; love yourself." – Debasish Mridha

"For years, I was emotionally unavailable to my kids. I was numb. The pain and depression of living in a violent intimate partner relationship was too much. Today my kids don't want anything to do with me. I hate myself for what I put them through. I recognize that in addition to asking them to forgive me, I have to forgive myself." –Alisha

We need to forgive ourselves when *our actions have hurt others and ourselves.* For example, the emotional damage done to our family/children by exposing them to fighting or abuse; for being afraid and not walking away or speaking up; self-abuse such as addictions, eating disorders, self-harm, etc.

If we're partially at fault, for example, if we retaliated or acted out in a destructive manner, that must be acknowledged. For example, if we've been living in addiction for any length of time, there are people we've offended. So, we'll need to ask for their forgiveness.

Most of us struggle intensely to self-forgive. It's often harder than forgiving another. We're good at beating ourselves with words of self-condemnation, remorse, guilt, self-doubt, and regret. We know God forgives us, but we just can't forgive ourselves. Unfortunately, until the road block of forgiving ourselves is removed, we won't go very far in the whole forgiveness and reconciliation process.

Perhaps, you've tried to let yourself off the hook but the self-condemnation and the consequences of the actions won't let go, such as the damage that's been done to your family. In some cases, we become abusive ourselves. How do we play two roles: the forgiver and forgiven?

We must surrender the situation over to God and ask for His forgiveness, which *He grants immediately*. I tell my right (emotional) brain what the left (rational) brain already knows: that if the great Almighty God can forgive me, then I can forgive myself.

In time, God will enable us to let go of the charges we've leveled against ourselves, as well as the blame, shame, guilt, and fear. This is the beginning of creating a mentally and emotionally healthy life for yourself.

Reflect: What do you believe is your biggest challenge or largest self-forgiveness obstacle to forgiving yourself?

Lost and Found

"But while he was still a long way off, his father saw him and was filled with compassion for him; he ran to his son, threw his arms around him and kissed him."
—Jesus, speaking in Luke 15:20

"The Parable of the Prodigal (or Lost) Son," found in Luke 15: 11-31, is about a young son who left home, wasted his life in extravagant and wild living, and then ended up in a literal pigpen. It's also a story about a party—a glorious party hosted by God. "Prodigal" means "wastefully, or recklessly extravagant." Many of us relate to the prodigal. I certainly do. Sadly, his label "The Prodigal" bars us from really understanding him. I get that too.

The younger son essentially said to his father, "I'd love to stay around until you die and get my inheritance then. But I want *right now* what's coming to me—the inheritance I deserve." By law the father could have simply disowned his son and been done with him. Even though the son was dishonoring him, the father graciously divided the property between the two sons. The younger son packed his bags and left. He lived an undisciplined life centered on doing whatever he wanted and on spending his money frivolously—until it ran out.

There were consequences. He was put in a position of feeding "unclean" smelly pigs. This young man degraded himself beyond belief. Hopelessly lost and insatiably hungry he desired to eat the pig slop, but no one would give him any. Talk about the "walk of shame!" Filled with guilt and shame, he humbled himself. He confessed what he'd done wrong.

Seeking healing and restoration, the son was willing to come back into his father's home as a slave. Imagine being in his shoes as he arrived at the outer gate; starved, dirty, haggard. The last time he passed through that gate, he had money and arrogantly thought he could make it in the world.

Humbled, he said, *"I am no longer worthy to be called your son; make me like one of your hired servants"* (*v. 19*). He thought his father would be very angry and punish him for his actions. He planned to give back to his father as a servant, thereby, acquiring his acceptance. However, the father had been waiting every day for his son to return home. When he saw his son, he could have said, "Hey son, you really messed up and caused me great pain." Instead, he was filled with compassion for him. He ran to his son (which was taboo for wealthy Jewish men to do), threw his arms around him, and kissed him. His son was home, which is all that mattered to the father.

Look at what his father did next. He said, *"Let's have a feast and celebrate"* (*v. 23*). His father's love and grace probably overwhelmed him. This too-good-to-be true feeling is common in the spiritual rebuilding process. *The son was always forgiven. But the son himself couldn't be healed until he returned, repented, and forgave himself.*

Jesus used this parable to dispel the lies and misconceptions about the character of His Father—that He is an angry punitive God who responds to sin with only judgment and punishment.

223 | The Perfect Counselor

The truth is that the Father delights to give good gifts to His children because He loves them immensely. God always waits with love and forgiveness for those willing to respond to His grace, and receive from Him. God's love makes no sense. His love is like no one else's.

Reflect:

- Do you believe the Father could forgive you without a condition attached? For example, "God will only forgive me if I do …" Might you believe there are no conditions to His forgiveness?
- Read Luke 15: 11-31. Put yourself in the son's place. What is God the Father saying to you about you?
- Now put yourself in God the Father's place. What does He see when He looks at you and thinks about the true you?

Release your guilt by thanking God for forgiving you for the offenses you're holding against yourself.

Asking for Forgiveness

"Forgiveness ought to be like a cancelled note—torn in two, burned up, so that it never can be shown against one." –Henry Ward Beecher

Think of a time when you experienced the grace of being forgiven for an offense you committed. How did that make you feel?

Alisha recognized there were things she did that required her asking her children for forgiveness. Jesus tells us to go to the persons we offended and make things right before we go to worship God (Matthew 5:23). Remember, our forgiveness doesn't depend on the other person. All we can do is the right thing. How they react to our effort is a matter between them and God. If we caused anguish, then we ask ourselves how we best can repair the damage. Restitution is required, even if we cannot completely restore the damage.

We must be willing to take full responsibility for our actions, and subsequent consequences. This requires prayers, wisdom, courage, and steadfastness from the Holy Spirit.

We need His wisdom so as not to create more harm, and to know when and where and how to make amends.

We need His courage to be honest and not become over-focused on ourselves.

We need His steadfastness when the other person doubts our sincerity.

The person you are seeking forgiveness from may likely bring up the past and ask the "why" questions, such as, "Why weren't you there for me? Why did you let this happen?" Sometimes all we can say is, "I'm sorry. I can't change what's happened in the past. I admit I [*name the offense*] and would like to change it, but I can't. I ask for your forgiveness and desire we move forward. I want you to know I truly want to earn your trust." Let the person vent, cry; whatever they need to do. Be still. Respect their feelings.

Reflect: Have you possibly turned a guilty or shaming belief into a reason to condemn yourself, therefore, not giving yourself permission to be forgiven? If the answer is yes, the reality is these are lies you've been telling yourself. Apply the *Change Your Self-Talk—Change Your Reality* to each belief. You may also revisit the "Six R's to Freedom" (see page 200).

Forgiving Our Parents

Lucie wept uncontrollably as she envisioned restoring her relationship with her dad. "My is a compulsive liar. He shows no remorse. I've been told to "let it go" as if nothing ever happened. I just can't do that!"

Quite often, the people who are responsible for our emotional issues are our parents. In some cases, they aren't even aware of their hurtful actions. We can't imagine honoring them because they've done nothing to deserve honor. Ephesians 6:1-4 gives instructions to children and parents:

"Children, <u>obey your parents</u> because you belong to the Lord, for this is the right thing to do. "<u>Honor your father and mother.</u>" This is the first commandment with a promise: If you honor your father and mother, "things will go well for you, and you will have a long life on the earth." Fathers, <u>do not provoke your children to anger by the way you treat them.</u> Rather, <u>bring them up with the discipline and instruction that comes from the Lord.</u>" (NLT)

First, the instructions are to children. The word "honor" means "to esteem at the highest level." It would be much easier if God asked only we "esteem at the highest level" our parents *if* they are good, kind, and loving to us. Yet, I don't see in Scripture where God tells us to honor an abusive mother or father. They misused their power and authority, and disobeyed God—they did not bring their children up with *"the discipline and instruction that comes from the Lord."*

The second set of the instructions are to parents. Parents are to treat children as Jesus treated children. No way can a parent ever justify being given permission to abuse, neglect, or abandon a child.

Honoring a Controlling or Abusive Parent

My dad was a controlling and often bullying father, the opposite of my quiet, godly, and meek mother. I resented Dad for calling all the shots of my life. (Today I can be quite the controller, just like my Dad.) Yet I always loved him. Healing meant setting boundaries with him.

The Bible commands honoring our parents—but it doesn't command remaining a prisoner in a dysfunctional family. Honoring a parent doesn't mean we allow them to treat us as doormats for them to wipe their feet on. It doesn't mean we don't confront them about their behavior, or set boundaries, or urge them to seek help. If a family is abusive, then strategies and boundaries must be developed to limit or completely restrict contact with abusive members.

Honor is not the same as loyalty, trust, and obedience. We can honor a parent, but not be loyal to him or her. They must earn our trust. If we have a parent who does evil before God, we don't have to honor them in their evil. We're not commanded to go along with their sin. If we do, this is *codependency.* Pastor Henry W. Wright calls codependency: "Calling evil good in the name of love."

We still love our parents, but we can choose not to be victimized or hurt deeply by their sin. Living in an environment of sin is usually unsafe and dangerous. Separate from the person and remove yourself if you must; it's not ungodly. Those who break free can find safety in God's family (the church). They can fill us up with the love and safety we need.

To honor our parent *and* set strong boundaries may look like this: I acknowledge my parent's sin of, for example, lying. I forgive the wrong, which is difficult, yet necessary for my healing and relationship with God. Without getting angry, I tell my parent I won't be lied to. My parent must comply and choose to speak truthfully to me or I will remove myself from the situation. I don't publicly demean my parent.

I'm not however, obligated to maintain a relationship with anyone who doesn't treat me as I should be treated, as a child of God. I can close the relational door. I don't want to lock it as the person's heart may change, thereby creating an opportunity for the relationship to be restored.

The next step is to be willing to forgive. This may seem utterly impossible, particularly if you don't receive any kind of acknowledgment or apology. Yet, *all things are possible with God* (Mark 10:27).

Reflect: How do you feel about your parent (or parents or caregiver) causing you pain? After you answer this question, answer: Do you believe they intended to cause you pain? Why or why not?

Healing Activities

Ask yourself, *"Am I willing to endure whatever consequences are necessary, and humbling myself and confessing, or facing the fear and accusations straight on?"* If no. Keep praying until your mind changes. Pray about how you intend to make the necessary act of forgiveness. Restoring a relationship and "fessing up," as they say, should be done face-to-face if possible—and *not* by a text, email, or on social media. If distance is a problem, make a phone call or write a letter.

Make the Call or Write a Letter: Some of us can accomplish safe and truthful confrontation through a phone call or letter. I suggest first writing down what you want to say before making the actual phone call. This will allow you to communicate exactly what you need to say and help you stick to your points. Pray about whether you should speak to this person or just send a letter. I suggest you read your letter to a trustworthy friend or group for constructive feedback. Remember, use "I" statements versus "You" statements.

14

Take Control of Your Life

She is like a well-watered plant in the sunshine ...
she danced in the celebration. – *Job 8:16; Judges 21:23* (GW)

"**C**hange is an unwelcome guest in the home of familiarity," wrote Dr. Mark Baker. Emilee stated, "I keep my feelings bottled up because I don't want them to burden others."

Growing up, Emilee's mom communicated, "Don't bother me with your stuff." Her dad was flat and unengaged; there was no support from him. This unconscious belief that she was invisible caused her to be unsure of herself in all her relationships. Once Emilee understood her rights as a human being and began to assert boundaries by speaking up and expressing her opinions, her mom became angrier and angrier. Her dad remained unresponsive. Mom didn't see that there was any need for change.

Emilee has changed. She can never go back to the way things were with her mom. Sometimes we can't go back. She isn't giving up on her relationship, she's simply insisting on a better one. For growth to occur in this family, a radical change in perspective must occur.

The Family Show

When conflict arises within the family, a positive outcome can only be achieved when *each person* makes the choice to work towards restoration. Think of it this way: Every family has a script. Every person has a role. I call it the "Family Show." Meet the Whitehead family:

The plot: Chaotic drama.

Characters:

- Mother Whitehead: victim, martyr, "doormat."
- Father Whitehead: workaholic; an occasional guest on the show.
- 22-year-old son: is married and responsible; rarely visits the family—he's "too busy."
- 19-year-old daughter: lives at home, is family drama-queen; is popular and involved in college activities.
- 16-year-old daughter: rebellious, "mean girl," doesn't study, "bad girl," black sheep; trying to find her way through the family drama.

Where is God? He's rarely invited into this home. In the Whitehead Family Show the perception is that the youngest daughter is upsetting the family drama. Every member of the family wants her to change. The problem is: If they want to change the plot of the entire show, they cannot change just one character. Even if the youngest daughter changes her role from the black sheep to the good girl, the Family Show drama will continue. The whole cast must change if the plot is to change. And, God must be invited in.

Most likely, if the youngest daughter gets counseling and is brought back into a chaotic family with the same characters, she'll revert to her old character. The entire cast must change their dysfunctional roles. It's not solely one person's responsibility to change the plot of the show. Galatians 6:5 says, *"For each one should carry their own load."*

The objective is to create a new plot; a new script; a new history with a new cast of characters—with God at the head of the household. The family as a unit has that power! The miracle of the grace of God is that He can restore the years the *"swarming locust has eaten, the creeping locust, the stripping locust and the gnawing locust" has destroyed" (Joel 2:25, NASB).*

The Doormat

As a child, I learned if I was to receive my parent's (particularly my father's) approval and love, I had to say "yes" to them, no matter how I felt about the matter. In most situations, my unconscious mind always pondered, "If I say yes to your request, then will you love me, accept me, and value me?"

In other words, I had no concept of setting boundaries. They were non-existent. We *need* boundaries in our lives. Lack of boundaries allows others to manipulate, deceive, abuse, take advantage, even put us in harm's way.

Codependent relationships lack boundaries and, therefore, continue to feed destructive behavior. Many people think of boundaries as only setting limits, saying no, or trying to stop something destructive from happening. But having good boundaries is more than stopping bad things from happening. It's taking responsibility for the good things you want to happen.

Proverbs 4:23 states, *"Above all else, guard your heart, for everything you do flows from it."* Protecting our hearts is a phrase that is rarely understood. Ask yourself: "What does self-care for my heart and soul look like?" One answer is, "Telling someone *no* or *yes* in a healthy, proper manner.

The following statements reveal the choices we make to stay a "doormat" for others to walk on. How many of these apply to you?

> **D**oing things for others they should do for themselves—*because I need the praise; because I am their servant.*
> **O**thers make choices for me and direct my life—*because I need their acceptance; because I have no voice.*
> **O**thers determine my self-worth and define my identity—*because I don't believe I'm important; because I need to feel valuable.*
> **R**ejection is my greatest fear—*because I want to be loved and accepted.*
> **M**ad at myself for being weak, imperfect, and not measuring up—*because I need to feel appreciated; because I have higher expectations for myself.*
> **A**fraid of conflict and power—*because I don't believe I deserve to be powerful.*
> **T**rue love is what I crave—*for myself and from significant others.*

A doormat is a person with no sense of boundaries. Do you want to develop self-respect and worth? Yes. Learn to create boundaries.

Defining Boundaries

Having clear boundaries is essential to a healthy, balanced lifestyle. Christian women often have overly flexible boundaries —they're unwilling to say no, always accommodating others' needs; or they have overly rigid boundaries to the point of being righteous and judgmental.

In the literal sense of the word, a "boundary" is a dividing line which separates one area from another. We use the word "boundaries" to describe limits and rules in relationships, like property lines. A boundary is a "property line" that defines a person; it defines where one person ends and someone else begins. If we know where a person's boundaries are, we know what we can expect this person to take control of: himself or herself. We can require responsibility regarding feelings, behaviors, and attitudes.

We have all seen couples, for example, arguing with each other about "who's to blame," each avoiding responsibility for oneself. Boundaries describe what's acceptable and can be tolerated in a relationship. Healthy boundaries lead to healthy relationships with people who have your best interests in mind.

By setting healthy boundaries, you no longer allow others to take advantage of you, thereby, establishing your sense of self-worth. You find your voice and learn how to use it. Your communication with others improves as you express your thoughts and feelings. Boundaries are what define your identity. *This is me—what I value, like, don't like, am good at, believe, need, or feel—and this is not me.*

Some people think a boundary is a wall, especially if they've been hurt. They think, *I'm going to protect myself from ever being hurt again. I won't let anyone get close to me.* Compulsive overeating was the perfect wall for me. I'd feast alone for hours to keep the bad people out because I couldn't take any more shame or rejection.

Why do most of us dislike setting boundaries and confrontation? Let me suggest:

- We become convinced in our minds the results will be negative, such as, *If I say, "No more!" then I'll probably unleash a horrible nightmare.*
- Encountering the anger of others is uncomfortable.
- We fear rejection, push back, and/or hostile confrontation.
- The "what ifs" can overwhelm and paralyze us. We assume a negative outcome.
- We fear we can't control the outcome.
- Setting new boundaries can feel like a loss.

The truth is that the person we set a boundary with has the freedom to choose to respect or reject it. And no one wants their boundary rejected.

Reflect: Do you fear setting boundaries for any of these reasons? If yes, what do you conclude about yourself?

Healthy Boundaries

Shaking her head, Tanya said, "How can I set limits on the man who needs me? That would be living for me and not for God!" Tanya has been led to believe setting boundaries was self-centered. To her it meant that she was interested only in her own well-being, not others.

Setting boundaries is difficult, even when we know it's healthy. This is especially true when we've been conditioned to need a parent's approval. Ignoring the issue seems far easier than confronting it. But the consequences are often far worse because the problems continue to build.

The concept of boundaries is rooted in God. He defines and takes responsibility for Himself by telling us what He thinks, feels, plans, allows, will not allow, likes, and dislikes. God limits what He'll allow. He confronts sin and permits consequences for behavior. He will not allow evil entry, and invites people in who will love Him.

God made us, in His image, to rule, to reign, and to have dominion in a limited atmosphere. We can set strong healthy boundaries! David, speaking in Psalm 16:5-6, said God, *"set me up with a house and yard"* (MSG). God has set each one of us up with our own house and yard.

Jesus set healthy boundaries. He always said no to inappropriate behavior. Love yourself enough to say "no." The ability to discern what you should say yes and no to gives you back a measure of control.

A healthy boundary says, "This is what I will do and accept; this is what I will not do and not accept." Healthy boundaries enable relationships to flourish. Despite what someone else may say, it's not selfish or unloving to have boundaries and take care of yourself. The truth is: Appropriate boundaries increase our ability to care about others.

Drs. Cloud and Townsend wrote in their best-selling book *Boundaries,* "Boundary setting is a large part of maturing. We can't really love until we have boundaries. Otherwise, we love out of compliance or guilt."

Reflect: Everything on our "property," so to speak, is our responsibility. We choose to let whomever we want into our yard and then into our house. We don't allow them to trespass, nor do we trespass on their property. What is your reaction to this?

Telling People What You Want

Deidre and Mike had been dating for almost a year. Whenever Deidre expressed an opinion that didn't match Mike's, he'd become irritated and irate. When her opinion was the same as his, things were fine. As a result, Deidre began to withhold her opinions because she loved Mike. Yet, she could no longer be herself. She said before she met Mike she loved a good debate. Now she finds she can't talk about certain subjects. If she does, Mike challenges and belittles her.

Over time, Deidre shifted the responsibility for what she wanted from her to him; she thought her "wants" were his problem, not hers. When he didn't solve her problem, when she felt sad or resentful, she saw it as Mike's responsibility to figure out what she was feeling and do something about it. Ultimately, this proved too much for him to do.

Deidre had been a confident person with relatively high self-esteem. Before long, her self-image and self-confidence lay in ruins. Eventually, with the help of friends, she identified the problem. When she did, Deidre stood her ground. When Mike discovered he could no longer control her, he broke up with her.

In their book, *Boundaries*, Drs. John Townsend and Henry Cloud wrote:

"Many people think of boundaries only as setting limits, saying no, or trying to stop something destructive from happening. But having good boundaries is more than stopping bad things from happening to you. It is also taking responsibility for the good things you want to happen. When you take responsibility for your desires and communicate them well, a relationship has much more chemistry, connection, and mutual fulfillment.

To have a relationship that works well, we should have a "responsibility" talk with ourselves before we have a "talk" with another person. We need to:

- Own our "want"—be honest about what we want, and be aware that our desires are our responsibility.
- Own the feelings that occur when our desire is not getting met—if we're sad, we need to say so, not wait for the other to figure it out."[83]

Reflect: Describe a time when you responded like Deidre. What one thing can you do to begin to choose to communicate your desires and move toward other people to let your wants be known?

Communicating Healthy Boundaries

"People can only walk on your back if you're bent over." –Indian proverb

Boundaries help us guard our heart with diligence. We need to keep nurturing things inside our property lines, and keep harmful things outside; keep the good in and the bad out. Often, when people are hurt or abused, they reverse the boundaries. They keep the bad in and the good out.

When it comes to communicating your boundaries, work on stating them appropriately. Jesus said, *"All you need to say is simply 'Yes' or 'No'; anything beyond this comes from the evil one"* (Matthew 5:37). Learn to say: "No." Period. You don't need to explain or justify your no. "No, I don't feel comfortable with that." Period. "No, I don't want to or I won't do that." Period.

Other examples of how defining boundaries might be used in your relationships:

- *I* have a rule for those who live in this house which is ...
- *I* want you to tell me how you think we're doing in our relationship.
- *I'm* a night owl, so I prefer we not meet too early.

This is simply how you tell people who you are and how they tell you who they are. You clarify and define yourself. Notice I used *"I" statements over "you" statements.* Saying *"I" and "me"* diffuses the possibility the other person will get defensive or will choose to leave.

For example: Francine said to Mike, "*I* will not allow *myself* to be treated this way any longer." Francine has control over what she allows herself to do or not do—but she doesn't have control over Mike. If she says, "*You* can't treat me this way any longer," her statement has less impact because she can't control him. The only time the "I will not allow *you*" statement works is when we have power over someone and can enforce our expectations, such as parents can with their children, or a boss can with an employee.

Focusing on our feelings instead of pointing the finger at someone else will almost always decrease defensiveness and opposition. For example, "Please do not insult *me*. I will not be talked to this way." "Never touch *me* without my permission."

Practice "protective boundaries" which are designed to "guard your heart" (Proverbs 4:23), and your life, from danger or trouble. There are times when we must protect our values, emotions, gifts, time, and energy from people and situations that may waste or injure them. *Step back or out of a relationship when the outcome of that relationship is destructive.*

Protective boundaries mean we face the reality that talking hasn't fixed a situation, and we must set a limit. For example, "I want us to work this out, but nothing I've said has made a difference, so I'm taking a different route." If the person doesn't care, this won't have much impact. If married with children, implementing a separation and/or restraining order becomes complicated because of finances, children, as well as the Bible's teachings. This requires a lot of prayer.

The difference between a defining boundary and a protective boundary is: A *defining boundary* is forever and unchangeable, part of what makes you "you." For example, you indicate you will always follow God and be committed to personal and spiritual growth. Whereas a *protective boundary* can change if the other person responds to it in a healthy way.

Rejoice in the guilty feelings! As strange as it may seem, a sign that you're becoming a boundaried person is often a sense of guilt, or a feeling that you've broken some important rules. This is normal when we begin telling the truth about *what is* and *what isn't* our (biblical) responsibility.

Role play: This is when two or more people assume the roles of the person or persons they will be addressing. The conversation is based on their knowledge of the people's characters and possible reactions to the dialogue. Again, use

"I" statements versus "You" statements when you speak.

Define the Consequences

The Bible sets consequences for certain behaviors. Therefore, we need to back up our boundaries with consequences. Many marriages could have been saved if one spouse had followed through with, "If you don't stop drinking (or yelling at the kids), I will leave until you get treatment!" Think of the many lives of young adults who would have been turned around if their parents had followed through with, "No more money if you quit another job without having another job," or "You can't stay here if you continue to smoke marijuana in my house."

Learning how to set boundaries is to learn how to set and stick with consequences—and be a united front, if two or more people are involved in setting them. *A boundary without a consequence isn't worth much.* God held Adam and Eve accountable for breaking His boundary (big time!). If you have children, you (should) understand this concept. *Don't set a boundary unless you are willing to follow through with a consequence.*

People like to test boundaries. Therefore, don't keep changing them. Being told your boundary isn't very godly or that it's cruel can make you feel like you should take it back. If someone tests your boundary ask yourself, "Am I being told this because she/he is trying to control me into doing what they want?" "And, "Who is going to benefit if I change my boundary?"

You can do this! Speak Scripture, *"I have set the LORD continually before me; Because He is at my right hand, I will not be shaken"* (Psalm 16:8, NASB).

Reflect: Who is your number-one boundary-buster, the primary person in your life with whom it's difficult to set limits? Why do you think this person keeps breaking your boundaries? How can you turn this situation around?

Here's What Will Happen

Lorie's mother-in-law didn't approve of her son Trent's marriage to "that woman." She treated Lorie with disrespect and constantly instructed her on how to be a good wife and mother. Worse, she told Lorie and Trent "God told her to help them this way." Lorie felt helpless to confront her.

Trent decided it was time to set a boundary and a consequence; to speak up in a respectful way. He addressed his mom firmly, "Mom, I have never seen you treat Lorie with respect. In my opinion, you belittle her and give her unwanted advice. This can't go on. She's my wife, a wonderful woman, and a great mom. I love her and I want you to love her. I need you to treat Lorie with respect, just like you treat me, or my family won't come over any more, and you'll not be welcome in our home."

Mom first became defensive, and made several excuses for her behavior. She wasn't ready to apologize but she did agree, reluctantly, to back off.

Trent called for *"zero tolerance."* Ezekiel 45:9 says, *"You have gone far enough … Give up your violence and oppression and do what's just and right."*

Zero tolerance gently says something like, "I'm against this type of behavior. I don't deserve to be treated this way. I'm calling you to confess and repent. I'm on your side if you choose to work to change. A whole new life in Christ is possible but it will require your commitment and work." (Notice the "I" statements.)

Reflect: When it comes to your primary boundary-breaker, what emotions or physical sensations do you feel when thinking about setting a "zero tolerance" boundary?

Your Assertive Rights

People violate our assertive rights every day through manipulation tactics. *Manipulation* is when unnecessary rules are imposed upon us that we have not previously agreed to, and therefore violates our rights to do things for ourselves. We come to believe that an authority wiser and greater than ourselves has the right to tell us how to think and act. This is not God's plan.

We all have God-given "Assertive Rights." Here are eight of them. And keep in mind, growth in setting these types of emotional boundaries must consider past injuries. Start slowly; baby steps, or you could fail.

1—You have the right to judge your own behavior, thoughts, emotions, and to take responsibility to set them in motion and accept the consequences. This works for me. This doesn't. I like … I don't like. I need to … I shouldn't.

237 | **The Perfect Counselor**

2—You have the right to offer no reasons or excuses to justify your actions.

> *Salesclerk:* Why don't you like these shoes?
> *You (Customer):* They're the wrong shade of brown.
> *Salesclerk:* Nonsense! They're the perfect color. They match your hair!
> *You:* They're too loose and the heel straps keep falling off.
> *Salesclerk:* We can put a set of heal pads in for $3.95. Simple fix!
> *You:* Okay. I'll buy the shoes!

Let's try it again.

> *Salesclerk:* Why don't you like these shoes?
> *You:* No reason. I just don't like them!

3—You have the right to decide whether you are responsible for finding solutions to other people's problems. How do you respond to a comment like, "If you really cared about me, you'd make things easier for me!" An assertive response would be, "If you really feel you can't cope right now, perhaps you should (take responsibility for yourself) see a counselor."

4—You have the right to change your mind. Manipulation says: "You shouldn't change your mind after you make a commitment. If you do, something is wrong with you. If you're in error, then you've shown you're irresponsible." A big part of our healing journey is working to change our minds (Romans 12:2).

5—You have the right to make mistakes, and be responsible for them. To err is part of our human condition, and so is taking responsibility for our blunders. There is no need to feel guilty or try to cover up a mistake. Jesus said, *"Let any one of you who is without sin be the first to throw a stone at her"* (John 8:7).

6—You have the right to say, "I don't know" and "I don't understand." There is only one all-knowing and all-wise person, and that is God Almighty. (A narcissist would disagree.) Many of us have been trained to have the answers to all the questions, because if we don't have them, we're irresponsible, and therefore, unacceptable—which means you have the right to control me.

7—You have the right to healthy relationships; to be interdependent. We must choose people we'd like to inhabit our inner circle. If we can't cut out certain people from our lives, like family, then we consider how to limit time with them.

8—You have the right to say no—persistently. Saying no isn't easy. With practice, it does get easier. Start with "baby no's."

Confrontation

"Be strong and courageous. Do not be afraid; do not be discouraged, for the LORD your God will be with you wherever you go." –God, speaking in Joshua 1:9

Too many people are bound by illnesses because of unresolved issues. They have a pathological fear of confrontation. When you hear the word "confrontation" what comes to your mind? What do you feel? The thought of confronting can certainly be scary. Most of us avoid conflict, thinking life will be easier. The word "confrontation" isn't really a dirty word. Yet it's possible we could experience our richest friendships and growth opportunities when we step into the uncomfortable space of conflict.

Let me say upfront: You do not have to resolve an issue with someone who has victimized you. But you do need to resolve the issue with God. Remember, God already knows everything.

Some women find it hard to believe they have any right to say no, or to draw a line. Confrontation and conflict, however unpleasant, are important aspects of any healthy adult relationship. Avoiding confrontation, although a common way of coping, may do more damage:

- Stuffed emotions fester and come out in other negative ways, and
- The behavior goes unchallenged and will continue to hurt others.

David Reardon wrote in his book *The Jericho Plan*, "Love demands confrontation because it cannot rest if the beloved is entangled in evil." Many think of the price of confrontation, but forget that there is also a price to be paid for NOT confronting. That price is that evil continues to flourish; relationships become superficial and shallow."

Confronting an Abusive Person

Confrontation comes with no set rules or guidelines … and is unpredictable! Therefore, we must seek the guidance of wise counsel and examine our motives. Many offenders tend to deny the truth and become defensive. Probably, the person will attempt to be in a position of power. Yet, their manipulative and controlling behavior must be confronted—not only by you, but by a group of his/her peers, family, and church (see Matthew 18: 16-17).

Confrontation is for our healing. There are two valid reasons for choosing to confront an offender:

1. *Concern for the offender,* particularly if he/she is a family member or your spouse. You should desire for him/her to know the joy of godly forgiveness and restoration.
2. *Concern for others.* Offenders are likely to harm and abuse again. Not addressing their actions often allows the offender to re-harm.

Confrontation Isn't an Absolute Must

We need to—with God's guidance—do what's in *our* best interests right now. *Confrontation can sometimes be unrealistic, even dangerous.* If the person is in denial, or has a narcissistic or sociopathic personality disorder, reconciliation will most likely be impossible. In some cases, the offender will agree to meet in order to hurt us or gather evidence against us. Therefore, it's necessary to *pray about it,* and go back to biblical teachings. It takes advance preparation, and possibly months, to ensure all the possible outcomes have been considered. *Confrontations often don't work out as planned. Don't despair. While confrontation helps many survivors, healing does not require it.*

Reflect: What is your reaction to this material? What kinds of feelings or physical sensations arise at the thought of confronting your offender, or any non-offending person?

Facing Off

"... leave your sacrifice there at the altar. Go and be reconciled to that person. Then come and offer your sacrifice to God." —Jesus, speaking in Matthew 5:24 (NLT)

Whether you have decided to forgive your offender or not, you may feel the time has come to confront him/her. Get ready to move forward in faith. As you prepare for the meeting consider *every* angle before moving forward. Pray about this, and consider speaking to a counselor or pastor. Remember, often we're dealing with a person who doesn't think like we think. Proverbs 15:12 says, *"Mockers hate to be corrected, so they stay away from the wise"* (NLT).

Visualize and personalize 2 Thessalonians 3:3 and Luke 12:11-12: *"the Lord is faithful; He'll strengthen me and guard me from the evil one. ... do not worry about how you'll defend yourselves or what you'll say, for the Holy Spirit will teach you at that time what you should say."* What a relief!

When we invite the offender to meet, we need to be honest about the reason for the meeting. Often circumstances dictate that the meeting should be in a safe, public place. This is often best done in the presence of a pastor, or church leader, or counselor who may act as a mediator. If the situation may possibly get volatile, have at least one person present, a witness, perhaps even two or three people. They don't have to say anything during the meeting. Ask them to stay close by and be praying.

When Confrontation Doesn't Go as Planned

If after the initial confrontation, the offender totally denies their actions and its damaging consequences, then we should pray and seek counsel about pursuing the subject again, and the appropriate time frame.

Some women will feel the need to make it clear that they will not drop the subject to make the person "comfortable" and relieve the relational tension.

Often, a compromise simply will not be reached. If the offender continues to reject God's offer to repent—which is *the only way* to restore the relationship, we explain that even though we've forgiven them, we must sever the relationship.

241 | The Perfect Counselor

We explain the estrangement is reversible if they choose at some point to begin the restoration process.

Success Means Authentic Repentance

"Prove by the way you live that you have repented of your sins and turned to God."
—John the Baptist, speaking in Luke 3:8

It's a fact: *We can only change ourselves, not another person.* But the amazing thing is, when we change, we change the equation. A healthier relationship is possible when there is sincere repentance.

Authentic repentance cannot be fabricated. When repentance is real, there is a groaning from the spirit that truly means, "I'm sorry." Then a flow of completed forgiveness from the heart may begin to restore the relationship. There are evidences of a changed or repentant heart. If the person can do all these things, then there's a strong chance of reconciliation and restoring intimacy. A person with renewed beliefs asks, "What would Jesus do in this situation?" It takes a bigger man (or woman) to be like Jesus.

Restoring Trust

One Christian couple struggled for 22-years with addiction and codependency in their marriage. They were on their third separation and ready to divorce. The wife wanted out because of his abusive control; and he was "beat-up" from her addiction. He struggled a lot with anxiety around rebuilding trust. He believed they both needed to forgive and trust God. To him this meant jumping back in emotionally to a marriage that didn't feel safe.

To this couple, I say: There should be no guilt and/or shame in taking the time to let a person earn your trust. This isn't a result of lack of faith or forgiveness. It is where setting boundaries essentially begins.

Trust is very fragile and can be destroyed in an instant. Therefore, betrayed and broken abuse survivors find it difficult to build healthy relationships built on trust. Trust is not a natural response.

Exert your will to trust God first—one day at a time. To trust God is to believe He is good and *always* will be good to you.

The fact is: He cannot be otherwise! Psalm 107:1 and 145:9 says, *"The LORD is good to all; he's compassion on all he's made; his love endures forever."*

Trust is a two-way street which involves being vulnerable. *Trust is always earned.* To trust someone is to feel confident the person is who he/she appears to be. They must prove to be faithful, honest, and have integrity. Therefore, it takes time to rebuild, and requires patience … And we must first become strong and trustworthy ourselves before we can jump into a healthy relationship.

Trust takes time. Part of the process is to figure out patterns of trust or distrust in our relationships. Answer these questions:

- How do you decide to trust a person?
- What are realistic expectations for trusting a fallen human?
- The day has come when your offender has truly repented for his/her actions and/or crimes. How will you trust a person who has hurt you or who you believe really doesn't have your best interests at heart?
- How will you avoid being set up to be harmed again?

Resolve Situations Assertively

Use this "ASSERTIVE" reference to handle situations as they arise.

A: *Always* rely on the power of the Holy Spirit; *ask* questions which gives the person a chance to think before they answer.

S: *Stand up* for your needs and convictions; negotiate to resolve issues.

S: *Specify* what you will and will not accept—your boundaries.

E: *Evaluate* the importance of how and what you'll talk about.

R: *Respect* others and ask for the same respect.

T: *Think* before you act and speak; *thank* this person for the things they did right in your relationship, even if it's only one thing.

I: *Initiate* action instead of reacting later.

V: *Verify* what you are being accused of; *value* the relationship.

E: *Encourage* Christlike, meaningful conduct.

15

Love Like You've Never Been Hurt

Place me like a seal over your heart, like a seal on your arm; for love is as strong as death, its jealousy unyielding as the grave. It burns like blazing fire, like a mighty flame. *—Song of Songs 8:6*

Some day my prince will come, Some day we'll meet again,
And away to his castle we'll go, To be happy forever I know,
Some day when spring is here, We'll find our love anew, And the birds will sing, And wedding bells will ring, Some day when my dreams come true.
 — *"Some Day My Prince Will Come" from Snow White*

Who doesn't long for a lasting, deep, passionate, and Snow White kind of relationship? The problem is many of us think that getting married will fill our soul hole and solve all our problems. I did. My only desire for going to college was to get a MRS. Degree (which I didn't receive). We might find someone, our prince, who makes us feel all tingly inside … for a short time. But this isn't real love. Real love is like God—pure, just, and perfect.

We receive messages all our life about what love is. Most of those messages are based on feelings and are lies because our world has a Hollywood shallow and selfish view of love. We don't seek to love others, but instead are driven to get what we can for ourselves. This view has contaminated the biblical meaning of love. We're set up to be vulnerable.

Galatians 5:1 states, *"It is for freedom that Christ has set us free [past tense]. stand firm, then,* [present tense] *and do not let yourselves be burdened again* [like in your past life] *by a yoke of slavery."*

244 | The Perfect Counselor

We know God has given us a spirit of power, *love*, and sound mind. God originally designed His created to be free—not to be enslaved by another person or by each other, but to love each other freely. Any violation of god's law of love damages our ability to love. Christ has *already* liberated us from the bondage in which we were born—not to bring us into another form of bondage—but free us completely from the bondage which ultimately leads to destruction.

Where there is power and control in a relationship, or the perception of power and control, there is no love, only bondage. Love only exists where there is a spirit of freedom. Freedom is necessary for love to develop. Freedom creates a safe and secure environment for a couple to love, trust, explore, and deepen their experience of each other. Each person is free from the other, and therefore, free to love the other.

Reflection Questions: If you are presently in a romantic relationship, how free do you feel? On a scale of 1 to 10 (1 = total bondage on; 10 = completely free). If you are not in one, or don't desire to be in one, how content do you feel living for "an audience of One?"

Fatal Attractions

"Our dependency makes slaves out of us, especially if this dependency is a dependency of our self-esteem. If you need encouragement, praise, pats on the back from everybody, then you make everybody your judge." – Fritz Pearls

In 1986 songwriter Robert Palmer made these words famous, "You're going to have to face it, you're addicted to love." Addictive relationships are common in our society. *Relationship dependency* (a.k.a. *Dependent Personality Disorder*) occurs when a person enmeshes an unhealthy self-identity with an equally unhealthy need for connection. It may be to a lover, spouse, friend, parent, or child. The person becomes dependent on the relationship to function in life. She/he will put up with the terrible because one, the alternative—being alone—is scarier and unthinkable, and two, to reduce their anxiety, yet avoid their own feelings and needs in relationship.[84]

Dependent relationships are very powerful, seductive, and hard to resist. The focus on the other person is usually obsessive; meaning you're constantly preoccupied with the person—while neglecting to care for or value yourself. One or both persons feel they cannot live complete without the other, nor walk out on the person. *Isn't this the definition of true love?* Not when each person encourages the other's dependency out of fear of being left alone. This is codependency; *a fearful reluctance to act independently.*

Reflect: Fear of abandonment usually drives the obsession. Did you experience abandonment, neglect, or inattention in childhood? Are you terrified of being alone? If yes, do you think you might allocate too much time, attention, and value to the other person, thereby, neglecting yourself?

Relationship Dependency versus Healthy Love

If a person's identity is in crisis, it will be difficult to love others in a healthy way. When a dependent person chooses someone else to fill their void; to fill their internal security and sense of wellness, they create *relationship dependency.* Unconsciously she says, "I can't love myself so you've got to love me for me." Words like *clingy, suffocating,* and *controlling* describe the relationship. Her mantra is, "Whatever you want. You decide for me."

Loving or helping others is not always done with the right motives. Passive people who have a shattered self-image and low self-esteem will often connect with others out of an unhealthy need to be loved, and/or accepted, and/or to feel competent. They may be "codependent. "

The term "codependency" refers to a relationship where one or both people "enable" the other person to act in inadequate and self-destructive ways, thereby, protecting their partner from the consequences, even though they believe they are just trying to help. *Codependent* means "dependent with."

The codependent person has built-in radar that leads her/him to other half available persons in an attempt to make a whole person. They give control of their identities over to the other: "I need *you to define* who I am." She sincerely believes she cannot survive without the relationship, or the other person cannot survive without her.

It's like Siamese twins. If they attempt to break their attachment it feels like they're losing a part of themselves. This results in resistance to separating, and is why so many remain in an abusive relationship.

Codependency complicates all relationships, including the relationship with God. The codependent hands over authority to others because of a deep distrust in their own abilities. Somewhere in their pasts they've learned that "alone" is not safe; they've learned they are not enough. This also has spiritual consequences: God may be seen as a condemning judge. There is no grace and forgiveness. (Spiritual counseling is vital for healing.)

A codependent relationship can range from one person feeling anxious and responsible for another person's well-being; to believing, *I need to manipulate and control this other person for their own benefit.* For example, there is a difference between seeing someone as your project (self-oriented), versus having a healthy vision for them (other oriented).

Reflect: What experiences have you had with dependency?

Interdependence

The opposite of codependence is "interdependent." The word *interdependent* means to "depend on others" in a healthy way. For example, I depend on my husband to bring home a paycheck. He depends on me to grocery shop for the family. When we marry someone, we take on the burden of loving them deeply and caring for him as no other. We care about their welfare and feelings. Yet, we can't cross the line of responsibility and not take ownership for our mate's life. We are responsible *to* each other, but not *for* each other. Two persons can become one without losing their identities.

Characteristics of healthy loving interdependent people:
- They are independent; can separate; know where proper boundaries begin and end.
- They refuse to rescue or enable the sinful or immature behavior of their partners. They set limits on each spouse's destructive acts or attitudes; don't try to solve the other person's problems; allow the person to experience the consequences of his/her behavior.

- They know their "true self" and don't have any expectations that another person can complete them.
- God is #1 in their lives.

Reflect: On a scale of 1 to 10, where would you rank yourself when it comes to your *primary* intimate relationship? (1 = dependent on; 10 = completely interdependent.)

The In-Love Brain and Mind

"… Dark is the night; Deep cuts the knife; No way I'll get away; Memories here to stay; Deep cuts the knife; Lately, I see your face in everything I do. Sleepless nights I lie in bed just thinkin' of you; I can't pretend that I don't need you back again. Did you love me? Did you need me? Well alright, but what's so wrong? This memory haunts me forever; Better run for my life; Hide from the light; Dark is the night Deep cuts the knife; No way I'll get away. Memories here to stay. Deep cuts." –Lyrics, *Deep Cuts the Knife* by Helix

Do you ever feel, *I hate him … I love him … He hates me … he loves me.* Here are two common scenarios:

1. You have cut the ties with your beloved, but he won't leave you alone. He pursues, hassles, even stalks, his "beloved," often with disastrous or violent results.

2. Many women one minute hate their partner (or ex), then the next minute love him and feel sorry for him. Then they hate him … then they love him and don't want to break up.

Let me offer two explanations. The first one is: "Cognitive Dissonance." This is when our mind tells us two different and competing things. We have inconsistent thoughts, beliefs, or attitudes. In an intimate relationship, even though our conscience and spirit is telling us something is wrong, part of us still desperately wants to believe in the perfect soul mate. Therefore, we want to "give it one more try." This is natural in a dysfunctional relationship because we're used to repeatedly being promised and told things by the other person——versus seeing and perceiving things with our own minds.

There's a saying that goes, "Don't believe everything you think." You could say we've been brainwashed. Our minds need to be re-washed in truth. The solution is washing our minds with God's Word. As truth grows stronger, wrong beliefs and lies grow smaller.

Addicted to Love

The second explanation is we've literally become *addicted to love*. In the *Psychology Today* online article "Can Love Be an Addiction?" Lori Jean Glass, revealed she was diagnosed with an addiction to being in love. For her, the addiction involved being completely absorbed in someone else's life and the feeling that someone else needed her and admired her. Someone, anyone; it didn't matter who it was as long as it was a warm body capable of overflowing her brain with love chemicals.

I'm not the first person to draw a comparison between the state of falling in love and the state of feeling high on drugs. Dr. Fisher, an anthropologist and relationship researcher, conducted a series of studies on the brain chemistry of love. She found the same brain neurochemicals are in play as with drug addiction (massive amounts of *serotonin, dopamine* and *norepinephrine*).

Many of the same brain pathways and structures are active when we're falling in love as when we're enjoying a high from a substance such as cocaine, alcohol, opioids, amphetamines, cannabis; as well as non-substance addictions, such as sugar, sex, shopping, exercise, or gambling. They both activate the same reward pathways in the brain.

Reflect: Love addiction is just as real as any other addiction in terms of its behavior patterns and brain mechanisms. Even when romantic love isn't harmful, it's been associated with intense cravings and anxiety, and can compel the lover to believe, say, and do inappropriate and dangerous things. Do you see it the same way? Why or why not?

Biblical Love

Someone in our life has manipulated our gift of love to cause pain. Now we need to know how to avoid toxic people so this will never happen again. Many build a permanent wall to protect themselves from any more harm.

This isn't necessary when we follow God's Word and His leading.

As human beings, we have this incredible gift from God—the ability to love and make another person feel wonderful with a kind word, a loving gesture, or a compassionate smile. It takes a long time to start building healthy relationships. It takes breaking old habits, developing a spiritual intuition about people, and coming to understand who we are in Christ.

1 Corinthians 13 is God's clearest picture of what agape love in action is and is not. Do you recall what *agape love* is? It's an "unselfish, thoughtful, unconditional, sacrificial love which doesn't expect anything in return." Too many people have a distorted definition of love, which is the total opposite of this passage. As you study each verse ask yourself: "How does the man I love, and who claims to love me, measure up to God's definition of love? Does this person create harmony or chaos?"

"Love is patient, love is kind. It does not envy, it does not boast, It's not proud. It's not rude, It's not self-seeking, It's not easily angered, it keeps no record of wrongs. Love does not delight in evil but rejoices with the truth. It always protects, always trusts, always hopes, always perseveres" (1 Corinthians 13:4-9).

I would add: "Love is not controlling; does not exert power over."

The Message version reads: "Love never gives up. Love cares more for others than for self. Love doesn't want what it doesn't have. Love doesn't strut, Doesn't have a swelled head, Doesn't force itself on others, Isn't always 'me first,' Doesn't fly off the handle, Doesn't keep score of the sins of others, Doesn't revel when others grovel, Takes pleasure in the flowering of truth, Puts up with anything, Trusts God always, Always looks for the best, Never looks back, But keeps going to the end. Love never dies."

I'm going to be bold and say that if the person you love expresses and lives out the opposite of each of these characteristics, such as extreme jealousy, possessiveness, anger, distrust, self-centeredness, is demeaning or depresses you, then you're in dangerous territory. This person won't meet every definition, but he should be willing to strive for all of them, as we should too. His focus should be on how he can serve you instead of on you serving him. Love is taking care of your partners needs before your own.

---

250 | The Perfect Counselor

Let me speak to "Love doesn't keep a record of wrongs." Some women say, "The Bible says *'love covers a multitude of sins; it covers all wrongs!'" (1 Peter 4:8)* In other words, "I love you so your bad behavior is okay. I'm going to expunge your records of wrongs." Love does cover a multitude of sins—but not all sins. Serious and repetitive sin is lethal to any relationship and should not be covered up. Then it becomes a "cover up." *Forgiveness doesn't mean we eliminate accountability and consequences.* We should never pacify a relationship just to keep the peace. This is called "pseudo peace." (Read 1 John 3:6-10.)

"Love never dies" means "Love never ends." It has staying power. Like God's agape love, our love—our actions—should benefit the other person, regardless of the cost or feelings. Real love happens when two people honor each other's values, standards, and purpose. They don't just talk about it. They live it. They "do" love. Real love says, "I've seen the ugly parts of you and I don't think any less of you!"

Just like any counterfeit object, it can be tricky to know and identify the real from the fake. Real love and false love can feel very similar. Being God-centered and familiar with His Word will enable us to navigate through a culture where false love is prominent. It requires wisdom and discernment which God is more than willing to give us; all we have to do is ask Him.

Reflect: Jesus demonstrated what agape love is by serving, listening, and meeting other people's needs. *"Christ loved us and gave himself up for us …" (Ephesians 5:2).* Does the person you love, truly love you with this kind of agape love? Can you say you both measure up to the *ABCDE's of love?*

- I **A**ccept you as you are.
- I **B**elieve you are valuable.
- I **C**are when you hurt.
- I **D**esire only what's best for you.
- I will **E**ndure through all things with you.

Submission versus Oppression

It's been said, "Love does not dominate, it cultivates." If what you have experienced in an intimate relationship doesn't line up with what God says love is, it's not love; it's most likely oppression.

Let's look at the difference between *godly submission* and *unrighteous oppression*.

The word "submit" is one of the most difficult, disliked, and divisive words in the Bible. "Submit" means to *willingly* line up under another's authority. Submission is an act of a person's free will. This means I voluntarily yield and limit what I naturally desire to do in this relationship to benefit you. Submission *isn't* about following "orders." It isn't translated as, "Just do it!"

Ephesians 5:21 gives us a command: *"Submit to one another out of reverence for Christ."* Let's say that I'm the one with more power (i.e. I make a lot of money); instead of using that power (money) to make my life easier, out of admiration and respect for Christ, I'll use my power (money) to serve and empower you. I'm willing to give up things I want to benefit you. On the other hand, if I'm the one with less power, submission means that instead of doing what I might do naturally, like fight you every step of the way, I choose to respect and honor your decisions. Dr. Gregory Jantz wrote,

"The power to demand obedience is a great responsibility. When we obey others, we submit to their will above our own. Therefore, this power should be used sparingly and only with the other person's best interests in mind."

On earth, Jesus submitted. He gave up His position and power to fulfill God's mission. Even today, He doesn't insist on having control or authority over us. He never says, "You'll submit to me! You must do it My way!" He gives us the choice if we want to follow and obey Him or not.

Self-centered men do the opposite. They twist the gift of submission to manipulate and control the other person into doing what they want, thereby, creating an unjust power imbalance called "oppression"—*The exercise of authority or power in a burdensome, cruel, or unjust manner; the feeling of being heavily weighed down, mentally or physically, by troubles, adverse conditions, anxiety, and the like.*[85]

Oppressive people demand others see and do things their way, bowing to their authoritarian ways. Their love is not self-sacrificing; it's self-gratifying. Think of oppression as *demanded submission*. Any type of headship that results in fear-based power and control is *not* biblical. God designed love so there will be no fear; no loss of freedom, for *"perfect [agape] love casts out fear"* (1 John 4:18).

It's our misunderstanding of what submission is that causes us to back down or give in—even when we know deep down the action is wrong and doesn't please God.

"The LORD works righteousness and justice for all the oppressed" (Psalm 103:6).

Reflect: Can you think of anyone in your life who presently oppresses you? Why shouldn't you suffer any kind of indignity or shame or disgrace?

Biblical Submission = Equality

Genesis 3:16 states, *"Your desire will be for your husband, and He'll rule over you."* If you are married, what is your response to this verse?

Many Christian women struggle with another tough word "headship." *Submit* and *headship* can imply a power differential. Sierra's husband's intention was "demanded submission." Some men may call themselves "spiritual leaders" but if they use intimidation, manipulation, anger, domination, and control to lead, then they are "oppressive leaders."

Contrary to what you've been told, both male and female are created equally in God's image. Whatever is true about the image of God in a man is true about the image of God in a woman. The female is made of the same spiritual stuff as the male.

A proverb goes, "Women hold up half the sky." Women are one of the world's most precious resources! Both Jesus and the early church elevated women.[86] Every woman was created by God equal to man.

Some men take Scripture out of context due to their need for power and control (2 Timothy 4:3). Genesis 3:16 was quoted by God because of Eve's disobedience. It was a consequence. God did *not* mandate for husbands to rule as masters with sovereign power over their wives like they were slaves. This wasn't God's intention. 1 Corinthians 7:23 says, *"... do not become slaves of men"* (NASB).

God is clear on gender equality. He created man in His own image; both male and female. He gave both sexes the exact same responsibilities (Genesis 1:27-28). The Bible records God's intentionality to reestablish the position of women to that of equality with men.

God's Son, Jesus Christ, not only bridged the gap between God and man through His death on the cross; He removed all barriers including that of gender, race, and nationality. The way Jesus acted towards women was revolutionary and shocking.

Relaxed and open with women, Jesus allowed them to touch and kiss Him, a rabbi. Accepting, sensitive, and affirming, He treated all women with the deepest respect. He is the kind of man God wants every woman to know in her life. You can trust Jesus with your heart.

Warning Signs of an Unhealthy Relationship

A push for quick involvement. This is when a person comes on really strong. He pressures you to be his wife/girlfriend immediately.

Lack of trust. Does your husband/boyfriend not like you to go out with others without them? Does he read your texts and/or mail? Every couple should be able to trust their partner; trust them not to cheat or poke around or spy.

Frequently insulting or verbal abuse. Does your relationship consist of constant criticism? Do you feel like you always must be on the defense? The person who loves you should make you feel amazing, and not be constantly putting you down. In the beginning of the relationship he is nice, but the longer you are together, the more he criticizes or yells at you, enjoys "pushing your buttons;" says mean, hurtful things; degrades, curses, or calls you ugly names. Another sign would be *no* communication; and/or changes in mood or behavior. For example, the person used to always talk but now rarely talks, leaving you feeling insecure and fearful.

Regularly picks a fight. Every relationship has its bumps, but if you're constantly fighting, particularly over small things, and you're frequently being picked at, this is a warning sign. The good days should outweigh the bad ones, not the other way around.

There is physical or sexual harm. Should anyone ever threaten you with physical or sexual abuse, or hit you; even kill or harm an animal, this is a *big* warning you're in a relationship with an unhealthy person.

Social isolation. Does your husband/boyfriend try to keep you from spending time with your family and friends? We need our families and friends. We need others' opinions besides our mate's. If you find that he expects you to only spend time with him, this is a warning sign.

Always blaming. Does your husband/boyfriend blame you for problems or mistakes? This type of person doesn't take responsibility for their mistakes. Instead, it's always another person's fault.

Lies or omits the truth. A person might not exactly be lying about something, but they aren't telling the truth either. While you don't necessarily need to tell your husband/boyfriend "everything," each person should be equally open with the other person. The Bible says, *"Do not be deceived: "Bad company corrupts good morals"* (1 Corinthians 15:33, NASB).

Attempts to control. We all appreciate being able to go to our boyfriend/husband to get advice but, if he continually advises or influences you to do certain things, it can be an attempt to control you. Does he tell you who to be friends with, what to wear, or what to do with your spare time? Does he feel he has the right to know where you are all the time? Red flags!

Keeps secrets. In a healthy relationship, couples should be able to talk openly with one another without having to keep secrets.

Lack of respect. Does your husband/boyfriend frequently break promises or criticize you? If yes, they are not showing you respect (means they do not hold you up in high esteem). No child of God should have to feel put down or feel like they're not valued.

It's all about sex. Sex is an important part of a married relationship, even then, it's not all of it. A person who loves and respects their partner doesn't push them to have sex. They don't make the other person feel they owe it to them.

Unhealthy jealousy and possessiveness. When your husband/boyfriend is envious of something you have or do, or doesn't like that you have friends, this is unhealthy. He should be happy for you and your accomplishments, and not feel like they're in competition with him.

No compromise. A big part of any relationship, romantic or not, is compromise. We can't always have things go exactly the way we want, so it's important to learn to compromise. If your husband/boyfriend can't make allowances for you, it's going to make your life and relationship very difficult.

255 | **The Perfect Counselor**

Love being in love. Might your husband/boyfriend "be in love with being in love" (but they are not really in love)? He may have come to believe that not having a romantic relationship means there is something wrong with him. He may feel that having a wife/girlfriend proves his worth. Some people feel a bad or violent relationship is better than no relationship at all. This is no way to live! You won't ever be happy.

Time-Out's: Many of us need to change the way we're doing relationships. We need to take a time-out to allow God to show us how to change our thinking and behavior to get a better result. Sometimes we need to take time away from relationship drama to see the mistakes we've made and to see God's perspective.

Jesus said, *"I am sending you out like sheep among wolves. Therefore, be as shrewd as snakes and as innocent as doves. Be on your guard"* (Matthew 10:16-17). Trust your instincts. You deserve a relationship in which you feel safe and respected.

Love Languages

Dr. Gary Chapman wrote a bestselling book titled *The Five Love Languages.* He believes every person functions best when speaking or using their primary "love language." The love languages fall into five distinct categories:

1. *Words of affirmation:* means compliments; words of encouragement. "I feel loved when I'm told I'm beautiful or did a good job."

2. *Quality time:* means receiving another person's undivided attention. "I feel loved when I get undivided attention; when that important person wants to hear about my day, and is really there for me."

3. *Receiving gifts:* means receiving symbols of love. "I feel loved when I receive a gift that interests me, like flowers or chocolates, or a person asks me to pick out a gift."

4. *Acts of service:* means doing things or small jobs. "I feel loved when my husband knows I've had a tough day and offers to cook dinner."

5. *Physical touch*: like holding hands, kissing, having sex. "I feel loved when my husband kisses my neck when I least expect it, or when I'm hugged by friends at church."

Abuse Distorts a Woman's Love Language

If you have a history of abuse, consider this. I have found that abused women's love languages change as their relationships become more manipulated, abusive, and/or violent.

- A woman may come into the relationship with the need for physical touch, but when the abuser distorts or destroys the gift of sex or hits her repeatedly she intuitively changes to another love language.
- If a woman's language is quality time, and she is neglected, she'll change to another.
- If her language is receiving gifts and the abuser makes up with gifts, and repeatedly uses gifts for power and control, she'll change to another love language.
- Perhaps her love language is words of affirmation. We know thoughtless and/or malicious comments do incalculable damage. Therefore, she'll seek another love language.
- To receive love, some women dabble with all the love languages.

For some women, their love tanks are completely dry and rusted, therefore, they cannot relate to any of the five love languages. When this happens, a woman must first learn to love God and allow Him to fill her love tank.

If your love language is physical touch, consider this regarding *sexual touch*. First, accepting healthy physical touch can be a challenge when all we've known is toxic touch. When physical touch is harming versus nurturing, a person's soul is endangered. It will take time, a mind renewal, and often counseling, to restore a sense of trust when it comes to healthy touch. *Never underestimate the importance of "proper" touch*. Ask yourself, "Could my view of sexual physical touch be distorted? Have I been using sex to feel loved and gratified, or for relieving stress or dealing with negative emotions?"

Reflect: Can you define a time when your love language changed due to abuse?

The Love Language Quiz

To discover your love language, take this short quiz. Choose only *one* statement in each pair that best represents your desire. Then circle the corresponding letter. Note: you may be so wounded by a man that when you read this list your only response is, "None of these!" Instead, replace "him" with your best friend or someone you feel close to.

1.	I like to receive loving and caring notes and cards.	A
	I like to be hugged by him (*or my best friend*).	E
2.	I like to spend one-on-one time with him.	B
	I feel loved when he gives practical help to me.	D
3.	I like it when he gives me gifts.	C
	I like taking leisurely visits and long trips with him.	B
4.	I feel loved when he does things to help me.	D
	I feel loved when he touches me.	E
5.	I feel loved when he puts his arm around me.	E
	I feel loved when he surprises me with a gift.	C
6.	I like to go almost anywhere with him.	B
	I like to hold hands with him.	E
7.	Visible symbols of love are very important to me.	C
	I feel especially loved when he tells me he loves me.	A
8.	I like to sit close to him.	E
	I like for him to tell me I'm attractive.	A
10.	Words of acceptance from him are important to me.	A
	I know he loves me when he helps me.	D
11.	I like being together and doing things with him.	B
	I like it when he speaks kind words to me.	A
13.	I value praise from him.	A
	Small, meaningful gifts show me how much he cares.	C
14.	I feel close to him when we are talking or doing something together.	B
	I feel closer to him when he touches me often.	E

15. I like for him to compliment my achievements.	A
I know he loves me when he helps me with something he dislikes.	D
16. I like to be touched as he walks by.	E
I like it when he shows genuine interest in what I'm saying.	B
17. I feel loved when he helps me with jobs or projects.	D
I really enjoy receiving gifts from him.	C
18. I like for him to compliment my appearance.	A
I feel loved when he takes time to understand my feelings.	B
19. I feel secure when he is touching me.	E
When he runs errands for me, it makes me feel loved.	D
20. I appreciate the many things that he does for me.	D
I like the thoughtful gifts that he makes for me.	C

Count the number of times you wrote down each letter. The dominant one is your love language:

- **A's:** Words of Affirmation
- **B's:** Quality Time
- **C's:** Receiving Gifts
- **D's:** Acts of Service
- **E's:** Physical Touch

16

Personal Power

I, yes I, am the LORD, and there is no other Savior. First, I predicted your rescue, then I saved you and proclaimed it to the world. No foreign god has ever done this. You are witnesses that I am the only God," says the LORD. —
Isaiah 43:11-12 (NLT)

In 1943, Rosa parks boarded a bus in Montgomery, Alabama. if you were black like Rosa, you entered the front door, paid the fare, exited the front door, and then had to reenter the bus through the back door, the accepted entrance for the "colored." one day Rosa paid her fare but didn't reenter in the back. she walked down the aisle and took a seat. the bus driver, James Blake, refused to drive the bus until she properly exited and reentered the bus in the rear. after Rosa exited, he drove off and left her.

Twelve years later, the same bus driver, was driving a bus Rosa got on (she didn't know it at the time). she paid her fare and sat in an empty seat in the first row of black seats in the "colored" section. as the bus traveled its route, all the white-only seats filled up. Blake noticed a few white men were standing. he then moved the "colored" section sign behind Rosa and demanded that she and three others give up their seats to the whites.

In her biography, my story, Rosa recalled, "when that white driver stepped toward us, when he waved his hand and ordered us up and out of our seats, I felt a determination cover my body like a quilt on a winter night. when he saw me still sitting, he asked if I was going to stand up, and I said, "no, I'm not." he said, "if you don't stand up, I'm going to have to call the police and have you arrested." I said, "you may do that."

Rosa Parks refused to be placed as "less than." She refused to be treated, in her own words, as a "second class citizen." By refusing her label, she showed others that they never must accept "less than;" that they always have a choice. What Rosa teaches us is:

No one can ever strip the image of God away from within us—no one can take our dignity away. No one—no one—can mess with God's workmanship!

We've come full circle. It's been rough but your courage and faith in God got you through. No doubt, God has demolished some big strongholds in your life. Praise Him for that. In the first chapter, we talked about the difference between power over versus personal power. we've all experienced power over—people who have changed our lives radically and crushed our spirits. Today we know what it means to exert *Personal Power* because we've been empowered through God's holy power.

"This makes it clear that our great power is from God, not from ourselves" (2 Cor. 4:7); *"Now all glory to God, who is able, through his mighty power at work within us, to accomplish infinitely more than we might ask or think"* (Ephesians 3:20, NLT).

Praise God for His power! There are four areas I'd like to address before we end this leg of our healing journey.

1: Radical Acceptance

We have reached the final stage in the grief cycle which is *radical acceptance*. This stage is one of stability, where you are ready and actively involved in moving on to the next phase of your life; when you have grasped your personal power. Many pray Reinhold Niebuhr's Prayer: *"God, grant me the serenity to accept the things I cannot change, courage to change the things I can, and wisdom to know the difference."*

Radical acceptance means accepting and enduring *all* circumstances, even the disastrous ones. It's a mindset that says, "I don't know the answer and it's okay." It's our faith in and relationship with God that helps us bear and grow from experiences which seem impossible to cope with.

Accept how the past has shaped you—this means both the negative and positive ways you've been shaped, trusting God to use all that raw material for your good as He promised (Romans 8:28). Jesus is saying to you,

"You're a woman with a future, a destiny! The negative messages from the world and people have probably robbed you of the knowledge that you're special, gifted, and talented. I chose you to be part of my family. You are included in My very important story. I have a great plan for your life—cracks and holes and all. You haven't seen anything yet!"

Accept what has happened to you in the past and how you have responded. You cannot go back and rewrite history. Your personal power is in writing your future story with God.

Accept what is. This is the point at which you start moving *toward* something new—creating your "new normal" based on godly positive changes. Remember, *could have, should have, if only I had,* and *would have* are dreadful companions. Personal power enables us to determine a clear course from where we are now—not where we wanted or thought we should be.

Reflect: Finish these sentences:
- One thing I can now accept which I couldn't accept before is:
- One way I have grown is:
- In the future when I'm confronted with painful memories or feelings, I will:
- I have accepted God's forgiveness for:
- I now have hope that:
- I am grateful for:
- I have joy in:
- I now want to ….

2: Monitor What You Worship

Did you know that human beings will become like whatever they tend to admire or worship? It's true. For example, when celebrities are recorded indulging in high-risk behavior such as binge drinking, having sex in public, drug abuse, or losing too much weight, they are doing what psychological professionals call "modeling" behavior. They broadcast an image that serves as a model for viewers.[87]

It is a fact: We will become like whatever we idealize. We adapt ourselves to whatever we focus on. If we focus on self, we become more selfish. If we focus on a guy, we become more relationship dependent. If we focus on money or status, we become more materialistic. As the mind is trained to focus on ungodly, unhealthy, and destructive elements, its dangerous power gets stronger and stronger. We lose personal power. The Bible calls this "idolatry," and it leads to distress in our minds and lives.

Whatever we choose to worship will change both our character and biology. We're not merely in a spiritual battle, but a biological one too. Our actions and choices result in physical changes in our brains and bodies, and relationships. The choices we make—what we think, believe, admire, and worship, as well as the behavior we engage in—all have profound effects on the development of our brains and minds, and thus our personalities and relationships. Personal power gives us the ability to choose the healthy alternative: focus on god and his word, and thereby, receive his divine power to follow through on all the other decisions we need to make.

Reflect: List five things/people, you idealize and/or admire. where is god on your list?

3: Seek Your Destiny

Theologian Howard Thurman wrote, "Don't ask what the world needs. Ask what makes you come alive, and go do it. Because what the world needs is people who have come alive."

For a long time, I looked back on my life and felt betrayed by myself— that I wasted nearly 40 years in the gutter. Today, I know those years weren't wasted. I've used those experiences to write this book and help many women. God knew I was going to mess up my life, and yet He had a good plan all along. The best part of the plan is knowing someday I'll meet Him in eternity, and will worship Him with all the women I helped.

Answer these questions: As a small child, what did you want to be or do when you grew up? As an adult, what wild and crazy thing have you always wanted to do? What promises did you make to yourself that, someday you'd have the guts or time to try? Without dreams we die.

You may say, "It's too late for me; I'm too old for this dream to come true." Colonel Sanders was 66-years-old when he fried his first Kentucky Fried Chicken. TV chef, Julia Child, didn't learn to cook until she was almost 40-years-old. She didn't launch her popular cooking show until she was 50.

Dreams which are God's plan have no age limit! Remember that Jesus took a fisherman and turned him into a shepherd! This is symbolic of what God does all the time.

Did you know before you began developing as a fetus in your mother's womb that God had created a plan specifically designed for you? It's true! David, speaking in Psalm 139:16 said to God, *"You saw me before I was born. Every day of my life was recorded in your book. Every moment was laid out before a single day had passed"* (NLT). You can never say you've wasted your life. None of us knows the larger story. Ask God to show you what makes you come alive—then go and pursue it—and don't let anything stop you!

Going forward, God will do with you, and in you, what He's not doing with any other person! The psalmist wrote, *"He'll instruct them in the ways they should choose"* (25:12). You're one of a kind, and God has specific tasks He's designed just for you. He's willing to guide you into His plans if you'll seek to know and obey Him.

Reflect: What did you want to be or do when you grew up? What wild thing have you wanted to do? What promises did you make to yourself? Are you ready to move forward with your dreams and plans? Why or why not?

4: Give Back God's Love

"Success has nothing to do with what you gain in life or accomplish for yourself. Success is what you do for others."—Danny Thomas

We can rest in God as He takes us through the healing process, but if we come out the other end and choose not to advance the kingdom of God, then we're retreating right back into ourselves. If we come out of this experience and neglect our spiritual purpose, we choke out all the good that has been planted and rooted in our souls.

The last step in most recovery programs is to help and comfort others. Personal power is something that grows in us and then we give it away to others. God did not just save us to only be His daughters. He intended we pour ourselves into one another. Personal power is power *with* other people, not *over* them; it's the power to identify and sympathize with others.

The Bible tells us God comforted us *"in all our troubles, so that we can comfort those in any trouble with the comfort we ourselves receive from God"* (2 Corinthians 1:4). Our faith and healing aren't complete until we take what we've learned and experienced, then give it to others in need. Our scars can give life to others so that their scars might be smaller. Our wounds may even turn another life around. God desires that we be His spiritual messengers. Since Christ is no longer on earth, all He has is our hands and feet through which to work. We're His representatives on earth.

"You are a guide for the blind, and a light for those who are in the dark" (Romans 2:19);
"You are the light of the world—like a city on a hilltop that cannot be hidden ...
let your good deeds shine out for all to see, so everyone will praise your heavenly Father"
(Matthew 5:14, 16).

Take the time to delight in your growth, your new relationship in Christ, and your success. *Celebrate who you are now*—a beautiful, spiritually healthy, delightful, joyous child of God; no longer shackled by the need to be better, perfect, or something you're not. *God makes beautiful things out of broken vessels!* You now have a radiant glow countless others don't have. Go shine and change your world! I'll be praying for you.

"No eye has seen, no ear has heard, and no mind has imagined what God has prepared for those who love him."—Paul, speaking in 1 Corinthians 2:9 (NLT)

Treasures by Janet Hansen

Jesus is *the* master Storyteller. Throughout His 3-year ministry, He revealed timeless truths through His parables and wisdom. Throughout the centuries, God has given people—Christians people like you and me, the gift of storytelling. Gifted storytellers add new meaning to the Bible, enabling the reader to draw closer to God. They transport you to the scene, captivating our hearts.

One such person is my mother, Janet Hansen. God has given her rare insights (treasures) into the God-man we know as Jesus, and his mother Mary. These two vignettes are a perfect way to end this book. Get comfortable, grab a cup of tea or coffee, and allow yourself to be carried back in time through Janet's words.

Jesus on the Cross

Oh! The pain, the pain. The physical shock of the nails entering my hands and feet. I can't put into words how awful it feels. Then the agony of being lifted on the cross. The pain is excruciating because my back is shredded because of the whippings. My "crown" pierces my flesh, and the blood runs down my face. Perspiration is pouring off my body.

Through my tear and blood stained eyes, I look down at the people milling around the crosses. Most of them are strangers. Some of them are taunting and reviling me. They tell me if I am so powerful, I would come down off the cross and save myself.

Where are my disciples? Where are my followers? Hardly any of them are here. More women than men have come to show their loyalty, and to suffer with me. They are the courageous ones.

Ah, I see my mother. She is being comforted, but she's crying and reaching out to me. She is so strong to be able to stay and witness my angst and death.

John is here too. It's my chance to give Mother to him. I know he'll care for her and keep her safe. From now on he is her son, and she is his mother.

I see the Roman soldiers casting lots for my clothes. They have now become valuable to them.

Death. It is the only thing we wish for on a cross. The agony and torture goes is endless, and death is the only way to end it.

My mission on this earth is over. I've done what my Father asked me to do. I've sown the seeds that will grow and continue to grow. I've taken away all the sins of the world, and they who believe in me will go with me when I leave this world.

But Abba, where are you? Why have you forsaken me? I'm dying and I need you more than ever, but you're not here. You're silent, and I'm alone.

It's getting darker. The atmosphere is changing. I can sense the presence of angels. They'll stay with me now and guard me in the tomb.

I took the drink they offered. The pain is fading away. I don't feel anything anymore.

"It is finished." *With that, he bowed his head and gave up his spirit (John 19:30).*

Mary's Perspective After the Crucifixion

It has been a dreadful day. My son Jesus was arrested, convicted, and nailed to a cross. Noon came, and it got dark everywhere. Three o'clock came, and my son gave up his spirit. The ground shuddered; the Temple veil tore from top to bottom; the heavens opened and it began to lightly rain.

I am now sitting near the foot of the cross—sitting because I just can't stand up any longer. The soldiers have just taken Jesus down and brought him to me. I'm cradling him in my arms—wailing and rocking back and forth, back and forth, as the rain softly washes my son's body.

They're coming now ... coming to take Jesus's broken body to the tomb, which has been graciously donated. I and a few others follow the men who are carrying Jesus. They lay him down, swiftly prepare his body, and wrap him in traditional burial linens. I remember wrapping him in swaddling clothes when he was first born.

They're now finished. The soldiers roll a stone over the entrance. One by one, bystanders walk away. I'm the only one left. Broken hearted and weeping, I lean against the stone for strength. But there is one person left. John. John comes towards me. He puts his arm around my shoulder and says, "Come Mother, I will take you home now."

Other Books by Kimberly Davidson

I'm Beautiful? Why Can't I See It? [2nd Edition]
Love Yourself and Love Your Body in 12 Weeks
(Addresses eating disorders & negative body image)

I'm God's Girl? Why Can't I Feel It?
Daily Biblical Encouragement to Defeat Depression & the Blues

Dancing In the Sonshine (Second Edition)
Restoration from the Wounds of Abuse
(Some chapters from The Perfect Counselor are also in Dancing in the Sonshine)

Something Happened On My Way to Hell
Break Free from the Insatiable Pursuit of Pleasure

Breaking the Cover Girl Mask: *Toss Out Toxic Thoughts*

Deadly Love: *Confronting the Sex Trafficking of Our Children*

Foundations
Empowering Youth to Establish Healthy Sexuality & Relationships
(A Parent's and Youth Leader's Guide)

Torn Between Two Masters
Encouraging Teens to Live Authentically in a Celebrity-Obsessed World

Connect with Kimberly

If you want to connect with Kimberly, you can through her website at *www.OliveBranchOutreach.com* or on Facebook. Or, email her at *kim@kim-davidson.com*. She'd love to hear from you or meet you at a future event.

Notes

[1] See: http://www.apa.org/helpcenter/choose-therapist.aspx.

[2] See: https://www.psychologytoday.com/blog/freudian-sip/201102/how-find-the-best-therapist-you.

[3] Daniel G. Amen, M.D., "Healing the Hardware of the Soul," http://www.amenclinic.com/bp/articles.php?articleID=20

[4] Philip Yancey, *Disappointment with God* (Grand Rapids: Zondervan, 1988), 105.

[5] Mark Driscoll and Gerry Breshears, *Vintage Jesus*, (Wheaton: Crossway, 2007), 31

[6] Philip Yancey, *Disappointment with God* (Grand Rapids: Zondervan, 1988), 118.

[7] Bishop Janes; Encyclopedia of 15,000 Illustrations

[8] See: Matthew 2:11; 14:33; 28:9, 17; Luke 24:52; John 9:38.

[9] C. S. Lewis, *Mere Christianity*, (San Francisco: HarperSanFrancisco, 1980), 56

[10] Stated by Larry Osborne, *Accidental Pharisees*, (Grand Rapids: Zondervan, 2012), 75.

[11] David W. Jones, *The Psychology of Jesus*, 2014; 110.

[12] See http://www.selfinjury.org/docs/brights.html

[13] Soul Care New Every Morning, March 4, 2010

[14] Philip Yancey, *Disappointment with God* (Grand Rapids: Zondervan, 1988), 253.

[15] Mark Baker, *Jesus: The Greatest Therapist Who Ever Lived*, (New York: HarperOne, 2007), 87.

[16] Henry Krystal, *Integration and Self-healing* (Mahwah NJ: The Analytic Press, 1988).

[17] Philip Yancey, *Disappointment with God* (Grand Rapids: Zondervan, 1988), 125.

[18] Dan Allender and Trempter Longman III, *The Cry of the Soul*, (Colorado Springs: NavPress, 1994). 26.

[19] Sharon A. Hersh, *Mom, I Hate My Life!* (Colorado Springs: Shaw Books, 2004), 40.

[20] Caroline Leaf, *Who Switched Off My Brain*, (Switch On Your Brain Pty; 2007), 113-114.

[21] Stated by Drs. Timothy Jennings and Caroline Leaf.

[22] *Life Today;* "Words of LIFE: The Desperate In-Between," September 25, 2016

[23] David Powlison, "In the Last Analysis," 2007 Leadership Conference, Sovereign Grace Ministries.

[24] See:
http://www.thepositivemind.com/tpm/aboutpainanddullnessarticle.html;
Accessed July, 2012.
[25] *Life Today;* "Words of LIFE: The Desperate In-Between," September 25,
2016
[26] *New York Times* 2011 report.
[27] Sociologist David Finkelhor conducted a massive study on child sexual
abuse; http://www.indiaparenting.com/raising-children/125_326/does-your-
child-know-about-sex-abuse.html
[28] Penny R. Smith, *The Second Woman Study* (Bloomington: WestBow, 2015)
111.
[29] Daniel Sweeny, Ph.D, *Traumatic Grief, Loss & Crisis 2.0,* "The Neurobiology
of Childhood," Light University, 2015.
[30] M.H. Silbet & A.M. Pines, "Early sexual exploitation as an influence in
prostitution," *Social Work* (1983); 285-89; C.S. Wisdom & J.B. Kuhns,
"Childhood victimization and subsequent risk for promiscuity, prostitution,
and teenage pregnancy," *American Journal of Public Health,* 86 (1996): 1607-12.
[31] K.A. Tyler et al., "The impact of childhood sexual abuse on later sexual
victimization among runaway youth," *Journal of Research on Adolescence,* 11
(2001): 151-76.
[32] Penny R. Smith, *The Second Woman Study* (Bloomington: WestBow, 2015)
109-110.
[33] Matthew Lieberman, *Social: Why Our Brains Are Wired to Connect,* xi.
[34] Studies stated in Lundy Bancroft, *Why Does He Do That?* (New York:
Berkley Books, 2002), 59.
[35] See also: Deuteronomy 22:25-26; Ezekiel 22:11, 13, 21; Lamentations 5:11,
21-22.
[36] Stephen R. Tracy & Celestia G. Tracy, *Princess Found,* Mending the Soul,
2011, 8.
[37] Ibid.
[38] Lundy Bancroft, *Why Does He Do That?* (New York: Berkley Books, 2002),
191, 200-203.
[39] Peter A. Levine, *Trauma and Memory,* (Berkley: North Atlantic Books, 2015),
xxi.
[40] Stated in Lundy Bancroft, *Why Does He Do That?* (New York: Berkley
Books, 2002), 130.
[41] Alan D. Wolfelt, *The PTSD Solution* (Fort Collins: Companion Press, 2015)
12.
[42] See: http://www.ptsd.va.gov/public/PTSD-overview/women/sexual-
assault-females.asp.
[43] Peter A. Levine, *Trauma and Memory,* (Berkley: North Atlantic Books, 2015),
45.

[44] Ibid, 40-46.

[45] Long-term exposure to high levels of cortisol is associated with low energy, poor concentration, elevated cholesterol risks, heart disease and hypertension, increased risk for strokes, diabetes, muscle wasting, osteoporosis, anxiety, depression, irregular menstrual cycles, lowered libido, and decreased fertility. | Daniel G. Amen, M.D., *Making a Good Brain Great*, (New York: Three Rivers Press, 2005), 168-169.

[46] Alan D. Wolfelt, *The PTSD Solution* (Fort Collins: Companion Press, 2015) 20-21.

[47] Oswald Chambers, "Daily Thoughts for Disciples," June 19.

[48] Katherine Wollard, *Body/Mind*, "Go Ahead, Cry Yourself A River," from William Frey II, *Crying: The Mystery of Tears*

[49] Alan D. Wolfelt, *The PTSD Solution* (Fort Collins: Companion Press, 2015) 100-105.

[50] Stated by David Johnson, *The Subtle Power of Spiritual Abuse* (Minneapolis: Bethany House, 1991), 125.

[51] Gerald May, *Addiction & Grace*, (New York: HarperOne, 1988), 3.

[52] W. E. Vine, *Vine's Complete Expository Dictionary*, (Nashville: Thomas Nelson, 1996), 547.

[53] Larry Crabb, *Finding God*, (Zondervan, 1995). 41.

[54] C. S. Lewis, "The Trouble with X," in *God in the Dock: Essays on Theology and Ethics* (Eerdmans, 1970) 155.

[55] See http://www.goodreads.com/quotes/tag/addiction; Accessed March 31, 2012.

[56] See http://christian-quotes.ochristian.com/Oswald-Chambers-Quotes/page-2.shtml.

[57] *SoulCare: New Every Morning*; December 6, 2012.

[58] Cecil Osborne, *The Art of Understanding Yourself* (Grand Rapids: Zondervan, 1982), 37.

[59] Peter A. Levine, *Trauma and Memory*, (Berkley: North Atlantic Books, 2015), 3-4.

[60] Tim Clinton & Mark Laaser, *The Fight for Your Life*, (Shippensburg: Destiny Image Publ., 2015), 60.

[61] Peter A. Levine, *Trauma and Memory*, (Berkley: North Atlantic Books, 2015), 135.

[62] Norman Doidge, "On Neuroplasticity."

[63] Source: Dr. Caroline Leaf; TBN, May 2, 2016

[64] Read more at http://www.relevantmagazine.com/god/how-your-brain-wired-god#eDU1WaAL7TGWzMDG.99

[65] Caroline Leaf, *Who Switched Off My Brain,* (Switch On Your Brain Pty; 2007), 113-114.

[66] Stated in Brennan Manning, *Reflections for Ragamuffins,* "June 11, Self-Condemnation."

[67] Oswald Chambers, "Daily Thoughts for Disciples."

[68] Caroline Leaf, *Who Switched Off My Brain,* (Switch On Your Brain; 2007), 8, 113-114, 94.

[69] Source: Dr. Caroline Leaf; TBN, May 25, 2016

[70] See: http://www.nytimes.com/2012/03/24/your-money/why-people-remember-negative-events-more-than-positive-ones.html?_r=0

[71] Ibid.

[72] Newberg and Waldman, *How God Changes Your Brain,* 39.

[73] Source: Dr. Caroline Leaf; TBN, "The Disordered Mind;" March 9, 2016.

[74] Stated by Dr. Paul G. Quinnett, *Counseling Suicidal People* (Spokane: The QPR Institute, 2000) 147-148.

[75] Stephen R. Tracy & Celestia G. Tracy, *Princess Found,* Mending the Soul, 2011, 8.

[76] David W. Jones, *The Psychology of Jesus,* 2014; 110.

[77] G. L. Jantz, *Hope, Help, and Healing for Eating Disorders* (Wheaton: Harold Shaw 1995), 125.

[78] Mark Baker, *The Greatest Therapist Who Ever Lived,* (New York: HarperOne, 2007), 56.

[79] Monique Sampson, "Rape," *Out of the Blues: Writing from the Women's Re-Entry Writer's Group at the Cuyahoga County Jail,* 28; 2002.

[80] See Leviticus 19:18; Deuteronomy 32:35; Proverbs 24:12; Romans 12:17-21; 1 Thessalonians 5:15; Hebrews 10:30.

[81] Cecil Osborne, *The Art of Understanding Yourself* (Grand Rapids: Zondervan, 1982), 87.

[82] Neil T. Anderson, *The Bondage Breaker,* (Eugene: Harvest House, 2000, 2nd Rev.), 69, 72.

[83] Henry Cloud & John Townsend, *Boundaries,* (Grand Rapids: Zondervan, 1992).

[84] Milan & Kay Yerkovich, *How We Love Our Kids* (Colorado Springs: WaterBrook Press, 2011), 281.

[85] See: http://dictionary.reference.com/browse/oppression?s=t.

[86] See: John 4:25-26; 11:1-44; 12:1-8; 20:1-16; Matt. 27:55-56; 27:61; Acts 1:14; 5:14; 8:12; 17:4, 12; 16:13-15; 1 Cor. 16:19.

[87] Drew Pinsky and S. Mark Young, *The Mirror Effect,* (New York: HarperCollins, 2009), 6-7.